32 in '44

Building the Portsmouth
Submarine Fleet in
World War II

RODNEY K. WATTERSON

NAVAL INSTITUTE PRESS
Annapolis, Maryland

Naval Institute Press
291 Wood Road
Annapolis, MD 21402

Library of Congress Cataloging-in-Publication Data

Watterson, Rodney K.

 32 in '44 : building the Portsmouth submarine fleet in World War II / Rodney K. Watterson.

  p. cm.

 Includes bibliographical references and index.

 ISBN 978-1-59114-953-8 (hardcover : alk. paper) 1. Portsmouth Naval Shipyard (U.S.)—History—20th century. 2. Submarines (Ships)—United States—Design and construction—History—20th century. 3. World War, 1939-1945—Naval operations—Submarine. 4. World War, 1939-1945—Naval operations, American. 5. Shipyards—New Hampshire—Portsmouth—History—20th century. I. Title. II. Title: Thirty-two in Forty-four.

 D783.W37 2011

 940.54'51—dc22

                        2010046867

Printed in the United States of America on acid-free paper

19 18 17 16 15 14 13 12 11   9 8 7 6 5 4 3 2 1

First printing

Contents

Illustrations

Foreword

Naval ships have been built on the shores of the Piscataqua River since before 1776. When the U.S. Navy Yard was established in 1800, naval ship repair and construction commenced as an operation of the U.S. government. A century later, the United States began building submarines, and in 1914 the Portsmouth Navy Yard received an order for the *L-8*, the first submarine built at the yard. Three decades later the Portsmouth Navy Yard set the pace for submarine construction and played a crucial role in the buildup of the underwater Pacific fleet during World War II.

This book is the story of a remarkable period of submarine construction in the Portsmouth Navy Yard during World War II. Rodney Watterson examines the history of the yard, from the earliest period of submarine construction there through the era during which it was the principal submarine design and construction yard in the country. The shipbuilding efforts prior to World War II are well described and easily identifiable as the building bocks upon which the outstanding performance described in this book became possible. Probably the most noteworthy feature was that the Navy Department wanted to retain Navy control over the design and construction of submarines, largely due to the earlier dissatisfaction with private shipbuilding companies.

The Portsmouth Navy Yard was built on a small island in the Piscataqua River, thus the area and facilities for shipbuilding were very small, while the infrastructure required for large-scale construction was limited in scope. Additionally, the size of the labor force was very modest prior to World War II. Shipbuilders were not just brought in from the street; new employees required considerable—often very precise—training in order to be effective contributors. These features—infrastructure, labor, and training—all loomed as major impediments to a large-scale buildup of submarine construction.

Following World War I and through the late 1930s, funds for Navy ship construction, especially submarines, were extremely limited. Fortunately, and with apparent good foresight, the Navy Department was able to keep a very modest submarine construction workload ongoing at Portsmouth Navy Yard. During these several years many private shipyards were forced to close, and for those in any way involved with submarine construction, know-how was lost. There were several years when the only submarine construction ongoing in the United States was at the Portsmouth Navy Yard. As the 1930s drew to a close, the threat of war drove the need for the construction of new naval warships, including submarines. Elements of the Navy Department directed shipyards to identify needed upgrades of infrastructure, and large-scale improvements were rapidly undertaken.

The fact that a submarine construction effort at Portsmouth continued during the decades preceding World War II placed the yard in the enviable position of having a management team and a trained, skilled workforce in place. Both were critical to the yard's many successes between 1941 and 1945. Indeed, the infrastructure, labor, and funding requirements were identified and Navy Department action was timely and responsive. The yard was able to proceed without impediment!

On the eve of the war, nearly four thousand people were on the payrolls at Portsmouth. Management realized, however, that far greater numbers were needed as new submarine orders poured in. Vast recruiting efforts were undertaken to increase the size of the workforce and improve training for new workers. As a result, by 1943 the number of men and women employed by the yard had swelled to more than twenty thousand.

During the early 1940s the Navy Department consolidated two of its existing "bureaus" into a single "Bureau of Ships" in an effort to eliminate the fragmentation of responsibilities. This new bureau was overwhelmed with its task of bringing new shipyards into the building business throughout the country. The impact on Portsmouth Navy Yard was most favorable. It was in the enviable position of not being overly managed by higher authority, thereby permitting many innovations by the challenged shipyard team. Many of these innovations are described in this book and, in some cases, are shown to be way ahead of their time.

Prior to World War II, the lifeblood of Portsmouth Navy Yard was its people. The managers and the workforce were made up of very experienced individuals, many of whom had stayed in their positions for lengthy periods of time. These individuals, in addition to supervising necessary training programs, were the ones who came forth with the ideas, challenges, and processes that led the yard to greater and greater performance. The yard was truly blessed with the caliber of its top leadership, both military and civilian.

In the concluding part of the book the author states, in part, that "remarkable production success can be achieved when bold and enlightened management leads dedicated and motivated employees and both are zealously committed to a common objective." Such was the case in the astonishing performance of Portsmouth

Navy Yard's submarine construction throughout World War II, especially the thirty-two boats delivered there in 1944.

—WILLIAM D. McDONOUGH,
Captain, U.S. Navy (Ret.)
Commander, Portsmouth Naval Shipyard
August 1974–August 1979

Acknowledgments

I want to thank the members of my dissertation committee who got me started on this work while I was a doctoral student at the University of New Hampshire. These include my dissertation adviser, Kurk Dorsey, and committee members Jeffrey Bolster, Ellen Fitzpatrick, Gary Weir, and Carole Barnett. Their comments were extensive, insightful, and helpful. Also to be thanked are Richard Winslow, author of several Portsmouth Naval Shipyard histories, and Jim Dolph, the Portsmouth Naval Shipyard historian, who read the dissertation and provided valuable comments. Thanks to Capt. Bill McDonough, USN (Ret.), for writing the foreword. I especially want to recognize the important contribution of Cdr. Vic Peters, USN (Ret.). He made many valuable professional and editorial recommendations that significantly improved the final manuscript. Finally, sincere thanks to copy editor Julie Kimmel.

Many contributed to the success of my research. Archivist Joanie Gearin was especially helpful in finding Portsmouth Navy Yard records and managing the carts of boxes and binders that I "mined" during my many visits to the National Archives and Records Administration (NARA) in Waltham, Massachusetts. Archivist Patrick Osborne provided the same support at NARA in College Park, Maryland. Nancy Mason, special collections assistant at the Milne Special Collections and Archives at the University of New Hampshire, was especially helpful in reproducing the shipyard photographs used in the dissertation. Thanks also to Tom Hardiman, the keeper at the Portsmouth Athenaeum, for making available the oral histories of shipyard workers collected as part of the Music Hall Shipyard Project. Walter Ross, William Tebo, and Dennis O'Keeffe were particularly accommodating, hospitable, and entertaining during my visits to the Portsmouth Naval Shipyard Museum.

I'm especially grateful for the individuals who consented to be interviewed for this work. The interviews with Frederick White, Percy Whitney, William Tebo, Eileen Dondero Foley, and Dan MacIsaac gave meaning and life to thousands of pages of yellowed paper and hundreds of old photographs. Their contributions added greatly to the quality of the book.

Most importantly, I want to thank my wife, Susan, for proofreading numerous drafts and offering recommendations and encouragement. I am deeply indebted to her for the patience and understanding she showed in granting me endless hours of our retirement time to pursue a dream. Lastly, I want to thank my loyal project assistant, Molly. Ever present during long hours at the computer, always eager to listen to new ideas, and frequently reminding me, with a nudge of her nose, when it was time for us to balance work with play, she was even more faithful and supportive than the average golden retriever.

Introduction

The enemy has struck a savage, treacherous blow. We are at war, all of us: there is no time now for disputes or delay of any kind. We must have ships and more ships, guns and more guns, men and more men—faster and faster. There is no time to lose. The navy must lead the way. Speed up—it is our navy and your nation.

—SECRETARY OF THE NAVY FRANK KNOX,
11 December 1941

On 27 January 1944 Portsmouth Navy Yard launched three submarines simultaneously and a fourth shortly thereafter. Prior to this, no shipyard had ever accomplished either feat. *Ronquil*, *Redfish*, and *Razorback* lifted off their blocks in dry dock #1 at 1:00 PM and the *Scabbardfish* slid down building way #4 into the Piscataqua River at 2:30 PM. These four submarines would be included in the record-setting thirty-two submarines that the yard completed in 1944. No U.S. shipyard before or since has built so many submarines in one year, hence the title of this study, *32 in '44*.[1]

Prior to the triple launching, Fred White, the shipyard's master rigger, had concerns about floating three 1,800-ton submarines off their blocks at the same time. The three submarines were jammed into the dry dock with little separation, and White and his line handlers were responsible for ensuring that the submarines did not damage each other as they floated free of the blocks. Photos 1 and 2 in the gallery show the tight conditions under which the three submarines were built and launched. White had made daily observations of the progress of the submarines' side-by-side construction since their keels were laid on the same day, 9 September 1943. Since that time, the submarines had grown in size and gradually filled the dock until only a few feet separated the hulls. At the points of least separation, one could almost step from hull to hull.[2]

White and the other civilian managers had already convinced the yard commandant, Rear Adm. Thomas Withers, that this should be the first—and last— triple simultaneous launching from a dry dock at Portsmouth Navy Yard. Having pushed the envelope this one time, the managers were convinced that working conditions were too tight and the risks too great to attempt to build and launch "three at a time." This was no easy decision because the managers at Portsmouth Navy Yard prided themselves on innovative submarine-building techniques and on their willingness to accept considerable risk for the sake of increased production.

Despite White's concerns, the triple launching went well. The slide of the *Scabbardfish* into the river shortly thereafter was equally successful. TM3 Dan MacIsaac watched the triple launching from the side of the dry dock that afternoon with a few other crew members of the USS *Redfish*. He recalled that the three sponsors carefully smashed the champagne bottles on the bows of the three submarines at precisely the same time to preserve the purity of the advertised triple simultaneous launching.[3]

Rear Admiral Withers had obviously alerted the highest levels of the Navy of the planned launchings because Secretary of the Navy James V. Forrestal sent a congratulatory message to the yard later that same day. Secretary Forrestal wrote, "In the launching of four submarines in a single day, the Portsmouth Navy Yard sets another record in the submarine program."[4] Portsmouth had set other submarine production records before this one and would go on to establish even more records before the war was over.

The quadruple launching on 27 January 1944 was a microcosm of events at Portsmouth Navy Yard during World War II. Innovative and creative management combined with a dedicated and very capable workforce to set submarine production records that brought great credit and recognition to the shipyard. This book tells the story of how Portsmouth Navy Yard was able to achieve such remarkable production performance.

—〰—

After completing on average less than two submarines a year in the 1930s, Portsmouth Navy Yard completed seventy-nine submarines between 1 July 1940 and 1 July 1945.[5] Similarly, the shipyard employed an average of about two thousand employees per year in the 1930s and grew to a peak employment of 20,445 in November 1943. Figure 1 shows the dramatic increase in employment and completed submarines during World War II. Clearly, something extraordinary occurred at Portsmouth Navy Yard during the war.

Figure 1. Employment and Submarines Built
Portsmouth Navy Yard (1930–50)

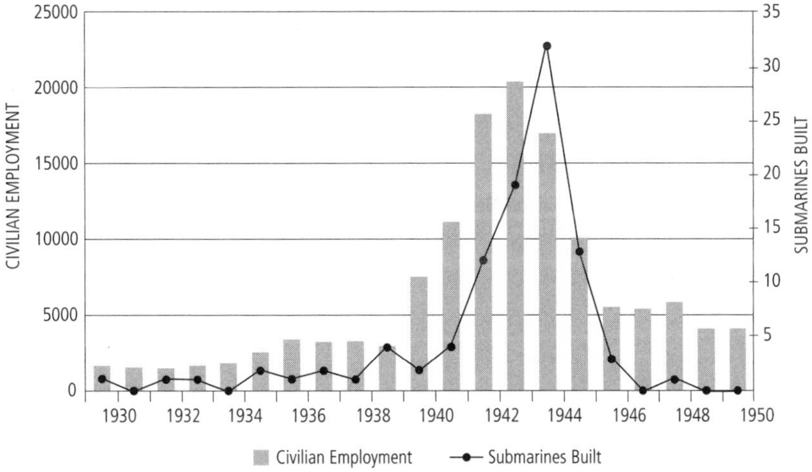

Source: From shipyard employment numbers and submarine construction records in *Cradle of American Shipbuilding: Portsmouth Naval Shipyard, Portsmouth, New Hampshire* (Portsmouth: Portsmouth Naval Shipyard, 1978), 76–83.

Portsmouth Navy Yard's outstanding performance was the direct result of a highly motivated workforce and innovative management techniques that thrived in the decentralized naval shipbuilding environment of World War II. The management of Portsmouth Navy Yard, either by design or necessity, successfully employed industrial management practices that were years ahead of their time. These practices included employee empowerment, special small teams, and mass production techniques to the extent that they could be applied to submarine construction at the time.

Portsmouth-built submarines made a significant contribution to the winning of the war. They sank 434 enemy ships totaling about 1.7 million tons.[6] This represents about one-third of the tonnage sunk by U.S. submarines during the war.[7] In its 27 August 1945 issue, the shipyard's newspaper, the *Portsmouth Periscope*, celebrated the yard's wartime accomplishments with considerable pride:

> The war is over! And the part that Portsmouth played in the war is something that . . . every loyal workingman can look back on with a feeling of pride. . . . The Portsmouth submarine fleet was the scourge of the famed Japanese merchant ships. From the very darkest days of the war, Portsmouth started to swing at the little yellow men who had pulled the sneak attack on Pearl Harbor. . . .

They rained submarines on the men who started this (for them) fatal conflict....
They slaughtered a Jap fleet that had had a free reign.[8]

Looking beyond the emotion and racially charged language of the moment, the *Periscope* was accurate in reporting that Portsmouth Navy Yard's performance had contributed significantly to the winning of the war.

The wartime mobilization of Portsmouth Navy Yard was a vitally important part of a nationwide mobilization of shipyards. The history of that mobilization, according to historian Frederic C. Lane, falls into two parts. Under the first part, the U.S. Maritime Commission, newly created by the Merchant Marine Act in 1936, had the task of building merchant ships faster than they were being sunk. Lane's *Ships for Victory* documents the remarkable wartime success of the U.S. Maritime Commission and private shipyards in achieving that goal. After suffering shipping losses that exceeded new construction in 1941 and 1942, the trend was reversed in 1943 when 18 million tons of large cargo carriers and tankers were built, more than the total merchant fleet under the U.S. flag in 1939.[9] The second part of the mobilization saw the Navy Department, through the Bureau of Ships, deliver warships at equally impressive rates.

There were similarities between the operations at the high-performing shipyards under the U.S. Maritime Commission and the better-performing shipyards building warships for the Navy Department. Those similarities included standardization of product and various uses of modular construction and assembly line manufacturing. More importantly, the successful shipyards thrived in a decentralized shipbuilding environment that encouraged local decision making and an entrepreneurial approach to production. In the case of merchant ships, Lane noted, "This decentralization enabled managers of successful yards to go ahead without being hamstrung by interference from Washington DC."[10] This book will show that the Bureau of Ships granted Portsmouth Navy Yard a similar license to build submarines. Success bred independence, and independence led to record-setting wartime deliveries of merchant ships, warships, and, in Portsmouth's case, submarines.

One final note about World War II mobilization studies: these studies usually present top-down views from Washington, D.C., where strategic decisions were made and important policies were implemented.[11] Few studies of wartime industrial mobilization reach down to the internal workings of an industrial activity to examine the implementation of mobilization at the shop-floor level; the few that do primarily involve commercial shipbuilding on the West Coast.[12] One exception is Tony Cope's *On the Swing Shift: Building Liberty Ships in Savannah*, which examines the World War II mobilization of a private East Coast shipyard, the

Southeastern Shipbuilding Corporation.[13] This volume, *32 in '44*, an analysis of the industrial mobilization of an East Coast submarine navy yard, is unique.

According to mobilization historian Christopher Tassava, "Perhaps, because the war is such a towering subject of historical inquiry, few works on wartime industry concretely discuss war work itself."[14] This book does discuss war work in great detail by examining the day-to-day waterfront operations of Portsmouth Navy Yard. The remarkable production accomplishments during the war are analyzed in light of the management practices and production methods that led to those accomplishments.

This mobilization story is prefaced by placing Portsmouth Navy Yard in the context of broader national and international events of the 1920s and 1930s. The discussion will show that post–World War I U.S. Navy concerns about submarine construction in private shipyards, disarmament conferences, neutrality acts, the Great Depression, and New Deal recovery programs all contributed to setting the stage for Portsmouth Navy Yard's World War II story to unfold as it did.

32 in '44

Building the Portsmouth
Submarine Fleet in
World War II

Chapter 1

Between the Wars

The working force at the Portsmouth Yard has been unusually steady and the result has been an excellent product at reasonable cost. . . . The ability of the Portsmouth Yard to meet its completion dates has in recent years been amply demonstrated by the excellent and unique record established of meeting every contract date of delivery.

—REAR ADM. W. G. DuBOSN, Chief,
Bureau of Construction and Repair, and
REAR ADM. H. G. BOWEN, Chief,
Bureau of Engineering,
joint letter of 10 August 1938

Portsmouth Navy Yard's expertise in submarine design and construction at the start of World War II can be traced back to the U.S. Navy's dissatisfaction with the submarine acquisition process that it had experienced prior to, and during, World War I. Many thought that during World War I private shipbuilders were motivated more by profiteering than by providing the fleet with the ships that it needed. The excessive profits reaped by private industry prompted numerous congressional efforts to bring the situation under control. According to Robert Connery, "In the years between 1918 and April 1942, some 140 bills and resolutions to reduce or eliminate profits on war production and equalize the economic burdens of war were introduced into Congress."[1] The U.S. Navy, in particular, believed it paid too much for inferior and ill-designed submarines during World War I. Gary Weir's *Building American Submarines, 1914–1940* describes how the U.S. Navy, dissatisfied with private industry during World War I, made a commitment to strengthen Portsmouth Navy Yard's submarine design and construction capabilities during the 1920s and 1930s.[2]

During the period of early submarine development, private submarine builders Electric Boat Company (then the Fore River Shipbuilding Company) in Quincy, Massachusetts, and Lake Torpedo Boat Company in Bridgeport, Connecticut, controlled the design of submarines with little or no input solicited—

1

or accepted—from the U.S. Navy. As a result, Portsmouth received favored treatment from the U.S. Navy in the 1920s while Electric Boat and Lake Torpedo Boat were neglected and struggled to remain open. Electric Boat continued to build submarines after World War I, but only to complete contracts received during the war. The last of these was delivered in 1925, and the U.S. Navy did not award any new submarine contracts to Electric Boat between 1919 and 1931. Finally, in 1931 Electric Boat was awarded a contract to build the USS *Cuttlefish* (SS 171). By that time the total workforce at Electric Boat had dropped to two hundred employees.[3]

Electric Boat Company survived during the 1920s by completing thirty-two cargo ships, which were still under contract at the end of World War I, and by taking on any work it could get. This included overhauling thirty S-class submarines; building pleasure craft, ferries, tow boats, and trawlers; and constructing four submarines for the Peruvian navy.[4] The Lake Torpedo Boat Company, however, folded in 1924 because, unlike Electric Boat, it was not successful in diversifying or finding other work. Thus, by 1930 Portsmouth Navy Yard was the only shipyard constructing submarines for the U.S. Navy.

Portsmouth Navy Yard Competes with Private Industry

How did Portsmouth Navy Yard become the sole provider of submarines to the U.S. Navy? Capt. Andrew I. McKee, planning officer at Portsmouth Navy Yard during World War II, explained the process in an article he wrote in 1945 for *Historical Transactions 1893–1943*, a fiftieth anniversary special publication by the Society of Naval Architects and Marine Engineers: "For fourteen years, from 1919 until 1933, all the submarines ordered, and there were only nine . . . were built to plans prepared by Portsmouth." The nine submarines are commonly grouped together as the Victory class, but as McKee notes, they were at the time considered to be five different classes because the characteristics varied considerably between submarines. The first Electric Boat submarine ordered after World War I, the *Cuttlefish*, was also required to be built to Portsmouth plans, with only minor departures.[5]

McKee went on to describe how the Navy used Portsmouth Navy Yard to wrest control of submarine design from the private yards during and immediately after World War I:

> As the first step in familiarizing its personnel with submarines and their designs, an order was placed in June 1914 for the building of the *L-8*, to the design of the Lake Torpedo [Boat] Company, at the Navy Yard Portsmouth, N.H. Two years later, the *O-1*, of the Holland type, was ordered built at Portsmouth to the design of the Electric Boat Company. Late in 1916, the Navy Department decided that Portsmouth had acquired enough experience in its work on these two ships to be trusted with the development of the working plans for a

third design, the preliminary design of which had been prepared by the Navy Department, and [the Navy Department] placed an order for one submarine, the *S-3*, at Portsmouth. At the same time, orders were placed for the *S-1* with Electric Boat and the *S-2* with the Lake Torpedo [Boat] Company.[6]

In effect, the Navy had set up a design competition between the two well-established private submarine design shipyards and the newcomer, Portsmouth Navy Yard. Portsmouth's design and workmanship were ultimately judged superior to the others. According to the S-Class Trial Board:

> Aside from all general features of design, a casual inspection shows a great difference in the care and thoroughness with which the three plants (Portsmouth, Quincy, and Bridgeport) design and work out the details of all interior and exterior arrangements and fitting. In this respect, there is no great difference in the product of the two private plants (Quincy and Bridgeport) that of the Lake Torpedo Boat Company being perhaps somewhat better. But the Navy yard (Portsmouth) built boats are far superior to the others, particularly in the interiors. In the *S-3* to *S-9* (Portsmouth-built boats) there is full evidence of careful design by personnel that know what is best, followed by good workmanship, everything being done in a painstaking manner.[7]

Vice Adm. George C. Dyer, then Lieutenant Dyer, reported to the *S-2* at the Lake Torpedo Boat Company in August 1919 to be the executive officer. According to Dyer, during a full-power run "a cylinder of one of the [diesel] engines dropped a spray valve smashing everything inside the cylinder." On a subsequent full-power trial "the engine labored terribly [but] we got through the engine test." Finally, prior to delivery the main motors burned up, causing about a four-month delay for repairs.[8] Such was the performance of the *S-2* and Lake Torpedo Boat Company, which the S-Class Trial Board judged to be the better of the two private yards.

Citing the trial board's report noting preference for Portsmouth Navy Yard's work, the chief of naval operations' annual report for 1923 stated, "Analysis of results obtained shows beyond question that submarines can be more economically and expeditiously overhauled at Portsmouth than at any other east coast yard within the limitation of size of yard force."[9] Early recognition for high quality, low cost, and short building periods reinforced the Navy's plan to develop an in-house submarine design and construction capability at Portsmouth Navy Yard. However, with the nation focused on disarmament during the 1920s, Portsmouth's design team had limited opportunities to design submarines. Electric Boat and other yards had no opportunities at all.

The yard's in-house design capabilities were aptly demonstrated by repairs to the *S-48* after she had run aground on a shoal outside Portsmouth Harbor in 1925. According to Rear Adm. William D. Irvin, USN, then Lieutenant (jg) Irvin assigned to *S-48*, the submarine was so badly damaged that "the Navy was going to abandon her, but the shipyard workers brought so much pressure to bear that it forced the Navy to take action, bring her into Portsmouth Navy Yard, and put her back in shape again. In 1927 and 1928 she was repaired, and the shipyard put a twenty-five foot section in the middle, so that she was much longer than when she started."[10] Even with limited opportunities during the 1920s, shipyard managers found ways to develop the yard's in-house design capabilities and, in the process, increase its reputation as the premier U.S. submarine design yard.

The post–World War I slump in shipbuilding was the death knell for a number of private shipyards. According to the Bureau of Ships' self-history, "By 1933, only six private yards remained in operation: the 'Big Three,' Bethlehem, New York, and Newport News; and three smaller companies, Bath Iron Works, Federal Shipbuilding and Dry Dock Company, and Electric Boat Company."[11] As noted by maritime historian Frederic C. Lane, "In the lean years from 1922 to 1938 only the very strong shipbuilding companies were able to keep going." Lane summarized well the state of shipyards between the wars when he wrote, "Dominating the clatter and seemingly random dispersion of a shipyard, guiding the work of its huge cranes, heavy presses, and other special equipment were the calculations of highly trained engineers and experienced managers. Their practical and theoretical knowledge had to be kept employed if the industry was to survive and have in it the possibility of sudden growth to meet a new emergency."[12] This was precisely the case at Portsmouth Navy Yard between the wars. The U.S. Navy, despite a budget that was severely constrained by economic depression, politics, and foreign policy, kept naval architects, marine engineers, and experienced managers employed to the maximum extent possible. In the end, Portsmouth Navy Yard not only survived, it actually improved its design and production capabilities throughout the 1920s and 1930s. As a result, the yard was more prepared than most shipyards for the industrial mobilization that immediately preceded World War II. In the simplest of terms, Portsmouth Navy Yard merely had to expand existing facilities and resources to meet the increased demands for a very familiar product, while other shipyards had to struggle to define new facility and resource needs to build new products.

Portsmouth Navy Yard's fate between the two wars was, to a large extent, determined by the U.S. Navy's commitment to develop it as competition to private industry. However, the Navy's ability to do that was heavily influenced by larger national and international events. Disarmament initiatives and neutrality, in conjunction with very limited naval appropriations during the Great Depression, restricted the number of submarines that could be built. This in turn limited the submarine design and construction experience that the yard could acquire during this interim period. The National Industrial Recovery Act (NIRA) kick-started the nation's naval shipbuilding program in 1933. NIRA authorizations included the construction of two new submarines at Portsmouth Navy Yard. These projects were crucial to the yard's stability between the wars. Funding through NIRA and other New Deal policies shaped Portsmouth Navy Yard's internal development in the years leading up to World War II.

Submarine Disarmament

Submarine numbers and tonnage were not restricted by any of the disarmament conferences between the wars. The primary participants (Great Britain, France, the United States, Japan, and Italy) were never able to compromise their own self-interests to the point that a consensus could be reached on any serious proposal for submarine disarmament. Nevertheless, attempts to include restrictions on the number and sizes of submarines in the various disarmament treaties discouraged support for any U.S. submarine rebuilding programs prior to the mid-1930s.

Even though unrestrained by treaty limitations, the United States voluntarily restricted submarine construction during the 1920s to a rate of less than one submarine per year, all at Portsmouth. The first four years of the 1930s were particularly lean for Portsmouth Navy Yard. Employment averaged a little over fifteen hundred, about the same as in 1916, before the buildup for World War I. During those four years the shipyard built only three submarines, the last of the V-class submarines, and the last surface combatant the yard would ever deliver, the Coast Guard cutter USS *Hudson*.[13]

When ex-Assistant Secretary of the Navy Franklin Delano Roosevelt assumed the presidency in March 1933, some legislators began to search for ways to reverse the U.S. Navy's decline and move the fleet toward the limits of the Washington and London Naval Treaties. Increased Japanese militancy and national economic needs provided what little impetus Roosevelt needed to move forward with substantial naval expansion. Japan officially withdrew from the League of Nations in March 1933 and announced intentions to abandon the naval limitations agreements. In the summer of 1933, the United States learned that Japan had increased its naval budget by 25 percent, and the sense that a Russo-Japanese conflict was inevitable was strong.[14]

With Roosevelt's support, NIRA provided authorization and funding to increase the Navy by thirty-two ships, including four submarines. Two of the four were assigned to Portsmouth Navy Yard. The year 1934 saw the passage of the Vinson-Trammell Act, which authorized the construction of another 102 ships, including twenty-eight submarines. This action was designed to bring the fleet up to the limits of the Washington and London Naval Treaties by 1942. Having been favored with the V-class submarine building program during the 1920s, Portsmouth Navy Yard greeted the renewed naval shipbuilding programs with an experienced submarine design team and a stable workforce experienced in submarine construction. The yard was well positioned to capitalize on the naval shipbuilding programs of the mid-1930s.

Another important factor contributed to the revitalized submarine construction program. After extensive debate during the 1920s about how best to employ submarines in battle, the Navy had decided to use submarines in long-range, independent operations similar to the German wolf-pack operations of World War I. Previously, U.S. submarines had been employed only as support elements of a large task force and in coastal defense. Having redefined the submarine's tactical role, naval authorities could now agree on the design characteristics needed to fill this new role. Thus, when the nation's leaders decided to rebuild the fleet, the submarine force had a much better idea of the kind of submarine they wanted. Designs could be standardized to a certain extent, multiple submarines of the same class design could be built, and the opportunities for constructing something other than one-of-a-kind, custom-built submarines were increased.

Cdr. Thomas Withers is given much of the credit for this major change in strategic planning. Commander Withers is the same Rear Admiral Withers who commanded Portsmouth Navy Yard during most of World War II. According to naval historian Gary Weir, "The climax of this dispute [about how best to employ U.S. submarines in battle] occurred between 1928 and 1930 when Commander Thomas Withers, commanding officer of Submarine Division 4, with the support of the Naval War College and the Submarine Officer's Conference, proposed imitating the offensive strategy and solo tactics employed by the Imperial Navy during the Great War. Only then did the major authorities begin to consider seriously the prospect of independent submarine operations and a vessel design suitable to the task."[15] During World War II, U.S. submarines effectively employed the offensive strategy and independent actions championed by Commander Withers and others, and they played a decisive role in winning the war in the Pacific. As commandant of Portsmouth Navy Yard, Rear Admiral Withers ensured that the submarines the yard designed, constructed, and sent to war incorporated the latest design innovations and met the reliability and durability standards needed to achieve their long-range, independent missions.

Neutrality

The same political climate and national attitude that had encouraged disarmament conferences and international peace movements also led to the enactment of a series of five neutrality acts, between 1935 and 1939, designed to distance the United States from entangling events that might lead to another war. Disarmament, while it certainly affected the ongoing workload and future of Portsmouth Navy Yard, took place on distant stages with indirect results. Neutrality, on the other hand, was woven into day-to-day occurrences at the shipyard and in the local community by the late 1930s.

Portsmouth area residents showed strong support for neutrality in the early years of the war in Europe. During the late 1930s and early 1940s the editorial page of the *Portsmouth Herald* boldly and repeatedly proclaimed "The *Herald*'s [3-Point] Platform," the first point of which was "Keep the United States of America out of War." The other two points of the platform were local civic-minded initiatives.[16]

In January 1941, after blackout drills had been conducted at the shipyard and in the city of Portsmouth,[17] and with Great Britain being heavily bombed, the *Portsmouth Herald* conducted a poll of its readers. Poll results showed that 32 percent of the readers favored no help at all for Britain, 18 percent favored limited help short of war, 28 percent favored all help short of war, and 22 percent favored all help possibly including war.[18] The poll had been conducted as a follow-up to President Roosevelt's fireside chat in late December during which he voiced his strong support for Great Britain. Thus, contrary to the president's convictions, 78 percent of the local citizenry still remained opposed to direct U.S. involvement in the war.

These attitudes began to change shortly after the *Herald* poll. President Roosevelt continued to show his strong support for Great Britain and the Allied forces in his weekly radio addresses and by signing the Lend-Lease Act on 11 March 1941. U.S. entry into the war seemed inevitable. The *Portsmouth Herald*, in a major departure from its longtime commitment to neutrality, replaced the antiwar plank in its platform with one calling for "A united effort in behalf of the Democratic nations to win the war and establish a just and lasting peace." Referring to a recent FDR address, in which the president called for a total victory, the paper reported, "After serious reflection, we sadly have realized that, on Saturday last, President Roosevelt delivered the funeral oration on the number one plank in our platform and with sincere regret it is herewith buried." With that statement, complete with a sketch of an RIP tombstone, the *Portsmouth Herald* abandoned its strong stance on neutrality.[19] On 27 May 1941, the *Herald*'s editorial went one step further and demanded an end to the neutrality deception that the president's administration had been practicing: "Let us no longer be deceived by words—by leases that are more than leases; by lending that is more than lending; by patrols that are more than patrols; and in this speech by an 'unlimited emergency' that is actually war."[20] With those words, the *Herald*'s editor had concisely summarized U.S. foreign policy for the first half of 1941.

In late March 1941 President Roosevelt took the nation one step closer to war when he extended Lend-Lease to include the repair of British vessels in American shipyards.[21] Starting in the summer of 1941 and continuing through the rest of the year, three British submarines and one Free French submarine were overhauled at Portsmouth Navy Yard.[22] These submarines were HMS *Truant*, HMS *Pandora*, HMS *Parthian*, and the *Surcouf.* Curiously, no mention of the foreign submarines appeared in the *Portsmouth Herald* until 21 September 1941. On that date, a front-page article with a Washington dateline revealed that more than a dozen British ships were being repaired in U.S. shipyards, including HMS *Pandora* at Portsmouth. An editor's note indicated, "This has been common knowledge in Portsmouth for many weeks, but the *Portsmouth Herald*, in co-operation with the Navy Department's request, has refrained from publishing it."[23] It is clear that Lend-Lease activities had been ongoing at Portsmouth Navy Yard for some time before the local press felt free to acknowledge it.

Not mentioned in the article or press release from Washington was the fact that the Free French submarine *Surcouf* was also in the yard at the time. Eleven days earlier, on 10 September, seventeen men who "had been working on the bottom of a French ship," removing hull paint, were treated at the shipyard hospital for skin and eye irritations.[24] Photo 3 in the gallery shows the *Surcouf* in dry dock #2. If the *Pandora*'s stay at the shipyard had been common knowledge, the *Surcouf*'s visit must have been even more obvious because of its size.

The *Surcouf* was the largest submarine in the world with a displacement of four thousand tons, two eight-inch guns, an airplane, and "more decks than the average city hotel has floors."[25] With over twice the displacement of the fleet-type submarines being built at the navy yard at the time, the *Surcouf* could hardly have transited up the narrow confines of the Piscataqua River to the shipyard without being noticed. Yet the Free French submarine was at the yard for some time before it was mentioned in the press, and only then after authorization by the U.S. Navy. Such was the world of secrecy and intrigue that surrounded events at Portsmouth Navy Yard in the fall of 1941.

On 3 October 1941 the *Portsmouth Herald* further lifted the veil of secrecy about foreign submarine visits when it published an interview with the commanding officers of the *Surcouf* and HMS *Parthian*, the next British submarine to be overhauled at the yard. The interview was complete with pictures of the *Parthian* in dock at the yard and several of the foreign officers seated at a table. The *Portsmouth Herald* reporter was especially captivated with the *Surcouf*'s acting commanding officer, Lt. Cdr. Louis G. Blaison. When asked if the *Surcouf* had sunk any enemy ships yet, Blaison replied, "We've been unlucky," meaning they had not yet engaged the enemy.[26] *Surcouf*'s luck changed and then went bad. The *Portsmouth Herald* sadly reported on 18 April 1942 that the Free French had announced that the *Surcouf* with its crew of 150 men was long overdue and presumed lost.[27]

Prior to these articles in late September and early October 1941, there had been only rumors of a British submarine at the yard. But front-page headlines and pictures in the *Herald* replaced rumor with fact. Portsmouth, like the nation, was slowly but surely dropping the pretense of neutrality and beginning to embrace the Allies.

The New Deal

In the early 1930s, during the Great Depression, funding for maintenance and upgrade of navy yard shops and facilities was virtually nonexistent. New Deal policies eventually changed that. The Bureau of Yards and Docks' self-history of operations during World War II credits New Deal programs with accomplishing limited, but important, rehabilitation, modernization, and improvements at navy yards during the 1930s. According to that report, the yards would have been "critically unprepared" for World War II without these programs.

Figure 2. Public Works Expenditures
Navy Yards (1933–39)

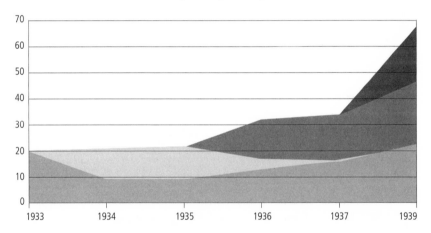

U.S. Navy   National Industrial Recovery Act
Emergency Relief Act   Public Works Administration

Source: From the *Bureau of Construction and Repair's Annual Reports*, NARA Waltham, RG 181, Portsmouth Naval Shipyard General Correspondence (Central Files), Box 22, Folder A9-1/EN 7, "Annual Reports Bureau of Construction and Repair."

The importance of the New Deal programs to the navy yards is obvious from figure 2, which shows the various funding sources available for the upgrade and maintenance of navy yard public works during the 1930s. The figure shows that the entire $19.8 million allocated in 1933 to navy yards for public works projects was from naval funds. In 1934, after passage of NIRA, the annual public works budget increased slightly to $20.3 million with $11.4 million (56 percent) of that total being funds appropriated for NIRA-designated projects. This funding trend continued throughout the 1930s, first under NIRA, then under the Emergency Relief Appropriations Act (ERA), and finally under the Public Works Administration (PWA). These sources provided well over 50 percent of the annual funding for navy yard public works projects. Despite modest Navy appropriations for shipyard projects between 1933 and 1939, the navy yards experienced a 348 percent increase in public works expenditures. Also important is the fact that public works expenditures more than doubled between 1937 and 1939 thanks to large PWA and NRA funding increases. These two New Deal programs helped pave the way for the massive navy yard facility upgrades that followed when the funding floodgates were opened with the naval expansion acts in 1940.

Keeping with the required NIRA split of work between private and navy yards, Portsmouth Navy Yard and Electric Boat Company were each awarded two submarines in 1933. The orders for the Portsmouth submarines, USS *Porpoise* (SS 171) and USS *Pike* (SS 172), were placed on 19 June 1933.[28] Photo 4 in the gallery shows the laying of the keel for the *Pike* with a proud banner that reads, "Second Navy Yard Man of War Keel under NIRA, Submarine Pike, Dec. 20, 1933."

The first man-of-war under NIRA, the USS *Porpoise*, was commissioned 15 August 1935. The secretary of the navy complimented the shipyard on the completion of *Porpoise* ahead of schedule: "The *Porpoise* was authorized and appropriated for under the National Industrial Recovery Act of 1933, and the Department notes, with pleasure, that this vessel is not only the first vessel of this 1933 program to be completed but also that it has been completed fifteen days ahead of contract time."[29] With *Porpoise*, the yard began using an innovative and more efficient sectional construction process that contributed to its early delivery. Instead of custom building the submarine at one site, sections were preassembled in various locations of the shipyard and transported to the building ways for assembly prior to launching. The yard continued to perfect this process during the 1930s. *Porpoise* was but one of many early completions to follow. These accomplishments enhanced Portsmouth Navy Yard's reputation for timely construction, helping to ensure a steady flow of new construction contracts to the shipyard. This process, critical to the yard's success during World War II, will be discussed in detail in chapter 5.

The Works Progress Administration (WPA), part of the Emergency Relief Appropriations Act of 1935, was much more manageable than earlier New Deal labor programs, which were plagued with excessive bureaucracy and overlapping jurisdictional authority. Significant public works upgrades were possible under WPA projects, not just labor-intensive housekeeping chores as with the earlier programs. Over the next five years the shipyard became very adept at working with the WPA, and the WPA became very accommodating in meeting the needs of the shipyard.[30] New employees hired to perform WPA projects learned construction skills through on-the-job training programs and acquired important shipyard experience. The combined effect was to create a valuable and growing workforce, in place and capable of meeting the challenges soon to arrive.

By January 1941 it was impossible to distinguish civil service employees from relief workers in the shops at Portsmouth Navy Yard. The WPA assigned allotments, not workers, to the shipyard, and it became an accounting exercise to ensure workers were charged to the proper WPA budget line items.[31] As war approached and Defense Department budgets increased, the authorized shipyard employment ceiling was raised, and many employees moved from the WPA relief worker category directly to civil service status.[32] Hundreds of skilled relief workers, with several years of experience in the shipyard, were hired as permanent shipyard employees with a stroke of the pen and no disruption to shop projects or schedules. The WPA projects had been excellent on-the-job training for these workers.

Portsmouth Navy Yard Performance (1920–40)

It was not just the U.S. Navy's desire to develop the yard as a competitor for private industry that placed it in the preeminent position of submarine design and construction by the start of World War II. The shipyard's management team and skilled workforce demonstrated consistent, superlative performance. At the same time, it became management's strategy during the mid-1930s to optimize the new construction workload at two submarines per year and shed as much of the disruptive multiship repair and overhaul work as possible. This streamlining philosophy prevailed during World War II, undoubtedly aided by the geographical location of Portsmouth Navy Yard, remote from the heaviest action in the western Pacific Ocean. Unlike Mare Island Navy Yard in Vallejo, California, which became heavily involved in submarine repair and refit during the war, Portsmouth was able to focus its efforts on new construction.

According to the Bureau of Ships' World War II self-history, "At one time or another during the period after World War I new construction disappeared from every Navy Yard except Portsmouth."[33] This steady new construction workload enabled the shipyard to maintain a well-trained and stable workforce during the 1920s. Table 1 shows the number of employees at each of the navy yards between 1917 and 1929. The percent change in employment during that period shows the workforce stability that Portsmouth Navy Yard enjoyed over other navy yards. The employment levels at Portsmouth Navy Yard stayed remarkably constant from 1917 to 1929, when other navy yards showed great fluctuation, which would be expected when transitioning from war to peace. The employment at East Coast yards, with the exception of Portsmouth and Philadelphia, dropped precipitously, while the West Coast yards moved as dramatically in the positive direction. Because Portsmouth Navy Yard enjoyed some measure of stability during the declining period of the U.S. Navy (1922–31), it was poised and ready to capitalize on the awakening period (1932–36) and then perform with distinction during the rebuilding years (1936–45).

Table 1: Navy Yard Employees (1917–29)

	1917	1924	1926	1929	% Change
Portsmouth	1,650	1,600	1,950	1,700	+3%
New York	6,800	3,100	2,750	3,400	−50%
Norfolk	4,350	2,100	2,800	3,500	−20%
Philadelphia	3,350	3,000	2,750	3,100	−7%
Boston	2,950	2,050	2,600	1,550	−47%
Puget Sound	1,600	2,700	2,550	3,250	+103%
Charleston	1,700	400	450	450	−74%
Mare Island	2,900	2,350	2,450	4,350	+50%
Pearl Harbor	0	1050	950	800	—

Source: Assistant Secretary of the Navy, letter to Commandants Navy Yards, 7 July 1930, NARA Waltham, RG 181, Formerly Confidential Correspondence, Portsmouth Naval Shipyard, 1930–50, Box 3, Folder L5-3/NY, "Navy Yards Inspection of Equipment Machine Tools."

As requested, the Navy assigned Portsmouth Navy Yard an optimum workload of two submarines a year from 1934 through 1938. The secretary of the navy, impressed with Portsmouth's performance, assigned two submarines, USS *Sculpin* (SS 191) and USS *Squalus* (SS 192), under the 1937 appropriation; two more, USS *Searaven* (SS 196) and USS *Seawolf* (SS 197), under the 1938 appropriation; and two more, USS *Triton* (SS 201) and USS *Trout* (SS 202), under the 1939 appropriation. Table 2 compares new construction assignments at Portsmouth, Mare Island, and Electric Boat Company, the only shipyards involved with submarine construction immediately prior to World War II. The submarine workload, as required by law, was evenly divided between public and private yards, with Electric Boat getting all the private yard work. Electric Boat had reestablished itself as the preeminent private submarine yard by the mid-1930s, but with much less leverage over the Navy than it had enjoyed prior to 1920. This was in part owing to the emergence of Portsmouth as the preeminent submarine design yard. According to naval historian Gary Weir, "Electric Boat would still play a vital role in the submarine construction program, but would now do so within the context of both the Navy's expertise in submarine technology and its substantial design and construction capability at Portsmouth. Hence from 1931 to 1940 teamwork with the Navy was EB's only option."[34] The eve of World War II found Portsmouth Navy Yard filling the lead submarine design role that the Navy had envisioned for it at the close of World War I.

Table 2: Submarine Construction Shipyard Assignments (1934–39)

	1934	1935	1936	1937	1938	1939
Portsmouth	2	2	2	2	2	3
Mare Island	1	1	0	1	1	1
Electric Boat		2	3	3	3	3

Source: Bureau of Construction and Repair and Bureau of Engineering, joint letter, 15 September 1934; Secretary of the Navy, letter, 14 June 1937; and Bureau of Construction and Repair and Bureau of Engineering, joint letter, 10 August 1938, NARA Waltham, RG 181, Portsmouth Naval Base General Correspondence, Box 1, Folder A-1, "New Construction (1932–40)."

Portsmouth Navy Yard's design role had expanded even more in 1935, when the yard was funded for the "preparation and reproducing of working and finished plans, ordering materials, preparing war plans and booklets of general information, planning and clerical work," to support Mare Island Navy Yard for the construction of submarines SS 185, 186, and 187.[35] Portsmouth Navy Yard continued to expand its role as lead design yard for Mare Island Navy Yard such that by 1940 much "Portsmouth procured material" was being pushed to Mare Island for submarine construction.[36] Shortly after the war started, Portsmouth provided the same lead yard service for Cramp Shipbuilding Company of Philadelphia, Pennsylvania, to support the submarine contracts that had been awarded to that company.[37] Electric Boat provided similar submarine design support for Manitowoc Shipbuilding Company in Wisconsin during the war.

While Portsmouth Navy Yard was completing submarines ahead of schedule in the late 1930s, other yards were having difficulty completing ships on time. For example, in August 1938 the Bureau of Construction and Repair, in noting the yard's outstanding performance relative to contracted delivery dates, wrote, "The ability of the Portsmouth Yard to meet its completion dates has in recent years been amply demonstrated by the excellent and unique record established of meeting every contract date of delivery."[38] However, a few months later Secretary of the Navy Claude A. Swanson wrote that shipbuilding delays were "a matter of grave concern" and that the situation was "decidedly unsatisfactory." Swanson was especially disturbed about the late delivery of destroyer construction contracts in the navy yards.[39] The average construction period had increased to forty-four months with little sign of improvement.

Portsmouth Navy Yard commandant Rear Adm. C. W. Cole took advantage of Secretary Swanson's concern about shipbuilding delays and on 11 January 1939 responded with a letter that advertised Portsmouth Navy Yard's recent early deliveries. The same letter also rescheduled three additional submarines for early completions and strongly suggested that Portsmouth should not be grouped with those yards having problems meeting scheduled completion dates. Cole's letter stated, "This yard has consistently met or anticipated its completion dates on new construction during the past four years. . . . With close attention to detail, cooperation of all hands, and Portsmouth Navy Yard's established skillful workmanship, the new dates can be met, and the shipbuilding record continued that is unequaled elsewhere in this country."[40] During the late 1930s Rear Admiral Cole and his management team conducted a justified self-promotion public relations program that emphasized the yard's superior performance and solicited a continued optimum workload of two or three submarines per year.

Portsmouth had been on a five-year roll of early deliveries when on 23 May 1939 disaster struck. While on predelivery sea trials off the Isles of Shoals, the USS *Squalus* (SS 192) sank, losing twenty-six officers and men. Subsequent investigation revealed that the main air induction valve had failed to close when the submarine submerged. The cause of the failure was never conclusively established. Thirty-three survivors were brought to the surface on 25 May 1939 in a historic rescue operation. The submarine was successfully raised on 13 September 1939 and eventually recommissioned as USS *Sailfish* (SS 192). She would become the first American submarine to sink a Japanese aircraft carrier.[41]

Five years of superlative shipyard performance had been instantly clouded by the sinking of the *Squalus*. The incident slowed, but by no means stopped, the mobilization rush at the shipyard. By late 1940 the naval expansion acts had significantly accelerated the Navy shipbuilding program.[42] The Bureau of Yards and Docks urged shipyards to pull out all the stops to complete those public works projects needed to support the ship construction program.

Chapter 2

Ramp-Up

We have drawn the sword. That sword will not be returned to its scabbard until our enemies who would destroy liberty, have been themselves destroyed. Under these grim conditions which call forth our resolution, our outrage, and our spirit of self-sacrifice we face, unafraid, those dangers that lie ahead.

—SECRETARY OF THE NAVY FRANK KNOX,
Washington, D.C., January 1942

Portsmouth Navy Yard ramped up for war during the two years between June 1940 and June 1942. Massive facility upgrades were started and many completed, thousands of new employees were hired, and orders for dozens of new submarines were received. This transition period was extremely challenging and chaotic, but eminently successful.

The need for the unprecedented rapid buildup of shipyard infrastructure and labor can be traced back to the nation's reluctance to shed its strong stance on neutrality during the late 1930s and a general belief that preparations for war might, in fact, precipitate war. Historian Robert Dallek wrote, "Roosevelt [in late 1939] resisted pressure for substantial increases in national defense forces and rapid industrial mobilization . . . fearful that these actions would agitate suspicions about his peaceful intentions and make any neutrality change appear as a step towards war."[1] In January 1940, when President Roosevelt did seek to increase the total national defense appropriation from $1.5 billion to $1.8 billion for the 1941 fiscal year, Congress "whittled away, even at that modest sum." In addition, historian David M. Kennedy wrote, "The Nye Committee's sensational accusations of World War I profiteering left many corporations [as late as January 1940] gun-shy about accepting orders for armaments."[2] Five months later the passage of the 11 Percent Naval Expansion Act signaled an end to congressional whittling of defense budgets and corporate reluctance to accept armament orders.

When urging the passage of the increased naval appropriation bills in 1940, the chief of naval operations, Adm. Harold R. Stark, warned Congress, "Dollars cannot buy yesterday."[3] Yet, with the bills' passage, the nation's shipyards were able to recover from years of inadequate funding during the eighteen months preceding the attack on Pearl Harbor. In an unprecedented burst of industrial activity, the shipyards overcame two decades of fiscal neglect by expeditiously completing facilities and doubling or tripling workforces as needed to construct large numbers of ships and submarines.

The national industrial mobilization escalated with each passing German advance in Europe. The president declared a limited national emergency on 8 September 1939, when Germany began aggressive actions in Eastern Europe. The fall of France in June 1940 motivated the passing of the 11 Percent Naval Expansion Act on 14 June 1940 and the 70 Percent Naval Expansion Act on 19 July 1940. The 11 Percent Act authorized increasing the fleet by 167,000 tons, including aircraft carriers (79,500 tons), cruisers (66,500 tons), and submarines (21,000 tons).[4] The 70 Percent Act authorized increasing the fleet by 1,325,000 tons, including aircraft carriers (200,000 tons), cruisers (420,000 tons), destroyers (250,000 tons), submarines (70,000 tons), and capital ships (385,000 tons).[5]

Midway between these two acts the Navy's leadership transitioned. Frank Knox became the secretary of the navy on 11 July 1940, and a month later James Forrestal became undersecretary of the navy.[6] Thus, the summer of 1940 brought new naval leadership and a surge of new construction contracts for naval ships and facilities unlike anything ever seen before.

The steep ramp-up of facilities and labor continued in 1941 as shipbuilding and other industries were flooded with orders for armaments. Events in Europe continued to escalate, causing President Roosevelt to declare an unlimited national emergency on 27 May 1941. Germany invaded Russia in June 1941, an event signaling a major expansion of the war. Japanese forces then attacked Pearl Harbor on 7 December 1941. The United States was finally at war. The eighteen-month period preceding the attack on Pearl Harbor was a time of industrial turmoil as the nation reluctantly turned from neutrality and hopes for peace to full mobilization.

The summer of 1941 was concurrently a time of great transition and adjustment in the Navy Department and the navy yards. After years of struggling to manage with too little funding, the Navy suddenly had more funding than it could manage effectively. Robert Connery wrote, "In the pre-war years of peace the Navy's chief problem was to obtain dollars with which to purchase manpower, munitions, ships, and bases. . . . When the war came, and even to some extent before December 7, 1941, Congress voted huge sums of money without question. The House of Representatives, in one instance during the war, passed a 32 billion dollar appropriation bill in twenty minutes without debate and without a single question from the floor."[7] Portsmouth Navy Yard and the other mobilized shipyards were challenged to quickly convert the sudden funding bonanza into the facility and personnel resources needed to accelerate production.

In the early months of the conflict, it was uncertain at best whether the rapidly expanding war in Europe could be contained to that continent and the Atlantic Ocean. According to Rear Adm. Maurice H. Rindskopf, then a junior officer on the *Drum*, under construction at Portsmouth Navy Yard, "I rushed back to the ship [on 7 December 1941] and learned that *Drum* was supposed to provide the sole antiaircraft protection for the shipyard. We quickly had a 3-inch gun installed on the after deck. The administration building had a captain's walk on the tower. It was manned around the clock because of the expectation that German bombers would be along any moment."[8] A continued fear of enemy attack on the mainland accompanied the increased activity and building at the yard after 7 December 1941. On the day before Christmas 1941, the industrial officer, Capt. H. F. D. Davis, reminded his employees that any attack would most likely come on a Sunday or holiday so workers should be especially vigilant on those days.[9] The commandant, Rear Adm. John D. Wainwright, likewise reminded his managers in February 1942 that "The Axis Governments have used bombs ranging from 100 to 3000 pounds in their attacks on England," and consequently, "vessels in the yard should be berthed singly if possible, and as widely dispersed as feasible, commensurate with dock space available and repair facilities along the docks."[10] In this highly charged and threatening environment Portsmouth Navy Yard brought thousands of new employees on board and upgraded the facilities as needed to achieve the production demanded.

Facilities Ramp-Up

After two decades of neglect the shipyard infrastructure was transformed in a matter of months as the funding floodgates were opened and contracting rules were relaxed to accelerate mobilization. Twenty-one million dollars of infrastructure upgrades were authorized for Portsmouth Navy Yard between June 1940 and December 1941, and another $1 million was authorized for upgrades in January 1942.

Previously, in late November 1939, the Bureau of Construction and Repair anticipated the approaching war despite the nation's strong neutral stance. The bureau asked Portsmouth Navy Yard to identify what additional facilities, if any, it would need to build three or four submarines annually, for a total of eighteen, finishing in 1946.[11] Drawing on the experience gained during the 1930s, Portsmouth requested a fourth building way, an upgraded machine shop, and other miscellaneous needs, including continuation of the project converting the shipyard from DC to AC power.[12] Until 1940 the shipyard was supplied with direct current electrical power only. Conversion to AC was needed to more efficiently supply the increased electrical loads that would accompany the new and expanded facilities. Funding was quickly provided for these upgrades.

In June 1940 Portsmouth was authorized to construct eight submarines with building periods ranging from twenty-one to thirty-eight and a half months. Activity at the navy yard increased in the summer of 1940, but production expectations remained low compared to the construction rates that would be achieved just two years later.

A presidential visit on Saturday, 10 August 1940, highlighted the increased activity at the yard that summer. Ten motorcycle officers of the New Hampshire State Police and a dozen others of the Maine State Police escorted President Roosevelt and Secretary Knox in a parade of thirty-one cars from the Portsmouth train station to the shipyard. At the shipyard, the presidential party met briefly with the commandant, department heads, and others and then took a short tour of the yard. Photo 5 in the gallery shows FDR touring the shipyard. Figure A-1 in the appendix shows the route of the shipyard tour. During the tour, several stops were made to inspect work, ships, and shops. The president did not leave his car.

At the completion of the tour the president boarded his barge *Potomac*, which had docked at the yard the previous evening, and sailed for Boston Navy Yard. The president boarded his yacht just fifty-five minutes after he had arrived at the train station and just forty minutes after he had entered the shipyard's main gate. He was not able to see much shipyard activity during the expedited visit because the yard had been closed at 7:30 AM that Saturday to all but selected employees and visitors.[13] As short as it was, the visit was an important reminder to shipyard employees that the Navy's expectations of them were on the rise. August 1940 was a big month for Portsmouth Navy Yard. It received orders for the construction of eight submarines, millions of dollars for facility upgrades, and a visit from President Roosevelt. The ramp-up had started, but few at the time appreciated where it would lead them.

In October 1940 the chief of the Bureau of Yards and Docks urged the navy yards to take all measures possible to accelerate the completion of the public works projects in view of "the recent developments in the international situation." After the fall of France, it looked like it was only a matter of time until Germany and its allies invaded Great Britain. Navy yards were told, "Even if those facilities are only partially completed or if the design and construction are not to the usual Bureau standards, it is more important to have them available than it is to spend the additional time which might have to be expended in order to achieve a strived for, but impossible, perfection." Contractors were to be given "considerable latitude for the exercise of their judgment" and permitted to "proceed without the detail of inspection which the Bureau ordinarily exercises."[14] Empowerment of contractors and a willingness to sacrifice quality of product for timely project completion were critical to Portsmouth Navy Yard's ability to undertake and complete massive upgrades to facilities while simultaneously increasing the rate of submarine production.

By the spring of 1941 Congressman Carl Vinson of Georgia and other national leaders who recognized the inevitability of war moved to appropriate funds to increase shipyard employment and upgrade facilities. Vinson, chairman of the Naval Affairs Committee, queried the yard in March 1941 about its problems with material deliveries, its current capabilities, and what it needed to accelerate delivery dates by 20 percent. Captain Davis replied that material deliveries were under control, a third building way had been completed in August 1940, and the fourth building way was nearing completion.[15] The yard had identified a need for these additional building ways shortly after the Franklin Shiphouse had burned to the ground with its two building ways on 10 March 1936.[16] That the building ways were not replaced until late 1940 is further evidence that minimal investment in needed facilities was provided Portsmouth Navy Yard during the 1930s. In his response to Vinson, Davis added that the yard had studied "the possibility of laying down one or two more temporary ground ways between the present ways" should they become necessary. Congress wanted to accelerate submarine building rates, and Portsmouth Navy Yard was already looking for opportunities to meet and exceed expectations.

On 29 June 1941, with the shipyard mobilization nearing its peak, Portsmouth Navy Yard was further challenged with another submarine sinking. Just two years after the *Squalus* disaster, the submarine *O-9* sank off Portsmouth Harbor on a test-dive shortly after its arrival from New London, Connecticut. Unlike the *Squalus*, which sunk in 200 feet of water, recovery operations were impossible because the *O-9* sank in water 370 feet deep. Thirty-three men were lost on the *O-9*. Tragic as it was, the loss of the submarine did not slow the shipyard's mobilization.[17]

The First Supplemental National Defense Appropriation Act, approved 25 August 1941, appropriated $160 million for equipment and facilities for the repair and conversion of ships and increased the appropriations for the construction of new ships from $5 billion to $8 billion.[18] The next month Secretary Knox approved Portsmouth Navy Yard's request for $7.662 million for facility upgrades, including a new fitting-out pier ($1.5 million) and power plant upgrades ($1.5 million). The approval process that brought the $7.7 million to Portsmouth was the height of bureaucratic efficiency as the necessary approvals that normally took weeks—if not months—to obtain were acquired from the chief of naval operations, assistant secretary of the navy, and secretary of the navy in four days. There appeared to be no end to the congressional commitment to fund upgrades to shipyard facilities or to the Navy's commitment to expedite those funds to the yards. Both the commitment and funding would moderate a year later when an urgent need developed to funnel critical materials and other resources directly to weapons and armament rather than to facilities. By that time, however, Portsmouth Navy Yard was well on its way to becoming a transformed shipyard.

The power plant upgrades authorized in the fall of 1941 accelerated the conversion of the shipyard from DC to the much more efficient AC power. This conversion started before the war, continued during the war, and remained incomplete in some areas at the end of the war.[19] The second major project, the fitting-out pier, involved reclamation of twelve acres of shoal water and wetlands on the corner of the shipyard directly across the river from Portsmouth's Strawbery Banke. This project permitted the remarkable increase in building rates achieved during the war.[20]

Construction of a new fitting-out pier was an enormous task to undertake during this period. Filling in Pumpkin Island Shoal created the portion of the pier closest to the Portsmouth side of the river (seen at the top of photo 6 in the gallery). Without the new fitting-out pier, there would have been insufficient pier space to accomplish the postlaunch work required on the increasing numbers of submarines coming off the ways. The new pier accommodated up to a half dozen submarines in various stages of construction as they were advanced from berth to berth for the postlaunch work required prior to dock trials and completion.

Prior to the construction of the new fitting-out pier, the submarines were completed at a much smaller pier, known as the flatiron pier, shown in figure A-2. In October 1941, about the time that the new pier was authorized, the superintendent of the flatiron pier became alarmed when the number of submarines at the pier increased from two to four; fitting-out work was not being completed owing to a lack of labor. He proposed that the pier workforce be doubled to 1,010 and that the submarines remain on the building ways longer to minimize the work that had to be done at the pier.[21] This, of course, was contrary to the "push 'em off the ways" strategy that carried the yard to production records a few years later. On the eve of the attack on Pearl Harbor, the four building ways were launching submarine hulls faster than the available space and workforce at the flatiron pier could handle. Had it not been for the spacious new fitting-out pier and the capability to more efficiently sequence the postlaunch-to-completion process, the yard would never have been able to achieve the building rates that it did.

Robert Connery notes, "In the dark days that followed Pearl Harbor many Americans must have realized how fortunate was the decision to begin the expansion of the fleet in 1940."[22] Portsmouth Navy Yard certainly shared in that good fortune as many major projects were well under way before the war started. Immediately after Pearl Harbor, the shipyard sought further improvements to increase building rates. It requested and quickly received an additional $2 million for projects that included the construction of a shallow shipbuilding basin (later upgraded to dry dock #3) in which two submarines could be constructed at a time, the fifth building way, a subassembly erection shop extension at the shipbuilding ways, and a utility building at the new fitting-out pier.[23] All of this shipyard activity and more that followed in early 1942 was facilitated by the First War Powers Act of December 1941, which permitted contracts to be negotiated rather than awarded through the time-consuming, competitive bidding process.

In January 1942 the shipyard began work on a fifth building way in the building shed and a fifty-foot extension of the roof and crane runways to accommodate a sub assembly erection shop.[24] The first was a relatively inexpensive $75,000 project, but the second was a $1.1 million major construction project designed to further refine Portsmouth's sectional construction process, which had first been used on the NIRA submarines in 1934. Fred White recalled working on submarine keels on the building ways while engulfed in sparks from welding on the roof of the building shed.[25] It is a credit to the shipyard workers that increased submarine construction rates could be achieved in the midst of such massive facility upgrades.

By December 1942 the shipyard had created a number of opportunities for increased production. The five building ways were launching submarines at unprecedented rates, the new fitting-out pier and increased workforce had progressed far enough to keep up with the submarines being launched, and the new building basin was in operation.[26] With plans to launch submarines after only four months on a building way, the existing seven building ways could produce twenty-one submarines per year. However, shipyard management had bigger plans: "Our goal is 30 ships per year; this rate is to be reached by July or August 1943. Our obvious requirement is more building ways. At least 2 and preferably 3 ways will be needed by April [1943] in order to come anywhere near meeting the schedule." The shipyard had two options to obtain the additional building ways. Two side launching ways could be built at one of the berths in four or five months for about $90,000, or the new dry dock that had been designated by the Bureau of Ships and the chief of naval operations for war damage and emergency repairs could be used for construction of two, or possibly three, submarines at the same time.[27] The yard had started planning locally for the building of multiple submarines in the new dry dock #1 shortly after the Pearl Harbor attack.[28] This local plan was somewhat controversial because the Navy Department had authorized the building of the new dry dock for other purposes. The yard's performance during the war would have been average at best if this new dry dock had been used as originally intended and not for the construction of submarines.

A comparison of figures A-1 (1939 map of the yard) and A-2 (1945 map of the yard) in the appendix gives an overall sense of the transformation that occurred at the yard during the war years. The major differences between the lower left and upper right corners of the maps are noteworthy. The lower left corner of the 1945 map shows the new twelve-acre, trapezoid-shaped fitting-out pier, the new dry dock #1, the new building basin, and the upgraded building ways. The building ways were increased from three partially covered to five completely covered ways shielding the work from harsh New Hampshire winters. These sites became the heart of submarine construction operations during the war. Comparison of the upper right corners of the maps shows the filling of channel and shoal waters to connect and develop Jamaica Island as an ammunition storage facility (discussed later in the chapter). There were many other shipyard upgrades, but these were the most important.

The ramp-up in facilities at Portsmouth Navy Yard during the eighteen months preceding Pearl Harbor was by no means unique. According to the Bureau of Yards and Docks World War II history, "The public works programs at these [navy] yards, during the last eighteen months of peace was concentrated on providing, with the utmost dispatch, the vast expansion of facilities for the effective accomplishment of this Herculean task [building the two-ocean Navy]. . . . Many individual projects were already complete by December 7, 1941, well ahead of schedule. Their early availability contributed significantly to the rapid mobilization of the fleet and the speedy conversion of merchant vessels taken over by the Navy."[29] Large facility upgrades were under way at all navy yards and many private shipyards at the same time that Portsmouth Navy Yard was undergoing expansion of its facilities.[30]

At Mare Island Navy Yard, the other navy yard building submarines, a large dry dock, which would give the yard a total of four dry docks, was under construction, as were four additional building ways, increasing the total to eight. More remarkably, the shipyard's acreage would increase from 635 to 1,500 acres, including much reclaimed land, during the war years.[31] At the only private submarine shipyard, Electric Boat, expansion was also the order of the day. In early 1942 the North and South yards of the Electric Boat plant were expanded, and a total of eleven building ways were installed at a cost of nearly $5 million. A little later, the Navy purchased Groton Iron Works for use by Electric Boat, and ten more ways were set up. The Navy appropriated $9.5 million for this construction. This new yard, Victory Yard, was opened 22 July 1942.[32]

Thus, the numerous shipyards on both coasts duplicated the building boom that Portsmouth Navy Yard experienced in 1941 and 1942. As compared to 1933, when only six private yards and eight navy yards were in operation, "by December 1941, the number of yards engaged in new construction had expanded to 156 and those concerned with conversion and repair had expanded to 76."[33] The story of the Portsmouth ramp-up must be multiplied dozens of times to get a sense of the nation's rush to construct the long-neglected shipyard facilities that were going to be needed to build the fleet necessary to win the war.

In June 1942 the need to direct all available funds and critical materials to the fleet caused Secretary of the Navy Knox to require increased control and scrutiny of requests for shipyard facility upgrades.[34] In November 1942 Secretary Knox further shut down facility construction by establishing firm guidelines that permitted consideration of only the most urgent needs. According to Knox, "The rapid diminution in available and prospective supplies of raw materials and equipment and the vital need for conserving these and our critical manpower, dictate a drastic reduction of new facilities, both in prospect and in process, so that the maximum of men, material, equipment, and transportation resources may be utilized for the more important instruments of war."[35] In December 1942 the secretary sent his special representative, Rear Adm. Claude C. Bloch, to all continental naval districts with the message, "We are scraping the bottom of the bucket" and drastic conservation measures were needed to support the war effort. The admiral specifically highlighted the need to limit facility construction to only the absolutely necessary so that more of the Navy's funds could be channeled to fleet production:

> The increased demand for construction on shore by all departments, both military and civilian, as well as by the states, counties, municipalities, and private parties, has gone on apace. Recently, statistical data has been prepared which shows that the construction program desired for the calendar year of 1943 amounts to thirty-two billion dollars. The entire production capacity of this country for war implements is only estimated to be seventy-five billion dollars. Therefore it can readily be seen what a tremendous burden the construction program would impose on our war implement production. Drastic measures are in order to reduce the construction so that production of our war implements may proceed unimpaired.[36]

By the end of 1942, when the Navy moved to cut back on facility projects, Portsmouth Navy Yard had already received the infusion of facility improvement appropriations it needed to transform itself into a modern high-capacity shipyard.

According to Frederic C. Lane, "Before 1942, in spite of some temporary steel shortages, shipbuilding was limited mainly by shipyard facilities. But by June or July of 1942, facilities got ahead of steel."[37] By late 1942 facilities had also been completed at Portsmouth Navy Yard to the point that steel and other contractor-supplied material and components controlled the pace of construction. Facilities were nearing completion, employment was increasing, and most importantly, quality submarines were being delivered to the U.S. Navy. On Christmas Eve 1942 Commandant Rear Admiral Withers announced to his management team with considerable pride, "A Portsmouth boat [not named for security reasons] has just reported operating 210 days out of 245 since completion . . . inflicting damage on the enemy just 492 days after the keel was laid."[38] Portsmouth employees could indeed reflect with considerable pride on their accomplishments during the first year of the war.

Off-Yard Growth

Despite the massive ramp-up in facilities, the physically constrained island shipyard still required more industrial space to fulfill its mission. In addition to the twelve acres of industrial space and the creation of the new fitting-out pier, another twelve acres were claimed when the shipyard was joined through landfills to Jamaica Island to create an ordnance storage facility. The creation of an electrical shop in Somersworth, New Hampshire, twenty miles from the shipyard, added valuable off-yard shop space. At its peak, this shop employed as many people as the entire shipyard did in 1939. In addition, a large gypsum plant in Portsmouth was leased and converted to provide much-needed support for the shipyard machine shops.

In early 1941 the Bureau of Ordnance directed Commandant Wainwright to investigate the possibility of purchasing Jamaica Island for the purpose of ammunition storage. The twelve-acre island was a stone's throw from the northeast corner of the shipyard island, across a shallow inlet. Commandant Wainwright contacted the owner, Dr. W. B. Johnston, in January 1941 to gauge his interest in selling the island.[39] Negotiations took place over most of that year and had progressed far enough by October 1941 for Wainwright to provide the Bureau of Ordnance an estimated price for the ordnance storage facilities: $327,000, including $30,000 to purchase the island.[40] The deal was announced in the judge advocate general's message of 7 December 1941: "Johnston option [$25,000] Jamaica Island accepted today."[41] The purchase of Jamaica Island had been agreed to just a few hours before the Japanese surprise attack on Pearl Harbor.

Jamaica Island's subsequent development and its connection to the shipyard proper through the reclamation of channel and shoal waters with fill that included contaminated industrial waste products cast a dark shadow on the yard's otherwise brilliant record during the war. The dumping of contaminated industrial waste continued well into the 1970s. Environmental Protection Agency (EPA) studies in the 1980s found extensive evidence of disposal of hazardous materials, including chromium, lead and cadmium-plating sludge, asbestos insulation, volatile organic compounds, waste and paint solvents, mercury-contaminated materials, and sandblasting grit containing various metal wastes. According to those studies, many of these materials were dumped on the shipyard's tidal flats as part of land reclamation projects, with the Jamaica Island landfill being the most extensive and seriously contaminated. The Jamaica Island landfill and other contaminated sites caused the shipyard to be placed on the national priorities list for Superfund projects in 1994. Recovery actions to date have required the expenditure of millions of dollars in cleanup projects.[42]

The rapid relocation of the electrical manufacturing shop in early 1942 to a vacated plant in Somersworth, New Hampshire, is one of the shipyard's more impressive accomplishments during the war. The need for the facility was dictated by the expansion of naval orders for electrical hull fittings, the mechanical connectors that accommodate the passage of electrical cables through watertight bulkheads and tanks, from $175,000 per month in 1940 to $1.9 million per month in 1943. Accordingly, shop employment expanded from a prewar average of 400 to a peak of 3,600 in the winter of 1943.[43]

Portsmouth Navy Yard records indicate that the move of the shipyard's electrical manufacturing shop to the plant at Somersworth was accomplished so efficiently that "no machine was out of production for more than an 8-hour shift."[44] The facility performed with impressive results during the war and, having served its purpose, was made available for disposal in 1946.[45]

In December 1943 the shipyard leased buildings owned by the Atlantic Gypsum Products Company in Portsmouth. The yard needed additional space for the manufacture of machined parts and assemblies. Without the gypsum plant, the yard would have been forced to do considerable assembly work in areas outside the shops, with minimal protection from the weather. The gypsum plant consisted of sixty acres, thirteen buildings, and numerous docks for nine railroad spurs.[46] Used as a shipyard during World War I, this complex also served the nation and Portsmouth Navy Yard well during World War II. The Navy released control of the plant in late 1945.[47]

Figure A-3 shows the effect of the addition of the Somersworth Electrical Shop and the gypsum plant. In particular, the sharp rise in employees assigned to "manufacturing" and "miscellaneous" work from mid-1942 to late 1943 reflects the increasing workload at the Somersworth Electrical Shop.

Employment Ramp-Up

At the same time that the shipyard was being transformed geographically and structurally, thousands of new employees were being hired. The hiring began slowly in October 1939, when navy yard ceilings were eliminated.[48] Prior to that time, the shipyard was obligated to obtain the authorization of the assistant secretary of the navy to exceed 3,600 employees. On 2 August 1940, as the funding flood gates were being opened, the shipyard reported that employment levels had increased to 5,843, with plans to further increase to the 6,440 employees required to complete the assigned workload of eight submarines. Always looking for ways to do better, the yard volunteered that a building rate of six submarines a year could be sustained, without additional facility upgrades, with a further increase to 8,400 employees and by taking advantage of local commercial firms for selective farm-out work.

The rapid growth in employment was not without problems. In February 1941 Hull Superintendent F. A. Tusler made the following observation regarding the recent rapid increase in employment:

> During the past year or more the Yard has taken on a large number of new men, the training of whom differs widely. It is believed that these men can be adequately trained if placed with older men who are familiar with the work. . . . It is recognized that old men with a large amount of submarine experience are more valuable than green men, even though competent mechanics. . . . Helpers and helper-trainees who have been rated up to mechanic must necessarily be placed on tasks with which they are familiar.[49]

Tusler's comments, about the value of older men with submarine experience, illustrate the importance of the yard's maintenance of a satisfactory workload and a core workforce during the late 1930s.

Ramp-Up of Submarine Orders

During the three months prior to Pearl Harbor, the Navy awarded 1,625 contracts for purchases exceeding $50,000 each, totaling $1.47 billion dollars. During the three months after Pearl Harbor, 2,917 similar contracts that totaled $5.327 billion were issued.[50] Portsmouth Navy Yard shared in this ordering frenzy. The large number of advance orders for submarines permitted bulk ordering of material and development of repetitive work procedures that would be critical for the mass production of submarines.

Orders for new submarines started to increase rapidly as the threat of war increased. On 26 August 1940 the War Planning Office told the shipyard to "increase new construction activity until a maximum output of six submarines a year is attained."[51] One year prior to Pearl Harbor, the shipyard was increasing its building rate from two to six submarines a year, still very modest when compared to the building rates that would be achieved in the coming years.

In the spring of 1941, when Congressman Vinson queried the yard about the possibility of accelerating completion dates for the submarines under contract by 20 percent, Captain Davis responded with a schedule of accelerated delivery dates for fourteen submarines: nine to be completed in 1942 and five more by August 1943.[52] The yard would ultimately complete twenty-one submarines in that same time frame. The ramp-up in production planned in the spring of 1941 bore little resemblance to what actually happened in the first year and a half of the war. It is a credit to the management and employees of the navy yard that they could adjust so quickly to changing conditions.

In January 1942 the shipyard's mobilization was in full stride. While the yard was moving rapidly toward acquiring the infrastructure needed to accelerate production, much remained to be completed before major increases could be realized. The yard remained heavily burdened with miscellaneous work and the overhauls of British submarines, which detracted from the submarine construction tasks. Figure A-3 shows the high repair and miscellaneous workload that the yard experienced during the latter half of 1941.

On 2 January 1942 Commandant Wainwright reported to his superiors that one British submarine had been completed on 1 January 1942 and another would be completed on 22 January 1942. In addition, construction of the USS *Drum* (SS 228) was completed on 24 December 1941, the USS *Grayback* (SS 208) was on sea trials, and the USS *Flying Fish* (SS 229) was undergoing dock trials.[53] The three submarines were progressing toward completion on comfortable schedules that minimized mutual interference and competition for shipyard resources. The very high number of work hours expended per delivered submarine during the latter half of 1941, shown in figure A-4, suggests less urgency for submarine completions than would be the case a few months later.

Maximum building rates would require the assumption of more schedule risk and the multiple processing of submarines on other than a single file basis. A reduction of submarine repair work, both foreign and domestic, and sufficient new construction facilities to permit simultaneous construction processes would also

Table 3: Portsmouth Navy Yard Submarine Orders (1940–43)

Submarines	Order Quantity	Date of Order
SS 228–235	8	June 1940
SS 275–280	6	Sept. 1940
SS 285–291	7	Dec. 1941
SS 308–312	5	April 1942
SS 381–410	30	June 1942
SS 417–424	8	Feb. 1943
SS 298–299	2	Started at Cramp Shipbldg, completed at PNY
SS 475–515	40	June 1943
	106	

Source: *Administrative History: Portsmouth Navy Yard in World War II* (n.d., Portsmouth Naval Shipyard Museum Archives, Kittery, ME), 1.

be necessary for Portsmouth Navy Yard to achieve higher production rates. This streamlining of facilities and workload is exactly what happened as 1942 unfolded.

Portsmouth Navy Yard's can-do attitude and demonstrated performance during the early stages of the war quickly led to increased Navy Department orders for submarines, and this continued through June 1943. Table 3 shows submarine orders between June 1940 and June 1943. The fourteen submarines ordered in 1940 were the direct result of the naval expansion acts passed that summer. The next forty-two submarines ordered were part of the flood of contracts issued during the first six months of the war in a frantic effort to further accelerate war production.

—⁓—

Between the summers of 1940 and 1942, Portsmouth Navy Yard, along with the other navy yards and private shipyards, mobilized for war. The increased authorizations for naval construction during the late 1930s had infused the yards with work and increased employment. But it was not until the summer of 1940 that legislation for expanding the Navy provided the funds necessary for massive shipyard infrastructure upgrades. The need for infrastructure upgrades occurred simultaneously with huge increases in employment and orders for large numbers of new ships and submarines. At Portsmouth Navy Yard the successful integration of new facilities and personnel resources into the day-to-day shipyard operations, with minimal interference to production schedules, was a challenge that the yard readily accepted.

Chapter 3

Management

*Admiral Withers was a man whom everybody liked because he let
everyone do their job.*

—FRED WHITE, 3 April 2006

A t this point it is well to ask the question, What part of the shipyard's success
was owing purely to the stimulation of war and what part was owing to
other factors? This unanswerable question recognizes the special environment that existed at the yard during the war—a crisis-filled environment that rallied employees and management to the common objective of increased production
to defeat the enemy. While the atmosphere surely contributed to heightened performance and an increased willingness to embrace organizational and production
change, it alone did not increase production. However, innovative management
working with a skilled workforce in an environment ripe for change can lead to
impressive results. That is what happened at Portsmouth Navy Yard during World
War II. That said, the next three chapters examine those other factors that contributed to the yard's success.

On one level, Portsmouth Navy Yard's remarkable performance can be attributed to superior leadership, massive hiring, extensive facility upgrades, effective
training programs, innovative production techniques, and an intelligent and highly
dedicated workforce. Another level of analysis shows that each of these attributes
contained its own set of challenges. The massive hiring added large numbers of
women and untrained employees to the shipyard workforce. Training programs
were constantly disrupted by the loss of the younger and more physically qualified
workers to military service. The facility upgrades, funded in 1940 after two decades
of neglect and minimal investment in shipyard infrastructure, were extensive and
disruptive to the accelerated submarine construction schedules. Clearly wartime
mobilization brought with it a new set of unprecedented challenges for shipyard
management.

Industrial Surveys

This book draws heavily from four World War II industrial studies. Independent management consulting firms under the sponsorship of the Office of the Secretary of the Navy conducted two of the studies. The other two are self-assessments by a Portsmouth Navy Yard industrial survey team. Because of their importance to this book, a discussion follows providing background and context for the studies.

The first independent survey was a September 1942 review of four navy yards (New York, Philadelphia, Bremerton, and Mare Island) by Industrial Relations Counselors Inc. as directed by Assistant Secretary of the Navy Ralph Bard.[1] The study evaluated the production efficiency and needs of each yard. While Portsmouth was not included in the survey, the results permit comparisons of Portsmouth to the yards surveyed. The second independent study, also directed by the Office of the Secretary of the Navy, was an assessment of Portsmouth Navy Yard's Industrial Department completed in late 1944.[2] The results provide an independent assessment of Portmouth's industrial operations during the war and a balance to the wealth of archival shipyard self-appraisals cited throughout this book. These two external studies will be referred to as SecNav Industrial Survey #1 (1942) and SecNav Industrial Survey #2 (1944).

The two surveys had different purposes. SecNav Industrial Survey #1 (1942) was a cursory survey of four navy yards conducted to provide feedback to Secretary of the Navy Knox regarding the effectiveness of the millions of dollars that had been spent on facility upgrades over the previous two years. The nation was in the early stage of a war whose outcome was still in doubt, and the pressure to maximize the navy yards' capabilities was on. While the auditors were careful not to overly criticize or condemn the efforts of the mobilizing yards, they were also quick to point out areas needing improvement to maximize production at each yard.

On the other hand, SecNav Industrial Survey #2 (1944) focused more on postwar operations than on maximizing production to win the war. Although this survey congratulated Portsmouth Navy Yard for its war record, it emphasized the changes needed to adjust to the fast-approaching reduction in workload and workforce. Of paramount concern was a desire to end the crisis management modus operandi that had characterized wartime operations and return to more structured and disciplined management with emphasis on cost monitoring and control.

The third and fourth studies are Portsmouth Navy Yard Industrial Department self-assessments that were issued on 8 December 1941 and 6 June 1942. The 8 December 1941 report provides an extensive analysis of the yard's production status and needs to achieve increased building rates.[3] The 6 June 1942 report provides extensive analysis of the yard's first six months of operations after Pearl Harbor.[4] It is a much more refined assessment of the yard's capabilities with a confident prognosis for future success. These Portsmouth Navy Yard self-assessments provide insight into much of management's thinking and actions during the war. They will be referred to as Portsmouth Industrial Survey #1 (December 1941) and Portsmouth Industrial Survey #2 (June 1942).

In conjunction with an accelerated shipbuilding program, in September 1941 the secretary of the navy announced the inauguration of a shipbuilding competition to commence 1 October to evaluate the efficiency of the nation's commercial and government shipyards. Five categories were to be evaluated: work progress, work quality, yard improvement, yard spirit, and the overall opinion of the evaluating board of officers.[5] The first three categories relied on the typical indicators of shipyard performance as measured by schedule adherence, inspection records, and test results. The last two—yard spirit and overall opinion of the board—addressed the intangibles needed to build mobilization momentum.

The board, with Rear Adm. H. E. Yarnell as the senior member, visited Portsmouth Navy Yard on 5 November 1941 to kick off the competition.[6] Each yard was to be evaluated quarterly and awards would be given quarterly, semiannually, and annually. The annual award for the best shipyard of each group was to be known as the Victory Award. Private shipyards were assigned to one of four regions. All navy yards were grouped together for evaluation purposes. The competition, obviously designed to motivate all shipyards to review internal capabilities and processes to eliminate waste and improve efficiency, had exactly the desired effect at Portsmouth Navy Yard. Commandant Wainwright established a well-qualified local review board to recommend improvements to new construction processes and practices. The board was in the final steps of its review on the day Pearl Harbor was attacked and published its initial findings the next day, 8 December 1941.[7]

The board continued to function after the war started and issued an updated report in June 1942. It consisted of six officers under the leadership of the shipyard's planning officer, Capt. Andrew I. McKee, and showed a clear understanding of shipyard industrial management and Portsmouth Navy Yard's needs in particular. The 8 December 1941 and 6 June 1942 reports are comprehensive at fifteen pages each and provide a convenient firsthand summary of activity at Portsmouth Navy Yard at the start and during the first six months of the war. In addition to valuable facts and figures, the studies are rich in analysis of the shipyard's needs and opportunities. The two reports served the intended purpose of kick-starting increased wartime production at the yard. While no follow-on reports are extant in the archives, the modified wartime work practices and the yard's physical transformation indicate that the shipyard continued to aggressively pursue and improve upon the recommendations contained in these two reports.

A comparison of the tone of the two studies, six months apart, suggests an attitude change on the part of the board and shipyard management. The first study reflects confidence in the yard's abilities to make the necessary changes to ramp-up production to meet expectations but expresses concerns about the details of that transition. The second report takes considerable pride in the yard's demonstrated performance during the first six months of the war and aggressively proposes opportunities, not just to meet, but also to exceed expectations. The first report focused on potential production limitations owing to local restraints. The second report reflects great confidence that the shipyard's performance can be limited only by external factors, especially the contractors' ability to provide timely delivery of components to support accelerated schedules. However, the board refused to accept schedule delays for any reason and recommended ways to work around disruptive factors.

These two shipyard self-assessments are not self-congratulatory or self-serving. The immediate threat of war, in the first case, and the early stages of war, in the second case, had cut through any ulterior motives or conclusions. The teams consisted of representatives from various shipyard departments who had the same objective: to define those actions needed to enable their shipyard to do its part to win the war. Captain McKee, who had been the planning officer since March 1938, was very knowledgeable of the yard's practices and capabilities. The reports are more critical of the support departments than the Industrial Department, calling for better planning, provisioning of material, and liaison of the support departments with the industrial scheduling department. In effect, the team called for maximum streamlining of all shipyard functions toward submarine construction. That is precisely what happened in the months that followed.

Navy Department—World War II

The next several chapters often refer to various Navy Department bureaus and commands to which Portsmouth Navy Yard was responsible and deal considerably with a power struggle within the Navy Department for control of navy yards that can be confusing to the reader unfamiliar with naval matters and organization. Figure 3 is a chart showing the chain of command and organizational flow of responsibilities and authority from the secretary of the navy to the navy yard commandants and shipyard departments that existed during World War II. This chart will be referred to frequently to provide context and a clearer understanding of the complex, and sometimes confusing, organizational structure in which the navy yards were required to operate during the war. At this point, it is sufficient to note that Frank Knox was secretary of the navy for most of the war—from 11 July 1940 until his sudden death on 28 April 1944. Knox's undersecretary and assistant for procurement and production, James V. Forrestal, succeeded him (19 May 1944 to 17 September 1947). Knox's other civilian assistant was Ralph Bard,

Figure 3. Navy Department World War II Organizational Chart

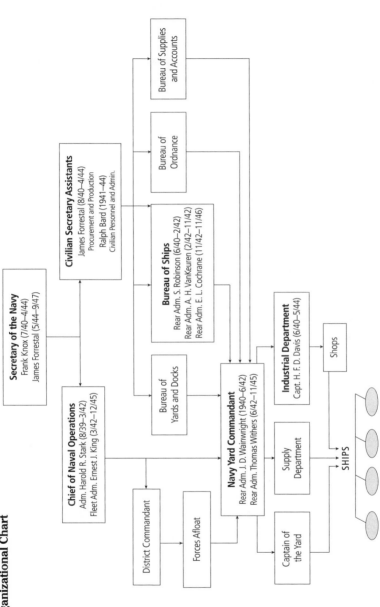

Source: *Administrative History: Bureau of Ships in World War II*, Naval Department World War II Admin History #89, 1946, Navy Department Library, Naval Historical Center, Washington, D.C., Chart 5, "Flow Chart—World War II"

assistant secretary of the navy for civilian personnel and administration. Two officers held the position of chief of naval operations during the war, Adm. Harold R. Stark (1 August 1939 to 2 March 1942) and Fleet Adm. Ernest J. King (26 March 1942 to 15 December 1945).

Robert Connery notes that on the eve of World War II Navy Department responsibilities for planning the Navy's industrial mobilization were ambiguous. According to Connery, "The Chief of Naval Operations, the material bureaus, and the Secretary's office all had some part in planning but their various roles were never clearly defined. The most serious consequence was lack of aggressive leadership in the industrial planning field. There were jurisdictional conflicts to be sure, but these were not nearly as serious as lack of interest arising from divided responsibility."[8] Things began to change for the better in August 1940, when Forrestal took office as the first undersecretary of the navy with responsibility for all material procurement. Forrestal, in time, did provide the leadership, structure, and clarification that the Navy needed for the industrial mobilization. However, the undersecretary was still organizing his new office early in the war, at the same time that the newly formed Bureau of Ships was struggling to get organized.

Figure 3 shows two primary paths from which authority flowed to the navy yard commandants. In the case of Portsmouth Navy Yard, the first path, through the chief of naval operations, primarily concerned the maintenance of the existing submarine fleet and the care and administration of the sailors and officers who manned those submarines. The chief of naval operations set priorities and schedules. The second path, through the undersecretary of the navy for procurement and production, primarily concerned matters pertaining to the construction of new submarines, including the oversight of navy yard management through the Bureau of Ships.

Conflicts between policies for the construction of new submarines and those for the maintenance and overhaul of existing submarines complicated operations at Portsmouth Navy Yard during the war. The tension created by these conflicts frequently left yard managers trying to please two masters as they sought to streamline operations for the construction of new submarines and avoid the assignment of additional repair and overhaul work. Management's ability to walk this political tightrope to the satisfaction of both masters was an essential element of the yard's performance during the war.

Before this discussion moves on to a detailed analysis of industrial methods and practices, it is important to understand the context of the times, beginning with the situation at the Bureau of Ships and working down through the shipyard leadership and management to the waterfront industrial operations.

Decentralized Shipbuilding Environment

The naval shipbuilding environment during the war was highly decentralized, and the Navy Department kept relatively loose oversight of navy yards, especially those that were performing well. This environment existed because the newly created Bureau of Ships was overwhelmed with other matters and was unable to devote the attention to the navy yards that it otherwise should have. Established in June 1940, the Bureau of Ships was quickly consumed with the administrative burden of organizing a rapidly expanding bureaucracy while mobilizing civilian industry to support a massive wartime shipbuilding program.

By 1940 decentralization was gaining in popularity in private industry but had not achieved the widespread application that it would find after the war. At the turn of the century American industry was characterized by little product diversification and strong central management structures. With the development of the automotive industry, diversification of product increased, and decentralization eventually became the model of choice for managing numerous product lines. According to management historian Alfred D. Chandler, after World War I decentralization was advanced when some companies began to reorganize so that operations were "handled by autonomous management units . . . supervised by a central unit consisting of a staff of specialists and an executive office of generalists." Decentralization was not implemented by a high percentage of companies prior to World War II, however. Reporting the results of a late 1950s management study of sixteen major firms in the chemical, electrical, and automotive industries, Chandler wrote, "Twelve [firms] have come since 1921 to such a decentralized structure. Eight have done so since 1940."[9] Debate about optimal industrial management structure was put on hold during the 1930s as concern about the availability of work took precedence over concerns about worker productivity. As World War II began, no management philosophy prevailed for how best to organize for maximum production.[10] The urgencies associated with wartime mobilization, especially the need to maximize production quickly, accelerated the move toward decentralization in the Bureau of Ships.

Frederic C. Lane, Christopher Tassava, and others have noted that wartime urgency demanded loose organizational structure and decentralization of the commercial shipbuilding industry.[11] According to Tassava, it was decentralization that freed Bechtel and Kaiser to build "breathtaking" numbers of commercial ships, especially Liberty ships.[12] In the case of Portsmouth, the yard was not just decentralized from the Bureau of Ships but released to operate as independently as possible. In the process, Portsmouth Navy Yard achieved its own breathtaking results.

In comparison to the detailed supervision and guidance imposed by the Naval Sea Systems Command on naval shipyards today, Portsmouth Navy Yard received relatively little direction from higher authority during the war. The navy yard's immediate supervisor during World War II was the Bureau of Ships, which spent a good part of the war in a crisis management mode and had little opportunity to oversee shipyard operations. To a large extent, each navy yard was an entrepreneurial operation whose success or failure depended on local management decisions and initiative.

According to the Bureau of Ships history of its operations during the war, "The role of the Bureau of Ships in management and supervision of the work in the naval industrial establishments had been restricted, in spite of its predominant interest, and had been subject to qualifications and limitations." The result was "decentralized, independent organizational growth" with each navy yard having different responsibilities and a variety of procedures to fulfill those responsibilities.[13] SecNav Industrial Survey #1 (1942) commented on the lack of coordination, communication, cross-training, and sharing of experiences between navy yards.[14] The Bureau of Ships might have been able to coordinate some activities between yards performing similar work, but it did not. In essence, each navy yard was left to independently develop and tailor processes and procedures to their own individual needs. Portsmouth Navy Yard's ability to develop processes and procedures that took advantage of existing facility and workforce attributes proved to be quite exceptional.

The change that left the navy yards lacking in organizational oversight during World War II had its roots in a long and tortured history of indecision about how best to manage and administer the yards. A 1945 survey of current navy yard operations, conducted by the Navy's Organization Planning and Procedures Unit, traced that volatile history to over a century of debate about the proper relationship between the secretary of the navy and the yards, the most efficient relationship between the Navy Department bureaus and the yards, and the optimum internal organization of navy yards.[15] According to the Bureau of Ships self-history, the tension can be traced to the post–Civil War alignment of internal navy yard departments to Navy Department bureaus, which created a lack of cooperation and a division of loyalties in the navy yards:

> The origin of many of the difficulties in defining the Bureau of Ships' role in Naval Yards goes back to 1 July 1868 when Secretary Welles extended the Bureau system [established in 1842] to the individual yards. In this action each bureau [Bureau of Construction and Repair, Bureau of Steam Engineering, Bureau of Ordnance, Bureau of Supplies and Accounts, and Bureau of Navigation] was assigned its own department in each yard and was permitted to handle its own supplies and materials. Each bureau dealt directly with its own department, with the result that cooperation often proved to be completely lacking. Although a Commandant commanded each yard, primary allegiance of department heads gravitated towards their [parent] bureau.[16]

Each Navy bureau received its own annual congressional appropriation, and each funded its corresponding navy yard department independently. This process commanded great allegiance from navy yard departments dependent on their parent bureaus for funds. Consequently, the internal navy yard departments were more loyal to their parent navy bureaus in Washington, D.C., than they were to their commandant at the navy yard.

The inefficient bureau system continued to be a major problem until a 1938 audit report by the firm Booz, Fry, Allen, and Hamilton noted, "In the gradual evolution of the two bureaus [Bureau of Construction and Repair and the Bureau of Engineering] the distinction between 'hull' and 'machinery' became increasingly obscure. . . . This resulted in overlapping and duplication of work, inefficiency, and confusion."[17] The inefficiencies became so bad that President Roosevelt intervened and, in a 16 March 1938 letter to Assistant Secretary of the Navy Charles Edison, complained of excessive delays in the cases of three cruisers under construction at the Philadelphia and New York navy yards. The president wrote, "In the case of the cruisers, the Philadelphia Navy Yard and, to a less degree, the New York Navy Yard need to be told that the Commander-in-Chief is much dissatisfied."[18] It should be noted that FDR added, "The record on submarines is not so bad." Congress became involved, and on 20 June 1940 it passed Public Law 644 abolishing the Bureau of Construction and Repair and the Bureau of Engineering and establishing the Bureau of Ships to consolidate navy yard operations under one bureau.[19]

Figure 3 shows the Navy Department organizational structure after the establishment of the Bureau of Ships. The technical and management responsibility for all naval ships and navy yards now resided in the Bureau of Ships instead of being split between the two feuding bureaus. However, the Bureau of Yards and Docks, the Bureau of Ordnance, and the Bureau of Supplies and Accounts continued to provide direction to their navy yard departments during the war. But, unlike the faulty bureau system that undermined the commandant's authority, the remaining independent bureaus were required to function through the navy yard commandant.

The establishment of the Bureau of Ships solved some, but certainly not all, navy yard problems. As late as December 1944 Secretary of the Navy Forrestal, who continued to be frustrated with the inefficient administration of the navy yards, wrote, "What I want is some man whose sole job is to examine the functions, to compare operations and handle difficulties [at navy yards]. We should have one man to go to."[20] Organizational revisions immediately after the war further consolidated many of these other bureau functions under the Bureau of Ships.

The consolidation of navy yard shipbuilding operations under one bureau in 1940 was a step in the right direction. However, the timing was bad as the new bureau rapidly grew from one thousand to six thousand employees and never had a chance to organize itself, let alone the navy yards. It soon became inundated with overwhelming wartime responsibilities.[21] The congressional hearings on further naval expansion, held during the spring of 1940, almost simultaneously with the birth of the Bureau of Ships, continued the mobilization of shipbuilding that had begun with the outbreak of the war in Europe in 1939. The fall of France stirred up demands for further increases in the strength of the U.S. Navy and, in July 1940, with the Bureau of Ships celebrating its one-month anniversary, the 70 Percent Naval Expansion Act was passed. This had the effect of substantially increasing the new bureau's workload. Bureau of Ships historians later admitted that "this rapid increase in the size of the shipbuilding program created a host of problems in the administration of the new Bureau's work. The Shipbuilding Program on the books on September 1, 1939 was 360 million man-hours; it had risen to about 2.25 trillion man-hours on January 1, 1942 and 3 trillion man-hours by 1 September 1942. Daily emergencies being the rule, little time could be devoted to the sort of work that would pay dividends only in the long-run."[22] As noted, the Bureau of Ships did little or no long-range planning. Rather, it fought day-to-day emergencies and settled into a crisis management mode that left the navy yards to fend for themselves. Concerning the Bureau of Ships' inability to function effectively during this period, Connery wrote, "The Bureau of Ships was going through a period of indigestion caused by the amalgamation of the Bureau of Steam Engineering and the Bureau of Construction and Repair and its administrative processes were confused."[23]

The bad case of indigestion at the Bureau of Ships was certainly aggravated by an unprecedented glut of shipbuilding contracts. Table 4 places the establishment of the Bureau of Ships chronologically with annual naval appropriations for ship construction and repair. This provides a sense of the overwhelming workload that the newly created bureau faced. The Bureau of Ships quickly found that it was responsible for managing budgets that were twenty to thirty times larger than those the Bureau of Construction and Repair had managed just a few years earlier. Concerning the Herculean task that the Navy faced, Connery wrote, "The year 1941, opening with the Battle of Britain, proved to be a challenging one for the United States Navy. Hundreds of millions of dollars had been voted by Congress in 1940 for a vast naval expansion program. . . . The new year was to test whether the Navy's administration organization would be able to turn these dollars into weapons of defense."[24]

Recognizing that the Bureau of Ships was overwhelmed with the nation's revitalized shipbuilding program, Secretary of the Navy Knox in January 1941 directed the navy yard commandants to operate independently of the new bureau to the maximum extent possible: "During the present emergency, it is directed that Commandants of all Navy Yards act with the full authority of the Bureau of Ships taking final local action to the greatest extent possible."[25] Knox further directed that

Table 4: Bureau of Ships' Naval Appropriations for Construction, Repair, and Engineering (1935–44)

	Bureau of Construction and Repair before 1940	
	Annual Appropriation	**Percent Increase over Previous Year**
1935	$29,204,200	—
1936	$39,490,233	35% increase
1937	$40,550,000	3% increase
1938	$41,559,300	2% increase
1939	$59,681,590	44% increase
1940	$84,072,000	41% increase
	Bureau of Ships established 20 June 1940	
1941	$228,898,180	**172% increase**
1942	$1,497,470,000	**554% increase**
1943	$1,708,979,935	14% increase
1944	$1,733,880,000	1% increase

Source: *Administrative History: Bureau of Ships in World War II*, Naval Department World War II Admin History #89, 1946, Navy Department Library, Naval Historical Center, Washington, DC, Table 2, "Decline and Renaissance of the Navy."

the only technical issues to be forwarded to the Bureau of Ships for concurrence prior to shipyard action were those deemed necessary by the shipyard commandant. Knox promulgated this policy to enable the navy yards to accelerate production to achieve the ambitious naval shipbuilding programs passed in the summer of 1940. It would become became the navy yard modus operandi for the duration of the war.

Not only were orders for new ships growing at an unprecedented rate, but changes to those orders were also frequently necessary to accommodate evolving war plans. On one hand, America's success during World War II was the direct result of an industrial flexibility that was able to shift production quickly from one goal to another. On the other hand, the shifting of workload priorities amid shipbuilding orders created an unmanageable situation for the fledgling Bureau of Ships. According to a Bureau of Ships report, "Not one month of the twenty-four under consideration [January 1942–January 1944] passed without the Bureau of Ships receiving at least one directive either ordering a ship to be built or canceling others previously ordered."[26] The chief of the Office of Procurement and Material, Rear Adm. Samuel M. Robinson, told the undersecretary of the navy in July 1942,

"Since the beginning of 1942, the Navy Shipbuilding Program has been in almost continuous turmoil."[27] There can be little doubt that, in the summer of 1942, when Portsmouth Navy Yard was ramping up facilities and employment to meet accelerated production schedules, it could expect little assistance from the Bureau of Ships.

In July 1942, "at a time when the production and scheduling of the Bureau of Ships was, for the first time, beginning to assume some semblance of order, following the initial wartime adjustment period," the Combined Chiefs of Staff decided to launch the North Africa offensive as soon as possible. Shipbuilding priorities had to be restructured to ensure that landing craft and support ships would be available to bolster the operation.[28] The chief of naval operations shifted ship construction priorities frequently, depending upon the war's progress, leaving the Bureau of Ships struggling to restructure and reassign shipyard workloads.

War by its very nature requires constant reassessment and revision of plans. The Bureau of Ships self-history of World War II, however, attributed the chaotic conditions in which it was required to operate to a lack of coordinated advance planning between the secretary of the navy and the chief of naval operations. The bureau believed that President Roosevelt's personal involvement in naval matters further added to the confusion: "The personal handling of many matters by President Roosevelt was well known and tended to give advantage to the individual who could get to him with his case." The end result was a failure to plan in advance that "led to haphazard development of requirements" that "made the job of the Bureau much more difficult than it would have been if greater stability had prevailed."[29]

The need for the newly created Bureau of Ships to come to grips with a vast array of material procurement issues also distracted the bureau's attention from navy yard management. The logistics problems associated with the mobilization of private industry, to provide basic components and equipment for shipbuilding, were especially taxing to the Bureau of Ships: "Although the most obvious interest of the Bureau of Ships was in the expansion of shipyards . . . its greatest headache centered on the problem of upland facilities capable of manufacturing the components and materials necessary to keep the shipyards supplied. It is not unreasonable to state that the Bureau devoted as much effort to the increase of production capacity in supporting industries as to the increase in shipbuilding facilities."[30] Again, the Bureau of Ships had pressing needs in several areas of responsibility that kept it from devoting sufficient attention to the navy yards.

Ineffective leadership also plagued the bureau during the hectic summer of 1942. The first chief of the new bureau, Rear Adm. Samuel M. Robinson, was widely respected and especially enjoyed the confidence of Assistant Secretary Forrestal. Historian Robert Albion described Robinson as "wise, shrewd, and technically competent." Forrestal promoted Robinson to head procurement operations for the entire Navy in February 1942. According to Albion, "His [Robinson's] successor [Rear Adm. Alexander H. VanKeuren] proved unable to hold in check the disruptive forces and ambitions within the Bureau of Ships and it was drifting into ineffectiveness."[31] In November 1942 Forrestal replaced VanKeuren—after only eight months in the job—with Rear Adm. Edward L. Cochrane, who proved to be much more capable and remained in the position until November 1946.

Looking up the chain of command from Portsmouth Navy Yard's vantage point in December 1942, one year into the war, it must have been obvious to shipyard management that they were on their own. The overwhelmed bureau to which they reported, and from which they should have received support and guidance, had been in existence for only eighteen months, and the admiral in charge had just been removed for ineffective performance. It would be a long time before the Bureau of Ships would assume any semblance of control over navy yard operations. In the meantime, Portsmouth Navy Yard had dozens of orders for new submarines and had to get on with the measures necessary to complete those orders and achieve its production goals.

Throughout 1943 and 1944, Portsmouth Navy Yard met its commitments and exceeded its production goals. This was not the case for many shipyards, as evidenced by a September 1943 Bureau of Ships letter that noted, "110 of the 342 [ships] actually scheduled for delivery in August did not meet their date."[32] The letter highlighted the need for the bureau to receive more accurate progress reports from the shipyards. Not only was the Bureau of Ships unable to actively manage the shipyards, it was also having difficulty keeping up to date on the progress of ships under construction at the yards. In late 1943 the bureau continued in a crisis-management mode with many shipyards adding to that crisis by failing to meet scheduled completion dates. What little attention the bureau could give to shipyards was best directed at the deficient yards and not at the better-performing yards.

Shipyard Management

Shipyard management includes both military and civilian managers. The naval officers, who hold the major leadership positions, turn over every few years. Consequently—as those who have served in navy yards know so well—the civilian managers provide the long-term continuity and the core industrial and technical expertise that defines the yard. Photo 8 in the gallery shows the shipyard's civilian management team.

The archives provide valuable insight into the military management of Portsmouth Navy Yard during the war, but much less insight into civilian management. This book includes the personal recollections of Fred White, a ninety-six-year-old shipyard retiree, who held a senior civilian management position during the war. As the master rigger and laborer, White supervised hundreds of employees and was heavily involved in important waterfront industrial events such as keel layings, launchings, dockings, undockings, and submarine movements. His recollections provided an invaluable contribution to this book. The family papers of a shipyard naval architect, Harold Sweetser, who worked at the yard from 1917 until 1958, and articles from the shipyard's newspaper, the *Portsmouth Periscope*, provide additional insight into civilian management at the yard during the war.

The managers at Portsmouth Navy Yard, by the summer of 1942, had successfully mobilized the yard and begun to increase production. About that time, U.S. submarines' success in sinking Japanese shipping was receiving considerable press coverage. Much of it advocated increased and accelerated production of submarines. Journalist David Lawrence urged that more emphasis be placed on submarine construction when he wrote,

> Why has the submarine been neglected in public discussions? . . . It takes about 11 months to build a large submarine nowadays. Can this time be cut by the various speedup formulas that have helped us to turn out planes and cargo ships at record production? Very little is known by the public of submarine construction. There has been a great deal of secrecy about it but, with the splendid work being done by American submarines in the Pacific, the opportunity for stimulating the whole submarine program would seem to be increased by disclosing more and more about our offensive operations with the submarine.[33]

Portsmouth Navy Yard management was in the process of doing much as David Lawrence was suggesting. It was accelerating the traditional production rate of submarines by employing new and innovative techniques. It was one thing to casually suggest the speedup of submarine production and quite another thing to achieve it.

Portsmouth Navy Yard's transformation, from the custom shop operation that built two submarines per year in the 1930s to a mass producer of dozens of submarines per year by 1944, required a unique industrial environment. That environment included exceptional leadership, innovative management practices, and a dedicated and empowered workforce.

Effective Military Leadership

Outstanding leadership is critical to the successful management of any industrial operation, and Portsmouth Navy Yard was blessed with one of the most respected leaders of the submarine community during the war, Rear Adm. Thomas Withers. Withers relieved Rear Admiral Wainwright as commandant of the Portsmouth Navy Yard on 10 June 1942. Photo 7 in the gallery shows Withers greeting the shipyard managers after the change-of-command ceremony. He remained in charge of the shipyard until late 1945. His assignment prior to coming to Portsmouth was as Commander Submarines Scouting Force, Pacific Fleet, and in this capacity he had witnessed the attack on Pearl Harbor and directed the first deployment of U.S. submarines in response to the attack.

As an eyewitness to the first minutes of the war, Withers reportedly witnessed the first Japanese "sinking" by a U.S. submarine when, on the morning of 7 December 1941, during the attack on Battleship Row, a machine gunner on USS *Tautog* (SS 199) downed a Japanese plane.[34] Rear Admiral Withers rallied the twenty-one submarines under his command at that time and sent them to sea to "commence unrestricted submarine warfare against all Japanese merchant and military units." In an inspirational message to the men of his command shortly after the attack, Withers wished them, "Good luck and good hunting, hit 'em hard."[35]

Prior to his assignment at Pearl Harbor, Withers had enjoyed a long and illustrious career in submarines. He graduated from the U.S. Naval Academy in 1906. A quote, attributed to the Earl of Claredon, appears with the picture of Midn. Thomas Withers Jr. in the 1906 U.S. Naval Academy yearbook, *The Lucky Bag.* That quote speaks to a side of his personality that would serve him well in the years to come: "He had a head to contrive, a tongue to persuade, and a hand to execute any mischief."[36] Indeed, throughout his naval career he proved to be a clear thinker able to inspire and convince subordinates to achieve the most challenging of tasks.

Withers assumed his first submarine command, the USS *E-1,* in 1914. After the war, he progressed through operational commands of ever greater responsibility, including commandant of the New London Submarine Base. He was assigned as Commander Submarine Scouting Force from January 1941 to May 1942. This command became Commander Submarine Force Pacific Fleet at the outbreak of World War II.

In 1928, as Commander Division 4, Withers advanced the argument that U.S. submarines should be used as independent commerce raiders, much as the Germans had used them in World War I, rather than as scouting units in conjunction with fleet or coastal defense. As a consequence, he is credited with helping change the strategic role of the submarine in the U.S. Navy. His concept of independent operations required submarine designs with longer ranges, better sea-keeping ability, and improved habitability.[37] U.S. submarines, designed and operated as Commander Withers had envisioned in the late 1920s, would go on to account for over 55 percent of all Japanese shipping sunk in the Pacific. Three hundred twenty-five submarines took part in the war. Fifty-two were lost with over thirty-five hundred of the brave men who operated them. The submarine force made up only about 2 percent of the U.S. Navy forces but certainly played a key role in winning the war in the Pacific.

It was fortunate that circumstances led the Navy to assign one of its most innovative thinkers, and an expert in submarine design, to head up the expanding submarine design and construction organization at Portsmouth Navy Yard. It was an added benefit that the trusting, low-key management style of Rear Admiral Withers was just what the shipyard needed to fully develop its production potential.

In the summer of 1939 Captain Withers had been a member of the court of inquiry that convened at Portsmouth Navy Yard to investigate the sinking of the USS *Squalus* (SS 192).[38] The investigation required several months to complete, and this gave Captain Withers ample opportunity to become familiar with the shipyard. By the time he assumed command of the yard in June 1942, he already had a good understanding of the shipyard and its operations. In its coverage of Withers' change-of-command ceremony, the *Portsmouth Herald* reported, "A man who has been associated with submarines during the better part of his career in the navy, it is expected that the new commandant will create new and powerful factors in production at the Portsmouth Navy Yard."[39] Indeed, under Withers, the yard would create new and powerful production factors. Rarely had a newspaper more accurately predicted the future.

According to a U.S. Navy press release, Withers apparently possessed what later management schools described as good people skills: "A kindly, soft-spoken officer, Radm Withers gained unlimited support and praise from his sailors after leasing the Honolulu Royal Hawaiian Hotel for permanent use as a rest camp deluxe for submarine sailors in port."[40] Gary Weir described Withers as "always quiet, and amiable—but perceptive and precise."[41] Fred White fondly remembered Withers and confirmed his popularity with shipyard workers. White said, "Admiral Withers was a much-respected man whom everybody liked because he let everyone do their job."[42] It is not a stretch to assume that Withers exhibited the same trust and confidence in his shipyard managers and workers that he had in the submarine officers and crews that he sent to war after the attack on Pearl Harbor. With little fanfare, he encouraged both to do their jobs independently and aggressively.

Rear Admiral Withers' inspirational, low-key leadership and the confidence he placed in his managers and employees were key to the yard's success. Under his leadership, managers and employees were empowered and encouraged to work more independently, perhaps more so than they would have been under a more authoritative shipyard commander.

Complementary Leadership Styles

One school of thought teaches that effective organizations often have executives with different, but complementary, leadership styles. One crude example is the good cop–bad cop police interrogator team that might question criminal suspects.

On board naval ships some think that the commanding officer and the second in command, the executive officer, work best as a team when one is a disciplinarian and the other a humanitarian. The top two executives at Portsmouth Navy Yard during the war, Commandant Withers and the industrial manager, Capt. H. F. D. Davis, had contrasting and complementary leadership styles.

It is important to note that the commandant and the industrial manager were members of two different naval officer communities. Rear Admiral Withers was an unrestricted line officer and, as such, had spent a naval career operating and commanding submarines and submariners. Captain Davis, on the other hand, was a restricted line officer, meaning that he was a specialist in a selected field. Davis' specialty was ship construction. In this capacity, he had spent most of his naval career in the shipbuilding industry in charge of industrial shops and large numbers of civilian employees.

Under the rules at the time, Captain Davis, as a restricted line officer, could never be promoted to command a ship, submarine, or navy yard. Before he reported to Portsmouth in June 1940, Davis had been the planning officer at Philadelphia Navy Yard, and when detached from Portsmouth in June 1944, he became the supervisor of shipbuilding at the Bethlehem Steel Corporation in Quincy, Massachusetts. While Withers was responsible for all facets of operations at Portsmouth Navy Yard, Davis was responsible for the Industrial Department, and to him goes much of the credit for the successful expansion of the yard and its outstanding productive performance. At the same time, Commandant Withers deserves much credit for giving Davis the freedom to, as Fred White put it, "do his job."

Figure 3 shows the three major department heads, all naval captains, who reported to the commandant during the war: the captain of the yard, the supply officer, and the industrial manager.[43] The captain of the yard was primarily responsible for the naval personnel attached to the yard and various administrative matters. The supply officer was primarily responsible for purchasing and managing material. The industrial manager was responsible for all the shops and industrial operations on the yard. In that capacity, he had two other senior naval captains reporting to him: Capt. Andrew I. McKee, the planning officer, and Capt. Sidney E. Dudley, the production officer.[44] While the industrial manager appears to share equal billing with the other two major department heads, such was not the case in the day-to-day business of the shipyard. On 15 November 1943, when the shipyard employment peaked at 20,445 employees, roughly 18,000 of those employees worked for the industrial manager; the remainder was split among the other shipyard departments. The shipyard mission during the war was to build as many submarines as possible as fast as possible. The task of carrying out that mission rested squarely on the shoulders of Captain Davis.

Whereas Withers managed the navy yard with a soft but firm hand, many shipyard workers came to believe that the "H. F. D." in front of Captain Davis' name stood for "Hell-fire and Damnation." Captain Davis' grandson, Stan Davis, remembers being in the presence of Withers, Davis, and other shipyard officers several times as a boy, when he "used to lean against the library wall and listen to them talk." According to Stan Davis, "The other guys were quite mild-mannered compared with my grandfather."[45] By all accounts, Captain Davis was always out-spoken and ever eager for an argument. The 1908 *Lucky Bag* notes about Midn. Henry Frederick Dilman Davis, "When engaged in an argument, [he] begins, con-tinues and ends with 'Oh, no! You're wrong.'"[46] Apparently Davis was never short on opinions, nor did he avoid controversy. These attributes would serve him well as industrial manager at Portsmouth Navy Yard.

Employee morale was always close to the top of Withers' priority list. For example, in an August 1943 memo to all shipyard supervisors that emphasized the need for efficient use of resources, Withers concluded, "Finally, that the human relations—the morale factors be made and kept as good as possible."[47] Davis, on the other hand, was more of a problem solver than a morale booster. On one occa-sion, when Cdr. J. H. Spiller suggested that employee morale was the Industrial Department's most important problem, Davis suggested that they first confine their attention to "concrete management problems" for which they were primarily responsible.[48] Concrete management problems included the improvement of work-ing conditions and the clarification of assignments and priorities. Davis' grandson remembers his grandfather telling him on more than one occasion, "You either suc-ceed or fail to make a delivery. It's binary. There's no mushiness about it."[49] Clearly, Davis was not a "touchy, feely" manager. Withers, however, was always sensitive to employee concerns and quick to address and resolve any personnel issues. Their management styles were a study in contrast.

Withers' directives were typically brief, clear, and to the point. He was a big-picture type of manager, in the style of Ronald Reagan, who set the tone and objec-tives for the organization but left the management of details to subordinates. Industrial Manager Davis, on the other hand, was a hands-on manager who rev-eled in the details of his responsibilities. His directives were typically long, if not verbose, with considerable explanation and detail to back up his position.

Captain Davis' effort in July 1943 to stress welding as the critical path to suc-cessful completion of the scheduled twenty-eight-submarine program is an excel-lent example of the attention to detail that he typically applied to his work. In a memo to shipyard managers, Davis began by telling his readers that 71,148 pounds of welding rod had been used on the recently completed SS 285 and concluded that 2 million pounds of welding rod would have to be laid to complete twenty-eight submarines in the next year. Following an analysis of sixteen months of personnel gains and losses in the welding shop, Davis determined that the welders then available would have to reduce nonwork days and weld at an average rate of 7,126 pounds per day to meet the schedule.[50] Such was Captain Davis' delight in details

Some of Stan Davis' recollections about his grandfather will help to complete this portrayal of Captain Davis as a firm, hands-on manager dedicated to detailed planning and innovation. According to Stan Davis, "His life's experiences taught him that making a big enterprise go, such as the enterprise of building ships, requires unremitting firmness, continuous oversight by knowledgeable and totally committed officers, detailed planning, a vivid imagination, etc. . . . Throughout his career he continually and maybe compulsively submitted detailed recommendations for new capabilities, enhancements to existing systems, and modifications in policy, procedures and organizations to various Navy Department authorities."[51] Having Captain Davis as a boss must have been an exhilarating, challenging, and demanding experience.

Fred White's assessment of the two leaders, as the result of personal experiences with both during the war, further highlights their contrasting management styles. Whereas Withers was respected and well liked, White remembers Captain Davis as "a meddler and a man of many ideas that seldom worked." When pressed for an example of one such idea, White told the story of a scheme Davis concocted to minimize inefficient use of riggers. In fairness to Captain Davis, needing a rigger and not having one, or having riggers in standby waiting to accomplish a job that ran late, can contribute significantly to great inefficiency in a shipyard. According to White, Davis sought to minimize that inefficiency by having all the riggers assigned to the fitting-out pier assemble in a central location to wait for a call for their services. The call would be made by the hoisting of a flag on specially constructed poles alongside each of a half dozen submarine berths. While the idea might sound quite reasonable, White and others were convinced that the daily informal communications on the waterfront were more than adequate to anticipate the need for riggers. As White recalled, a "standby shack" was built, but [lacking the riggers' enthusiastic support] the idea was abandoned even before the flagpoles were erected.[52] Nevertheless, Davis kept the waterfront supervisors on edge with his incessant suggestions and demands for improved performance.

While Captain Davis may have been somewhat of an irritant to Fred White and the other shop masters, there is little doubt that he was a presence and a force on the waterfront that kept the industrial pot stirring. If he was a man of ideas that did not always work, he was also a man constantly looking for another approach, a novel way to get the job done. Imagination and innovation thrive in organizations with leaders who practice and encourage such thinking. As this narrative illustrates, Portsmouth Navy Yard had an abundance of both during the war.

Senior Management Continuity

Both Rear Admiral Withers and Captain Davis held their shipyard leadership positions for most of the war years. Withers held command from 10 June 1942 until November 1945, and Davis served in his position from 28 June 1940 until 25 May 1944. As Table 5 shows, the other senior managers in critical industrial positions also experienced similar longevity in their jobs. The average tour length for the senior officers who served in the six critical industrial management positions in the shipyard was over fifty months. The officer who held his position for the shortest time, Captain Dudley, was promoted within the yard from production officer to industrial manager, replacing Captain Davis on 25 May 1944. Likewise, Capt. Homer Ambrose was promoted from machinery superintendent to production officer, replacing Captain Dudley on the same date. Such in-house promotions suggest that both officers had performed well in their previous assignments and proved themselves competent and capable of handling additional responsibilities.

Table 5: World War II Leadership Continuity at Portsmouth Navy Yard

Position	Person	Reported	Detached	Duration (mos.)
Commandant	Rear Adm. Withers	10 June 1942	Nov. 1945	41
Industrial Manager	Capt. Davis	28 June 1940	25 May 1944	47
Production Officer	Capt. Dudley	Aug. 1941	25 May 1944	34
Planning Officer	Capt. McKee	March 1938	20 Jan. 1945	82
Hull Support	Capt. Spiller	3 Sept. 1941	July 1945+	46+
Machinery Support	Capt. Ambrose	7 Dec. 1939	25 May 1944	53

Source: *Administrative History: Portsmouth Navy Yard in World War II* (n.d., Portsmouth Naval Shipyard Museum Archives, Kittery, ME), 66–68.

Captain McKee headed the local team that produced Portsmouth Industrial Surveys #1 (December 1941) and #2 (June 1942). These surveys established many of the concepts that later contributed to the shipyard's outstanding performance. McKee had already served as planning officer for forty-four months prior to leading that team. With his extensive background and experience, he obviously knew the shipyard well and was fully qualified to assess its needs and capabilities. Moreover, Captain McKee continued in his assignment at the shipyard for another forty-eight months, during which time he was able to monitor and implement the changes his team had recommended. McKee's tenure of almost seven years as planning officer undoubtedly was essential to the yard's success during the war.

Hardly overshadowed by Rear Admiral Withers and Captain Davis, Captain McKee enjoyed a well-deserved reputation as an expert in submarine design. In 1945, when the Society of Naval Architects and Marine Engineers published *Historical Transactions*, McKee was selected to author an article on the history of submarine design.[53] In the early 1950s Rear Admiral McKee, USN (Ret.), and Vice Adm. Ned Cochrane, USN (Ret.), Commander Bureau of Ships during the war, were members of a small committee under the auspices of the National Academy of Science that proposed to the chief of naval operations the development of "an attack submarine with a streamlined body, a single propeller and modified control surfaces."[54] This concept, of course, became the USS *Albacore* with the teardrop hull form and other technological innovations that became standard design features on the nation's emerging nuclear-powered submarine fleet. After retiring from the Navy, Rear Admiral McKee enjoyed a second career at Electric Boat as the chief design engineer. In recognition of his career accomplishments, a submarine tender USS *McKee* (AS 41) honored his name, and the A. I. McKee Award for academic excellence is presented to the most deserving officer in each graduating class of the Navy's Nuclear Power Training Course. Clearly Rear Admiral Withers was surrounded by a core of very competent and experienced managers.

As can be seen from Table 5, during the first two years of Rear Admiral Withers' tour as commandant, none of the critical management positions turned over. The rock-solid stability of a competent management team during the early stages of the war, when the shipyard was being transformed from a custom shop to a mass producer of submarines, was a significant reason for the shipyard's ultimate success.

Civilian Management

Another factor in the success of the yard was the contribution of a dedicated and talented cadre of civilian designers and managers. Having highlighted the lengthy tours of duty of the senior naval officers in the yard during the war, it is appropriate to note that the naval officer continuity paled in comparison to the civilian management continuity. While forty *months* was a long tour of duty for a naval officer, it was not unusual for senior civilian managers to complete forty *years* of service at the yard before retiring. Indeed, pictures of shipyard employees being presented forty-year pins during the war and postwar periods were common in the shipyard newspaper, the *Portsmouth Periscope*. For example, on 16 February 1945, Rear Admiral Withers presented no less than twenty shipyard employees with forty-year pins.[55] These twenty employees had hired on at the shipyard in 1905. These employees had been hired ten years before the yard started building submarines and had gained valuable experience in submarine construction during the 1920s, when Lake Torpedo Boat folded, Electric Boat was struggling for work, and other shipyards were closing down.

Harold Sweetser hired on at the yard in May 1917 and progressed through various draftsman jobs. In 1958 he retired as the supervisory naval architect after forty years of service. Likewise, Sweetser's compatriot, Chief Draftsman Robert Boyd, retired in October 1945 after forty-nine years of service. Another of Sweetser's friends, Carl Galle, began his navy yard career as a draftsman in 1918 and was promoted to senior naval architect during World War II. Galle was promoted to the position of head engineer of the yard in October 1951. The shipyard was fortunate to have many such experienced and competent civilian employees occupying critical positions at the start of and during the war.[56]

The shipyard would not have had the benefit of the extensive submarine design experience of employees like Sweetser, Boyd, and Galle had the Navy not decided to develop the submarine design capabilities of Portsmouth Navy Yard after World War I. Additionally, had the construction of new submarines at the yard been discontinued for any period of time between the wars, these naval architects would probably have been forced to seek employment elsewhere. As was noted earlier, all navy yards except Portsmouth experienced a hiatus in new ship construction at one time or another after World War I and before the rebirth of naval shipbuilding in the 1930s. With an experienced group of designers and industrial workers, it was no accident that Portsmouth Navy Yard acquired a reputation for building high-quality submarines.

Navy Department industrial strategy created the opportunity to develop submarine design capabilities at Portsmouth Navy Yard prior to the war, and naval officer leadership set the objectives during the war. However, most of the credit for the yard's outstanding production accomplishments must go to its experienced core of talented civilian designers and skilled shop employees. They put drafting pen to paper, welding rods to steel, and wrenches to valves.

Management Advantages

Portsmouth Navy Yard had two distinct advantages over the other navy yards during World War II. First, unlike the seven other navy yards (Boston, New York, Philadelphia, Norfolk, Charleston, Bremerton, and Mare Island) that dealt with multiple ship types and disruptive repair and overhaul work, Portsmouth was able to specialize in the design and construction of submarines. This specialization was the fruit of efforts to develop the yard's submarine design and construction capabilities during the 1920s and 1930s in order to compete with private industry.

Portsmouth's second advantage was its small size compared to the other navy yards. Despite expanding sixfold between 1940 and 1943, Portsmouth was the smallest navy yard in March 1943. At that time the yard had 20,445 employees, whereas the other seven navy yards averaged 38,377 employees.[57] A small shipyard with a specialized mission and a well-defined workload had a distinct advantage over larger shipyards with a workload of multiple ship types and the urgent and unpredictable need to repair battle damage to operating ships. This section will first examine the obvious advantages of being a small yard and then will present a more detailed analysis of workload specialization.

SecNav Industrial Survey #1 (1942) noted, "The expanse of the waterfront at all [surveyed] Yards [New York, Boston, Bremerton, and Mare Island] tends to retard the transfer of gangs between ships and makes for a more rigid operating situation than is normally found in commercial yards."[58] In comparison, Portsmouth Navy Yard had a rather limited and compact waterfront area that lent itself to the efficient transfer of teams from submarine to submarine and a high degree of flexibility not found in the other navy yards. Left to its own devices to manage its own workload, the smaller yard with the more homogeneous workload would have a much better chance of developing successful practices and processes than a larger shipyard with a complex workload.

SecNav Industrial Survey #1 (1942) noted that the industrial departments in all navy yards had increased three- to fourfold in less than two years. Such employment increases would pale in comparison to the peak employments reached at each yard later in the war. Table 6 compares civilian employment levels at each navy yard on 1 July 1938 with the peak employment reached during the war. The table shows that Portsmouth, one of the smaller navy yards in 1938, experienced considerably less growth during the war than did the other navy yards. Portsmouth increased by a factor of 6.25, while all navy yards increased by an average factor of 10.38. Relative to the other yards, Portsmouth's smaller, specialized, and concentrated workforce had better opportunities to optimize production than those at the other yards. Electric Boat, a relatively small private shipyard, enjoyed advantages similar to those of Portsmouth Navy Yard during the war. It grew from 2,900 employees in August 1940 to a peak of 12,466 employees during the war, a multiple of only 4.3. Electric Boat, like Portsmouth Navy Yard, also specialized in submarine construction.[59]

SecNav Industrial Survey #1 (1942) noted that much disorganization and confusion existed in other navy yards. It also highlighted the production control and scheduling advantages that private shipyards, engaged in only the new construction of ships, enjoyed over the navy yards surveyed. Those navy yards serviced the fleet with ship repairs and overhauls, often of an emergency nature. The study reported that private shipyards could build a more orderly and disciplined work environment, whereas the navy yards surveyed might have "thousands of employees thrown aboard a single ship to expedite the work by having men available when

Table 6: Navy Yard Employment (1938–World War II Peak)

Navy Yard	7/1/1938	Peak during WWII	Multiple Increase
Portsmouth	3,273	20,445	6.25
Boston	2,860	50,128	17.53
New York	6,876	69,128	10.05
Philadelphia	5,636	46,454	8.24
Norfolk	5,739	42,372	7.38
Mare Island	4,756	39,736	8.35
Puget Sound	3,469	32,643	9.41
Pearl Harbor	1,974	24,916	12.62
Terminal Island	—	15,971	(temporary)
San Francisco	—	17,174	(temporary)
Total	34,583	358,967	10.38

Source: *Administrative History: Bureau of Ships in World War II*, Naval Department World War II Admin History #89, 1946, Navy Department Library, Naval Historical Center, Washington, D.C., 145.

and where they are needed, [and] gangs are constantly forced to stand by waiting for other crafts to finish up or for servicemen to bring up necessary material or equipment."[60] In this regard, Portsmouth Navy Yard enjoyed the same advantages as the private shipyards and, for the most part, did not have to deal with the chaotic repair and overhaul work environment that characterized the inefficient operations at the other navy yards.

SecNav Industrial Survey #2 (1944) credited the Portsmouth Navy Yard for its ability to focus resources and streamline work practices toward a single objective, the construction of submarines. According to the survey, "Any present judgment of the organization, administration and control procedures of the Navy Yard, Portsmouth, N.H. must give great weight to the development of the Yard, subordinating all other considerations to the demands of the war effort, into a specialized construction activity for submarines only. All operating units have been streamlined for this sole purpose."[61] The U.S. Navy's goal of developing the submarine design and production capabilities of the yard between the wars and Portsmouth's strategy in the mid- and late 1930s to shed work other than submarine construction had been a resounding success. This strategy, which served the interests of the shipyard so well, served the war effort even more. Had Portsmouth Navy Yard not been able to perform as it did early in the war, the U.S. Navy would not have had the numbers of submarines that it did. One can only speculate what effect that would have had on the war in the Pacific, given the level of devastation that U.S. submarines wreaked on the Japanese merchant fleet and the Japanese Imperial Navy.

Table 7 shows the workload transition at the yard from a preponderance of ship overhauls in the early 1930s to submarine construction during World War II. During the early 1930s the shipyard overhauled many more submarines than it built. It also constructed surface ships and yard craft. Although not shown in this table, the shipyard built its last surface ship, U.S. Coast Guard cutter *Hudson*, in 1934.[62] During the wartime construction years of 1942–44, the shipyard overhauled far fewer submarines annually than it did in the early 1930s. The ratio of subs overhauled to subs built clearly shows the streamlining for new construction during the war years to which SecNav Industrial Survey #2 (1944) referred. With most of the U.S. submarine fleet deployed to the Pacific theater, the West Coast shipyards assumed a disproportionate share of the submarine repair and overhaul workload, leaving Portsmouth Navy Yard relatively free to concentrate on the construction of new submarines.

Figure A-3 in the appendix, Portsmouth Navy Yard Manpower Curves by Work Category (1940–45), shows the effects of the streamlining for new construction.[63] The curves show that the repair workload (shaded in the figure) was phased out between early 1940 and early 1942. In the second quarter of 1940 the fifteen hundred men per day expended on repairs approximated the number expended on new construction. By January 1942 only a few hundred men per day were assigned to repair/overhaul work and over six thousand men per day were working on new construction. As can be seen in Figure A-3, the workload of the shipyard continued

Table 7: Portsmouth Navy Yard Workload Mix (1931–45)

	1931	1932	1933	1941	1942	1943	1944	Aug. 1945
Subs Built	1	2	2	4	12	19	32	12
Yard Craft Built	2			1	2	7		
Overhauled Subs	7	8	7	2	5	4	10	19
Ships Overhauled	2				2	1	6	16
Yard Craft Repaired						3	1	
Subs Ovhld/Built	7	4	3.5	.5	.42	.21	.31	1.58
Yard Employment	1,552	1,477	1,595	11,142	18,326	20,445	17,102	10,133

Source: Data from the 1930s is from the *Industrial Manager's Annual Reports*, NARA Waltham, RG 181, Portsmouth Naval Shipyard General Correspondence (Central Files), Box 22, Folder A9-1/Y1, "Annual Reports Commandant First Naval District 1925–34." The data is a fiscal year summary ending on 30 June. Data from the 1940s is from *Administrative History: Portsmouth Navy Yard during World War II*, (Portsmouth Naval Shipyard Museum Archives, Kittery, ME), 3.

to reflect negligible repair work in comparison to new construction work until the end of 1944.

Not only could the shipyard concentrate on one type of work, it was protected from external changes in priorities for scheduling that work. Shipyards that handled a mix of ship types and work packages, including repairs and overhauls, were subject to ever shifting priorities that resulted in the need for frequent short-notice internal shipyard scheduling revisions. For example, Jeffery M. Dorwart, discussing the shifting wartime priorities at the Philadelphia Navy Yard, described how the workload shifted from the construction of battleships, to destroyer escorts, to amphibious ships, to heavy cruisers, to aircraft carriers: "In 1942, the Navy Department changed building priorities from battleships to destroyer escorts for an anti-submarine war in the Atlantic. . . . FDR announced an emergency program in April 1942 to build landing craft for North African, European, and later Pacific amphibious operations. . . . With victory in Europe becoming more certain by 1944, League Island [Philadelphia Navy Yard] turned to construction of heavy cruisers and aircraft carriers to fight the Pacific War against Japan."[64] Philadelphia Navy Yard found it difficult to aim at a moving target whereas Portsmouth Navy Yard could continuously improve its aim at a stationary target, submarine construction.

The chief of naval operations established a priority system for navy yard work. In order of precedence, the priority levels were overriding priority, first priority, second priority, and new construction priority. The first three priorities were all related to war damage and urgent repairs; each priority was then subcategorized according to urgency by ship type. Under the new construction priority, submarines were generally low on the ship-type list with landing craft, transport ships, and other surface ships high on the list to support the next invasion or coordinated assault. As a result, submarine construction was assigned a low priority—on paper.[65] For example, on a priority system ranking of 1 to 10, submarines were most often ranked seventh with the priorities 8 to 10 not used or assigned to "all other [miscellaneous] vessels."[66] While other shipyards were whipsawed back and forth with waves of changing priorities, according to the fortunes of war, the priorities of Portsmouth Navy Yard seldom wavered. The shipyard's charge for the entire war remained constant: to build as many submarines as possible as fast as possible. The ability to specialize in one line of work was, unquestionably, one of the keys to the success of the shipyard during the war.

Once Portsmouth Navy Yard started to deliver new submarines at record rates, the Navy Department made no serious attempt to direct other types of work to Portsmouth until the end of the war. The U.S. Navy had many material procurement problems, but getting submarines out of Portsmouth was not one of them. Rather than attempt to fix what was not broken, the Navy left Portsmouth free to do its thing.

Portsmouth Navy Yard was a CEO's dream. The shipyard, with its workforce and facilities aligned for submarine construction, consistently met schedules and achieved its production and quality goals with little or no investment of time or effort on the part of "corporate" management.

—∞—

During the war, Commandant Withers, Industrial Manager Davis, and Planning Officer McKee provided strong leadership for an experienced group of naval and civilian managers who enjoyed long and successful tours of duty at the shipyard. This stable and well-qualified management team led exceptionally motivated experienced designers and skilled shop tradesmen to tremendous production achievements. Portsmouth had the additional advantages of being a relatively small shipyard with a sharply focused and well-defined mission. This vital, but very specific, mission protected the yard from external forces and shifting priorities. As a result, the yard's industrial operations could proceed without interruption, with no need to deviate from the streamlined new construction processes that had been in development since the mid-1930s. All of these factors combined to enable the yard to excel in an industrial environment characterized by loose oversight. Portsmouth Navy Yard could not have written a better script for success.

Chapter 4

Employees

The workforce at Portsmouth is especially high grade. Top civilian
supervisors are alert, intelligent, and obviously proud of their Yard.

—SecNav Industrial Survey #2, 6 November 1944

This chapter may seem to lack balance in that it is skewed toward high praise for the yard's employees and their performance during the war. While it may have been desirable, from a literary standpoint, to provide more tension in the analysis, the fact is that the archives are filled with evidence of the high quality and cooperative nature of the workforce and very little evidence to the contrary. Suffice it to say that the archives would contain counterevidence aplenty if the workforce had faltered in any significant way.

A number of factors contributed to the harmonious relationship that existed between the workforce and management. As explained in the previous chapter, there was a definite lack of management oppressiveness, a mutually clear focus of efforts on a repetitive and familiar workload, and efficiencies gained from being a small shipyard. This chapter also addresses the homogeneity, intelligence, patriotism, and dedication of the predominantly Yankee workforce. Combined, these factors created a climate of cooperation and support that made the jobs of both management and employees much easier than might otherwise have been the case.

During the war the shipyard workforce grew to over 20,000 employees, including over 3,800 women. The assimilation of thousands of new employees into the shops and offices and the training of those employees was a major challenge. This was further complicated by the loss of younger and often more talented employees to military service. The analysis that follows examines workforce quality, the contribution of women to the success of the yard, and the impact of the Selective Service Act of 1940.

Workforce Quality

A prominent theme throughout the previous chapters has been the good fortune of Portsmouth Navy Yard to have been favored with submarine construction programs continually between the wars. As a result, the yard was able to maintain a nucleus of skilled employees that became the basis for the mobilization workforce. The observations of Admiral Stuart S. Murray, USN (Ret.), who reported to Portsmouth Navy Yard as a lieutenant in mid-1933 to be the assistant machine superintendent, highlight the experience and quality of the workforce at that time. According to Murray, approximately one-third of the navy yard workforce was laid off in 1933 as a result of the Depression, leaving only supervisors and rated civil service personnel to do the work. This honing of the workforce had its positive effects: "However, this made for very good working with the personnel, because you were working with well-trained and experienced men. No man on the yard had been there less than seven years and the average was about fifteen years of employment in that yard. These were men whose families had worked in that shipyard for generations, so they were well grounded in the type of work they were doing."[1] The eventual wartime contributions of these skilled workers, with shipyard ties that went back several generations, were characterized by an uncommon dedication and loyalty to the shipyard and the nation.

For the skilled workers at Portsmouth, work was often a family affair. Sons followed their fathers as shipyard employees. Fred White's father, Andrew White, was hired on at the yard around the turn of the century. After being laid off prior to World War I, he was rehired in 1916 as a machinist and continued to work at the yard until he retired in 1938. Andrew was one of the many employees who benefited from the Navy's decision to favor Portsmouth with new submarine construction between the wars. Fred White hired on at the yard in 1935, advanced to a shop superintendent position in 1944, and further advanced to a group superintendent position after World War II. Continuing the line, Fred's son, Stephen White, was later employed at the yard as a machinist until he retired.[2] The White family is one of many in the seacoast New Hampshire and southern Maine areas that have a proud history of many years of uninterrupted family service at Portsmouth Navy Yard.

It was obvious from the earliest days of the war that Portsmouth Navy Yard had an unusually patriotic and dedicated workforce. In mid-December 1941 all the employees at the yard announced their intention to work Sunday, 21 December, without pay. The idea for a payless workday had originated with a few workers after a war rally at the shipyard on Monday, 15 December.[3] Photo 9 in the gallery shows a shipyard rally at the start of the war. Much to the chagrin of the employees, Secretary of the Navy Knox later vetoed the idea because it would violate existing work statutes. Even though Navy officials would not go along with the idea, the gesture spoke volumes about the dedication and unity of the Portsmouth Navy Yard employees.

An incident involving a change in shift work hours in April 1942 further illustrates the employees' patriotism. It also shows that the employees were willing to exercise the power of labor to affect management decisions. Shift work hours were changed in the spring of 1942 so that the first shift started at 4:00 AM instead of 6:00 AM. The other eight-hour shifts were advanced accordingly. Management believed that the new shifts would increase productivity. However, members of Ranger Lodge 836, International Association of Machinists, believed there would be no productivity improvement and that the change would result in an unnecessary inconvenience to workers and their families. The aggressive effort of the machinists to have management reverse its decision was mitigated by a reaffirmation of their support for yard management. The following statement from Ranger Lodge 836 immediately appeared on the front page of the *Portsmouth Herald*: "We have the utmost confidence in the officers who have been designated by the Navy department to administer the policies at this yard and we pledge our utmost cooperation with their efforts to build our submarine navy quickly and efficiently, but we reserve our inalienable rights to protest any local orders that to us seem unnecessary to our country's war program."[4] Shortly after the machinists had voiced their displeasure with the new shifts, a yard-wide poll confirmed that a majority of the rest of the yard employees felt the same way. Management relented, restored the old shift hours, and the controversy was settled.[5] Mutual respect and open communications were a hallmark of management-employee relations at Portsmouth Navy Yard at that time.

Exceptional patriotism and employee-management cooperation were also evident when the yard set a national record for war bond participation in November 1942. The yard established the record when 100 percent of the yard's more than seventeen thousand employees pledged an average of 13.1 percent of their gross pay to the war bond program. Philadelphia Navy Yard held the previous record at 98 percent participation and 12.1 percent of gross pay.[6] Portsmouth Navy Yard management had solicited maximum employee support for the war bond campaign, and the employees responded beyond all expectations. Once the employees realized that 100 percent participation was possible, peer pressure and pride drove the final record-setting results.

Portsmouth Herald coverage of a union banquet in January 1946 offers further evidence that labor-management cooperation at the shipyard was high throughout the war. According to the newspaper, "Accenting the fine cooperation between labor and management at the Portsmouth naval base, more than 300 members of the Ranger Lodge No. 836, International Order of Machinists, and high-ranking officials attended an installation banquet and program held Saturday at the

American Legion hall." Rear Adm. John H. Brown, who had relieved Rear Admiral Withers as commandant a few months before, told the gathering that "he could plainly see that the cooperation in the yard during the war years was the reason for the success in production and other records."[7]

SecNav Industrial Survey #2 (1944) emphasized the high quality of the Portsmouth workforce and supervisory personnel: "The working force at Portsmouth is especially high grade. Top civilian supervisors are alert, intelligent and obviously proud of their Yard. Intermediate supervision of high quality is in general evidence. . . . Most of the mechanical employees have been recruited from nearby areas, normally non-industrial. The result is an average of unusually high type [sic] of personnel among this group."[8] Percy Whitney, hired in June 1940 as a trainee in the shipyard apprentice program, is an example of the high-quality worker to which the industrial survey refers. He applied for the apprentice program after attending Bates College for two and a half years.[9] Another example was Eileen Dondero Foley, a painter's helper at the yard during the war. She had graduated from Syracuse University with honors prior to seeking employment at the yard.[10] With intelligent, educated, and motivated young men and women such as Whitney and Foley working their way through the shops and training programs, there is little wonder that the SecNav industrial survey team would be so highly impressed with the workforce.

SecNav Industrial Survey #2 (1944) also noted, "The supervisory ratio is below the prewar standard of one to twelve, which is the exception rather than the rule in shipyards."[11] Portsmouth, unlike the other navy yards, did not increase the ratio of supervisors to workers to compensate for the addition of large numbers of inexperienced employees during the war. Several factors contributed to the low supervisory ratios at Portsmouth Navy Yard. The intelligent and self-motivated workforce required less direct supervision, specialized training created a pool of independent workers and teams, and managers trusted and empowered employees to do their jobs. The next chapter will show that self-directed small teams with specialized training were a key element of the production strategy of the yard during the war.

Minimal supervision is one indicator of worker independence and empowerment, but there were others. According to SecNav Industrial Survey #2 (1944), "There has been a notable simplification of paperwork and of routine reports. A minimum of management and shop conferences are held for coordination of work and dissemination of information."[12] The trained, trusted, and empowered workforce had little need for paperwork and meetings. Managers and supervisors obviously agreed.

Reducing paperwork and lightening administrative burdens were shipyard goals from the earliest stages of the war. Portsmouth Industrial Survey #1 (December 1941) noted,

The practice of holding a shop accountable for overexpenditures of estimates on a job order practically requires each shop to set up a small accounting system and requires a leadingman either to keep cost records or to furnish information to a shop clerk for such records. The effort now devoted to cost keeping could be better devoted to the supervision of men. It is recommended that this practice be discontinued and that all shops be informed that they will not in the future be held accountable for the expenditures on any job.[13]

In effect, shipyard management was saying that accomplishing work was far more important than accounting for the cost of doing that work. As will be seen later, Portsmouth Navy Yard was very cost competitive during the war despite, or possibly because of, its abbreviated cost-accounting procedures.

The decision to free supervisors of administrative burdens that detracted from the direct supervision and coordination of work can be found throughout all of the local board's recommendations for production improvements at the start of the war. SecNav Industrial Survey #2 (1944) critically confirmed the yard's success in this regard by observing, "Practically no regular records are kept of production, whether of individual workers, of shops, or by jobs."[14] Paperwork reduction and worker independence, both increasingly emphasized as keys to successful industrial management in the latter half of the twentieth century, were facts of life at the Portsmouth Navy Yard during World War II.

Teamwork, another attribute coveted by industrial managers, was much in evidence at the shipyard during the war. Noting "a spirit of teamwork and of harmonious cooperation was evident at all levels," SecNav Industrial Survey #2 (1944) observed that the Portsmouth Navy Yard was "unusually free from labor or other personnel difficulties."[15] The inspectors noted a very positive and healthy relationship between Portsmouth Navy Yard management and employees.

Orderly and harmonious management-employee relationships were not the case at many shipyards. SecNav Industrial Survey #1 (1942) noted extensive confusion and disorganization at other navy yards: "This rapid expansion has given rise to problems of recruitment, development of new sources of labor supply, and training, and these difficulties have been intensified by the fact that supervision has been thinly spread, inexperienced, and perhaps not sufficiently informed as to policies and procedures. Under these circumstances, the ordinary management controls in matters of discipline have been increasingly difficult to maintain." While the report did not cite specific employee discipline details at navy yards, it did note that "at Boston, yard management had taken a firm hand to control discipline and counteract any tendency towards loafing" and "at Bremerton the clarification of the jurisdiction and authority of officer personnel and civilian supervisors . . . deserve special commendation."[16] Portsmouth faced these same challenges of recruitment, training, and supervision. In all three instances, the challenges were not only successfully resolved, but turned into strengths.

Labor-management relations were more contentious in private shipyards than at navy yards. Maritime historian Frederic C. Lane compiled data relative to the percentage of time lost because of strikes during the war years in the U.S. merchant shipbuilding industry versus all U.S. industries, which is shown in Table 8. There was an initial flurry of serious labor strikes at civilian shipyards in 1941, during which nearly 250,000 production workdays were lost. After that, time lost owing to strikes in the merchant shipbuilding industry was approximately the same or less than in all other U.S. industries during the remainder of the war years. Not to be minimized is the fact that merchant shipyards experienced 148 strikes during the war that cost the nation 743,000 production workdays.[17] In comparison, the "no-strike pledge" that had to be signed as a condition of employment at the navy yards kept those yards free of strikes.[18]

Table 8: Time Lost Owing to Strikes during World War II

	U.S. Merchant Shipbuilding	All Industry
1941	1.26%	.32%
1942	.07%	.05%
1943	.07%	.15%
1944	.09%	.09%
1945	.15%	.47%

Source: Frederic C. Lane, *Ships for Victory* (Baltimore: Johns Hopkins University Press, 2001), 305.

Ninety percent of the more than eleven thousand production workers at Electric Boat Company, Portsmouth's prime competitor in submarine construction, went on strike on 15 August 1944 for higher wages.[19] The union presented a list of thirty-four grievances that it claimed had been originally presented to company officials the previous December. The company president, L. Y. Spear, insisted that "the strike was brought about by a small group of union officers in an attempt to hide the real issue—the two-day suspension of the union president for being away from his job without permission."[20] Not only did Portsmouth Navy Yard not experience any labor strikes during the war, the yard was essentially free of the haggling and contentious relations between management and employees that existed at Electric Boat Company and other shipyards.

Why was that the case? When interviewed, Eileen Foley repeatedly emphasized the exceptional patriotism and respect for authority that she and her fellow workers held during the war.[21] William Tebo expressed a similar sentiment about the shipyard managers.[22] One might be quick to dismiss such idealism in today's skeptical world, but there is no doubt in Foley's mind that two Yankee attributes—respect for authority and patriotism—were powerful forces at the yard during the war.

Also to be considered is that the increase in yard employees included few minorities and other workers relocating from distant parts of the country with different values and attitudes that might have caused tensions among locals with biases. Other shipyards, especially those on the West Coast, experienced the migration of large numbers of workers, including many African Americans and others who had moved great distances to find employment at shipyards. Lorraine McConaghy, in her study of the small shipyard boomtown of Kirkland, Washington, wrote that residents often complained of "the ignorance of Tarheels, Arkies, and Okies" and "traded stories about the arrogance of Texans and the streetwise savvy of Chicago city slickers."[23] Portsmouth residents and shipyard workers were not measurably exposed to such a variety of strangers. Consequently, they did not develop similar feelings, attitudes, and prejudices toward their brand of newcomers.

This is not to say that Portsmouth was not without ethnic diversity. Indeed, the city and the mill towns of New Hampshire experienced much immigration during the late nineteenth and early twentieth century that populated the state with many nationalities, including Italians, Irish, Greeks, Poles, and French-Canadians. According to historian David M. Kennedy, in 1924 "Congress choked the immigrant stream to a trickle, closing the era of virtually unlimited entry to the United States. The ethnic neighborhoods that had mushroomed in the preceding generations would grow no more through further inflows from abroad." Kennedy notes, "Of the 123 million Americans recorded in the census of 1930, one in ten was foreign born and, an additional 20 percent had at least one parent born abroad."[24] By the late 1930s the immigration wave had also subsided in New Hampshire, and many of the immigrants had become U.S. citizens.[25] While native customs and traditions remained strong in the ethnic neighborhoods of Portsmouth, the shipyard served as a melting pot to promote interactions and understanding between new workers with various ethnic backgrounds and between them and the yard's experienced workforce. The result was a more homogeneous workforce than found at most shipyards.

At Electric Boat, in the early days of wartime expansion, new workers came from local communities. But as production demands increased the company recruited from as far away as Pennsylvania, West Virginia, and Minnesota.[26] Portsmouth, on the other hand, attracted other New Englanders. Many of the new residents of the Portsmouth area merely relocated from other nearby towns and states. In fact, many relocated from the more distant parts of the same county, Rockingham County.[27] When asked about new shipyard employees who had not grown up in the local area, William Tebo responded, "There were a lot from towns in Down East Maine."[28] At the time employees from Millinocket and Damariscotta shared many of the same values and agendas as employees from Kittery and Portsmouth.

Loafing, observed to be much too prevalent in the shipbuilding industry during the early stages of the war, was not a serious problem at Portsmouth Navy Yard. Adm. Emory Land, the chairman of the Maritime Commission, was outspoken in his criticism of loafing in the shipbuilding industry during the initial months of the war. A March 1942 Maritime Commission investigation found eight yards rated satisfactory, seven rated fair, and eleven to be "unsatisfactory" or "downright disgraceful."[29]

SecNav Industrial Survey #1 (1942) noted a high prevalence of inefficient standby time in some navy yards caused by short lead time and unplanned ship repair work. Much less tolerable was the unethical behavior that included sleeping during working hours, leaving work places before quitting time, and loafing. The survey recommended firm supervisory control of work sites and timely discipline of offenders. According to the survey, shipyard workers that were short on work ethic could find ample opportunity to stand by, waiting for other support trades or supervision to provide direction. Worse yet, slackers could escape detection in ship compartments and tanks and other out-of-the-way work sites. As late in the war as January 1945, a Senate committee investigating war contracts reported an alarming condition of wasted labor at Norfolk Navy Yard and concluded that the yard's supervisory system required improvements.[30] Disturbing as these examples are, it appears that even a wartime environment can fail to motivate some of the less inclined workers. To be fair, idle shipyard workers did not always lack motivation. Idleness was often the result of shipyards being inundated with new and inexperienced workers and management's failure to efficiently make appropriate work assignments.

Portsmouth's small size and homogeneous workload enabled management to efficiently assimilate new workers and reduce idleness. In fact, Portsmouth's World War II history is remarkably free of any need to discipline workers for unethical work practices. Portsmouth Industrial Survey #1 (December 1941) reported, "The Board does not believe that loafing exists at this Yard to such a degree as to constitute a serious problem."[31] However, the board did recommend a number of changes to reduce the temptation for workers to loaf, including reduced hours for the shipyard restaurant and mobile lunch carts and improved staffing for both to reduce lines and time lost from the job. The same task force evaluated the established practice of monitoring shipboard job sites using checklists to ensure assigned workers were on the job. The board considered this practice to be inefficient and not commensurate with the administrative burden it entailed. It recommended that the practice be discontinued. All evidence points toward a level of mutual trust and confidence between managers and employees that started at the top and extended down through the workforce. The result was a cadre of independent and specialized workers routinely doing their jobs with minimal supervision.

Eileen Foley was a painter's helper during the war and later served as the mayor of Portsmouth for sixteen years. When interviewed about the relationship between management and employees during the war, she was most emphatic about the mutual respect that existed between the two groups. She remembered the civilian managers as being ever present in the industrial areas, monitoring the progress of work sites but seldom criticizing or interfering with the workers. Attired in coat, tie, and felt hat, their dress was a symbol of their authority, which Foley remembered as being exercised in a firm, fair manner.[32]

Shipyard employees apparently were not as dedicated to safety regulations as they were to the quality of their work and the timely completion of their job responsibilities. SecNav Industrial Survey #2 (1944) found, "The Yard has a creditable safety record although its ratio of lost time to all accidents has been high." The survey added, "Safety hats were noticeable by their absence," and "There was a noticeable neglect of using goggles on grinding operations."[33] William Tebo, who worked at the yard about the time of the survey, was issued a pair of safety glasses. However, he never wore a hard hat and does not recall any being made available. Tebo also recalled that earplugs were not available until late 1944, when, he suspects, authorities began to make an association between the growing instance of hearing loss and the intolerable noise that resulted from banging and chipping on a submarine pressure hull. Tebo also had a friend lose a few toes in a shop accident for lack of safety shoes.[34] The wartime environment at the shipyard, as in most other industrial sites, was filled with hazards that were simply classified as the cost of doing business.

SecNav Industrial Survey #2 (1944) also observed, "There seemed to be a feeling in some shops that all action in accident prevention is the sole responsibility of the Safety Engineer and his staff."[35] Without too much imagination, one can conjure an image of an employee, confident in his ability to get the job done, free of rules and restrictions, wanting to extend that same independence and freedom of choice to the observance of safety rules.

In summary, Portsmouth Navy Yard employees were intelligent, cooperative, independent, trusted, well trained, and able to accomplish their jobs with minimal supervision. Cooperative and self-motivated employees enabled managers to employ worker empowerment and other team-oriented concepts. There were no strikes or slowdowns at Portsmouth Navy Yard. Employee disciplinary actions were infrequent when compared to other navy yards. Loafing, prevalent at some shipyards, was not an issue at Portsmouth. The harmonious management-employee environment at Portsmouth Navy Yard during the war was the exception in the shipbuilding industry rather than the rule. The cooperative environment at Portsmouth was certainly a significant factor in the yard's success.

Female Employees

The mobilization of women across the nation during the war to fill industrial jobs for which there were not enough men was slow to develop. Such was also the case at Portsmouth Navy Yard. According to Alice Kessler-Harris' seminal study of female employees in America, "As government programs began early in 1942 to 'warm up' the unemployed to heavy industry, twenty men were offered places to every woman. Some workers received training in industrial skills in the last half of 1941. Only 1 percent of those were female. Employers believed women were not suited to most jobs and declared themselves unwilling to hire women for 81 percent of available production jobs. . . . Attitudes began to change after Pearl Harbor. . . . For the first time employers sought out women for nontraditional jobs."[36] The progress made by female employees in filling industrial jobs at Portsmouth Navy Yard during the war, as Kessler-Harris described on a national level, was initially resisted by management and, consequently, was slow in developing. In addition, Portsmouth and the other East Coast navy yards lagged behind their West Coast counterparts in hiring women to fill shipyard employment needs.

Frederic C. Lane writes that "the female invasion began in the fall of 1942" and reached its maximum in 1944 and 1945, when "female workers formed 10 to 20 percent in most yards." According to Lane, female employment during the war was lowest in the Northeast and the Gulf and highest on the West Coast. For example, the percentage of females employed at the Richmond Shipyard outside San Francisco was 20 to 23 percent in 1944, and the Oregon Shipyard peaked at 31 percent in 1945.[37] These, of course, were both private shipyards.

West Coast navy yards also had a higher percentage of female employees than other navy yards. The top two yards for female employment in March 1943 were Mare Island, California (19.6 percent), and Bremerton, Washington (16.8 percent).[38] At that time, Portsmouth Navy Yard had a workforce that included only 8.5 percent female employees, the second lowest of the navy yards. New York Navy Yard was lowest at 8.0 percent.

In September 1942 Captain Davis urged the Industrial Department to "more aggressively pursue training programs for women—as the West Coast shipyards have done so effectively."[39] At the high point for shipyard employment—20,445 employees in November 1943—3,832 women were employed, almost 18.7 percent of the workforce. Near the end of the war, in July 1945, women still made up about 18 percent of the 15,078-person workforce.[40] Even though Portsmouth Navy Yard got off to a slow start, by the end of the war the yard employed women at about the same percentages as other navy yards.

In general, New England society showed a reluctance to utilize female employees to the fullest extent of their capabilities early in the war. Perhaps, in the case of shipyards, it reflected a sincere desire on the part of the managers to keep women safe and protected from the rigors and unsavory aspects of shipyard industrial work. In January 1942 the commandant of the Boston Navy Yard issued a directive illustrating concern about the safety of female employees: "The Commandant considers that most clerical positions in the yard can be filled by female employees, except stockmen in the storehouse, clerks assigned to night shifts in the shops or in shops where a single clerk is employed, and messengers required to go in the shops or on the ships."[41] In short, women were not to be hired for jobs for which they might have to interact with men in out-of-the-way job sites without other women present, especially at night. Without a doubt, shipyard managers were concerned about the introduction of sexuality and its potential repercussions to the workplace.

Captain Davis encouraged the recruitment of female employees but also expressed guarded optimism about their limitations and potential contributions. In September 1942 Davis wrote, "In view of the increasing demands on the available manpower of the country for defense work and military duty, it is apparent that the services of women must be utilized in every type of work *for which they can be trained and for which physically qualified*" (emphasis added).[42] Implicit in the memo is the understanding that women could not be expected to replace certain male employees because of their inherent physical characteristics and training limitations. Specifically, Captain Davis stressed that women were not to be employed on board ships or as security guards.[43]

Foley recalls that she was permitted to work topside on submarines, but "never, never, never, in the compartments or tanks." She added, "They [the shipyard managers] were very strict about that."[44] Female workers were not prohibited from entering interior submarine worksites for the entire war. Tebo and Dan MacIsaac both remembered women working alongside men in submarine compartments and tanks toward the end of the war.[45]

Jeffery M. Dorwart found a similar reluctance to assign women to worksites on board ships at Philadelphia Navy Yard: "The Philadelphia Navy Yard never appeared entirely comfortable with female employees during World War II. . . . Supervisors would not allow women to work on board the battleship *New Jersey* for nearly a year. . . . Approximately 70 percent of the Navy Yard's female employees held clerical, office, or inside shop work."[46] Six months after the war started, the federal government, recognizing industry's reluctance to hire women for jobs they did not traditionally hold, increased the pressure to hire women. Kessler-Harris' study describes the government's actions to dramatically increase employment opportunities for the women: "By mid-1942, it was clear that this [the rate that women were entering the industrial workforce] was not enough. . . . The government lowered the age limit for employment of women from eighteen to sixteen years. . . . And in July 1943, the War Production Board declared itself in need of a million and a half more women."[47] Reacting to a secretary of the navy directive of 1 September 1942 that alerted the navy yards to hire women because all eligible males would soon be called by the Selective Service Administration, Captain Davis wrote a memo on 30 September 1942 that gives more insight into his sympathies regarding woman employees: "Seeing the trend of the movement [toward hiring women], it would behoove Portsmouth to take action to obtain the pick of women available as to avoid the serious dislocations which may occur if action is delayed and later forced upon the Yard in larger numbers and suddenly."[48] In this memo, Davis appears to be suggesting that it would be best to follow the secretary of the navy's direction and expeditiously hire women. By hiring women quickly the shipyard could get the pick of the talent available. If the yard could gradually increase the number of female employees, it might avoid being forced to hire them en masse at a later date. He seems to hold the fear that delaying the inevitable might later inundate the yard with large numbers of unqualified and untrained employees.

Captain Davis' concerns were realized in May 1943, when Assistant Secretary of the Navy Bard directed Portsmouth and the other East Coast navy yards to increase their employment of women, especially skilled women. According to Bard, "The Navy yards at Portsmouth, N.H., Boston, Mass., New York, N.Y., Philadelphia, Pa., and Norfolk, Va., especially should increase their employment of women to at least the average for all yards. The acceptance of women in private industry indicates that the continental Navy yards are not utilizing women on a comparable scale, particularly in the skilled Group III."[49] Bard's observation about the shortage of skilled female workers in navy yards was especially true for Portsmouth Navy Yard.

Foley was hired at the Portsmouth Navy Yard shortly after Bard's directive. During an interview with the master of the paint shop on her first day of work in 1942, she and another woman were told, "This is dirty work. You are here to paint the boats and not your faces." Such was the no-nonsense approach of shipyard management to the increased hiring of women on the yard. Foley reported to work at the paint shop the next morning, but she never saw the other woman again.[50]

While Foley may have interpreted the comment by her shop master to mean she should deemphasize her personal appearance for the sake of the job and production, Alice Kessler-Harris claims the opposite was often the case during the war. She argues that women often "found themselves facing male pressure to be feminine" and personnel managers preferred "the girls to be neat and trim and well put together," claiming that it helped the women's morale and brought prestige to the workplace. Another less welcomed consequence of the maintenance of a feminine appearance in the workplace, according to Kessler-Harris, was that "catcalls, whistles, and hisses faced women who walked onto production floors for the first time."[51] Neither Foley nor any of the other retired shipyard employees interviewed for this study alluded to the type of male behavior in the workplace described by Kessler-Harris. Rather, Foley's example with the master of the paint shop suggests the opposite.

Most women at the yard were employed as clerks or administrative assistants in offices, as mechanics' helpers in the shops, as shop cleaners, or as operators of shop equipment on which they had been specially trained. Hazel Sinclair, one of a few African American women at the yard, worked as a woodworker's helper for over two years during the war. Sinclair reported that "they didn't let women work on the machines," and consequently, she stacked wood during the period of her employment. Rosary Cooper, another African American woman, first found wartime employment at the shipyard as a file clerk and eventually qualified as a crane operator.[52] Anna Jones, also African American, began at the yard as a messenger and was in training to be a draftsman when the war ended. Ambitious and opportunistic, these women benefitted from a window of employment opportunity that opened for African American women during the war.

Nationwide, many African American women took advantage of industry's need for workers to enter well-paying jobs for which they had previously not been considered. According to Kessler-Harris, "For black women, the change was dramatic. For generations they had been denied access to good, skilled jobs that now opened to them. . . . About 20 percent of those who had been domestic servants found work in areas that had previously snubbed them. By war's end the position of black women had improved substantially. . . . Their movement into better jobs reflects not changed attitudes but their ability to take timely advantage of enlarged opportunities."[53] Portsmouth Navy Yard's Hazel Sinclair and Rosary Cooper were part of a national movement that saw African American women capitalize on unprecedented opportunities to improve their lives by moving into better-paying jobs.

Women hired into industrial shops most often found employment as helpers for welders, sheet metal workers, or foundry molders. While not a scientific approach, a review of Public Works records of upgraded women's toilet facilities gives indications of where the women were working in the shipyard in September 1942. Toilet facility upgrades were completed in the following buildings to accommodate the number of female workers indicated: Building #96, twenty-five core and molding workers; Building #55, fifty welders; Building #2, fifty welders; Building #74, fifty sheet metal workers; and Building #75, fifty sheet metal workers.[54] The shop distribution of female workers at Portsmouth was very similar to that at a private yard in South Portland, Maine, where half of the women employed were welders and the rest were assigned to trades that included shipfitting, pipefitting, burners, and crane operators.[55] According to Fred White, the female employees at Portsmouth Navy Yard were more likely to be assigned to secondary operations, such as punching holes for fasteners or grinding metal for welds, leaving the primary operation for the experienced male mechanics.[56] In her capacity as a painter's helper, Eileen Foley remembers being allowed to apply the primer or first coat of paint topside on a submarine, but the finishing coats were always left to the experienced and skilled male painters.[57]

Rosie the Riveter did not work at Portsmouth Navy Yard during World War II. First, the use of rivets was nearing extinction as submarine construction had moved from mild steel to all welded, high-tensile steel pressure hulls. Secondly, Portsmouth Rosie would not have actually driven the rivets; instead she would have punched the holes for the rivets. The assignment of women to secondary jobs at Portsmouth Navy Yard was typical of all wartime industry; as David Kennedy writes, "Women held just 4.4% of war jobs classified as skilled and a far smaller percentage of management positions." Kennedy claims that the emblem of Rosie the Riveter as a "denim-clad, tool-wielding, can-do figure" actually typified very few wartime woman employees. He suggests that Wendy the Welder, Sally the Secretary, or Molly the Mom might have been more appropriate labels for the typical wartime female employee.[58]

Private industries in the Portsmouth area were also slow to hire women. A Portsmouth Health and Welfare Survey conducted in June 1942 indicated that, of the three Portsmouth industrial plants engaged in defense work, only the Morley Company employed women. Morley employed 93 women, only 3 of whom were married. At the time, the navy yard employed 430 women, only 10 of whom were married. A later survey, between June 1942 and August 1943, found 470 female clerical workers at the yard and 400 female employees at the Somersworth plant.[59]

It is apparent that during the early stages of the war, a limited number of women were employed in an industrial environment and almost all of those employed were unmarried. The Portsmouth Defense Area Health and Welfare Survey concluded, "There has been no significant increase in the number of mothers employed since the inception of defense work." Also, "Because the Portsmouth Navy Yard is the major industry [in the area], and the only large one, it seems there will be no appreciable increase in numbers of employed women unless, and until, the Navy Yard employs women in large numbers."[60] Women in Portsmouth did fill a void in taxi drivers as male drivers went to war or took better-paying defense jobs. In the summer of 1942 Rosie was driving a taxi in Portsmouth, not rivets in the shipyard across the river.

Despite the slow initial progress in hiring women to fill jobs at the yard, the *Portsmouth Herald* periodically featured front-page articles and pictures that highlighted the advancements made by women. For example, on 18 May 1942 the paper reported on the employment of women as taxi and bus drivers: "No wonder people are beginning to wonder if it really is a man's world. First Portsmouth had a woman cleaning company driver, then a taxi driver, and now the Hill Transportation company has hired from the government employment agency two women for duty behind its wheels."[61] Six months after the attack on Pearl Harbor, the local hiring of women as replacements for men had progressed only to the level of replacing cabbies and bus drivers gone off to war—and this was front-page news. While not a particularly glamorous beginning, driving a taxi or a bus paid better than cleaning a house or performing most other jobs available to women at the time.

Over the next year and a half the *Portsmouth Herald* frequently carried pictures of women in training for, or being hired to perform, better-paying jobs traditionally held by men at the shipyard. The *Herald*'s coverage of events provides a chronological summary of the incremental progress that women made toward more meaningful industrial employment.

On 18 June 1942 the *Herald* published a picture of several Exeter girls "amid gears and belts of steel lathes," who were among the first women to enroll in defense mechanical training classes, with hopes of gaining employment at the shipyard.[62] The 22 March 1943 newspaper displays a picture of the first female navy yard machinist to apply for membership in the Ranger Lodge, International Association of Machinists. The article notes that the woman is currently a "checker of machines and other supplies," but her number one ambition is to become a "full fledged machinist."[63] The 12 May 1943 edition contains an article titled "School Aids Production of Navy Submarines" that credits the local Federal Vocational Training School and notes that 125 of the 322 students enrolled in the school are women.[64] On 11 November 1943 four shipyard "welderettes" are pictured with their supervisor. According to the *Herald*, the four women had patriotically completed 150 hours of electric welding training; "They have swapped the duties of housekeeping and the tapping typewriter for the glow of a blow torch and the clang of steel. They're laboring, sweating, amid steel beams and plates to build fighting submarines for America's safety."[65] Finally, in May 1944 a very important milestone was reached when the first women graduated from the shipyard supervisory training program. Four of the 195 graduates were women. Rear Admiral Withers' graduation address praised not just the women, but also the class: "Your class is different from any other class in that it is coeducational. I am proud that this navy yard recognizes the fact that women are capable of becoming supervisors and I cannot understand why other navy yards do not take advantage of the capable woman employees they must have."[66] Withers' remarks imply that the other navy yards had not yet trained any women for supervisory positions. Portsmouth Navy Yard, after a slow start, had made up a lot of ground.

Women had progressed from housewives at the start of the war, to bus and taxi drivers by May 1942, to machine operator training programs in the early part of 1943, to fully qualified sweaty welders by November 1943, and finally to trained shop supervisors by May 1944. Elsewhere at the yard, military women were also breaking new ground. In May 1943 the first class of fifty women accepted for voluntary emergency service (WAVES) arrived at the Portsmouth Navy Yard Hospital for four weeks of basic training. The first female doctor at the shipyard reported for duty on 22 February 1945.[67]

Mary C. Dondero, who had been a clerical helper in the Portsmouth Navy Yard Supply Department early in the war, progressed further than any other woman employed at the yard during the war when she was elected mayor of Portsmouth in November 1944.[68] Dondero was the first woman to be elected mayor in the state of New Hampshire and one of the first in the nation.[69] The progress in Portsmouth did not extend to the rest of the state, however. A little over a month after Mary Dondero became mayor of Portsmouth, the New Hampshire House of Representatives rejected a bill to allow women to serve as jurors by a vote of 181 to 174.[70] Thus, in early 1945 women could hold responsible positions at the Portsmouth Navy Yard and govern the city of Portsmouth, but they could not sit on juries in the state of New Hampshire.

Late in 1945 Fred White was faced with the need to terminate about sixty women working in the sail loft. This shop produced items such as torpedo restraining straps, bunk covers, cushions, and other canvas and leather products used in outfitting new submarines. Because all the female employees were in the category of wartime employees without rights to continued employment after the war, the shipyard had no choice but to end their employment. After careful consideration, and with the encouragement of the women involved, White decided to forgo the normal practice of terminating employees individually, according to hiring date. He released all sixty on the same day. The women, who did not want to experience individual firings and possible disputes about who should go next, met the decision with universal approval. According to White, the women celebrated together as they walked out of the shop on their last day of employment.[71]

Nationwide, women were quick to quit their jobs when war production ended. Kessler-Harris writes, "The rate at which women chose to leave jobs was at least double, and sometimes triple the rate at which they were discharged. And it was consistently higher than quit rates for men."[72] Many of the women who had found employment in the shipyard industrial shops during the war, like millions of women in comparable positions across the United States, were more than willing to leave their wartime jobs so as to make them available for returning veterans. The majority preferred to return to their homes and to other occupations.

Selective Service

That the younger, more adaptable and physically fit employees were routinely drafted or volunteered for military service became one of the more serious employment problems of the war. The Selective Service Act was passed on 16 September 1940. Soon, more than 16 million men between the ages of twenty-one and thirty-five were registered on the draft rolls. To further complicate matters, the Navy's well-advertised "choose while you can" program enticed a large number of patriotic young men of the seacoast area to volunteer for the Navy and Marine Corps during the early years of the war. Thus, fifteen months before the start of the war, at about the same time that the shipyard ramp-up was gathering momentum, many of the younger employees began to be siphoned from the shipyard's rolls. Over the next two years amendments extended the age limits for military service down to eighteen years and up to sixty-five years. However, the military wanted no men over forty-five and strongly preferred only those under the age of twenty-six.[73]

The shipyard apprentice program was especially devastated by the loss of men to military service. SecNav Industrial Survey #2 (1944) reported, "Just before the war the Yard employed some 400 apprentices. The present number is about 80. Some 240 former apprentices are in the armed forces on military furlough."[74] At the end of the war, in the summer of 1945, the shipyard reported "approximately 450 on military furlough, leaving less than 50 apprentices now employed."[75] The loss of skilled and experienced employees to military service was a continuing employment problem throughout the war.

Percy Whitney was one of the skilled shipyard employees lost to the draft in 1943. Whitney entered the apprentice program in June 1940 and graduated three years later. He believes he had the good fortune of being employed for three years before he was drafted because the work he was doing in the foundry was critical and because he was married.[76] Even so, he joined the long list of former apprentices and skilled shipyard employees on furlough to the military when he was drafted into the Marine Corps in 1943.

Attrition caused by the loss of employees to military service early in the war was particularly acute in the shipyard welding shop. First established in November 1939, the welding shop quickly grew in size and importance as submarine construction moved from riveted carbon steel (mild steel) hulls to welded high-tensile steel (HTS) pressure hulls.[77] By April 1942 the shop employed nearly a thousand workers and had a pressing need to hire many more welders. In early 1942 the shop was scheduled to lose twenty-five to thirty qualified welders per month to military service. Welders were being lost faster than replacements could be trained and certified.[78]

The welding shop was not the only shop to lose large numbers of trained employees to the service. Charles Downing, a group superintendent at the yard when he retired in 1973, was a journeyman machinist there when he was drafted in 1944. According to him, the inside machine shop was decimated when "forty machinists left Kennebunk on a train for Fort Devens on the same day." Many of them, like Downing, had completed the three-year apprentice program and were well into the four-year journeyman program when they were drafted. The requirement to constantly replace large numbers of trained workers was a never-ending challenge.[79]

The procedures of the Selective Service Administration (SSA) were a particularly difficult challenge for the shipyard throughout the war. The efforts of management to schedule the orderly release of employees with critical skills, such as welders, had to be coordinated with numerous local draft boards in all three of the states from which the yard drew most of its employees. In February 1943 the shipyard, under the leadership of Captain Davis, brought some order to this chaotic situation when it reached a precedent-setting agreement with the SSA. The SSA agreed that the shipyard could release workers in accordance with a long-range, predetermined plan. The New Hampshire deferment rules would apply to all yard employees subject to the draft. According to the *Portsmouth Herald* of 5 February 1943, "This establishes the yard as the first employer in New Hampshire and, it is believed, the first navy yard in the United States to reach [such] an agreement with the Selective Service System." Explaining the advantages of the agreement, the *Herald* reported, "The naval authorities will no longer be required to deal with many local boards in several states in the cases of individual employees whose services they desire to retain for occupational reasons. . . . A single deferment policy, that which prevails in the state of New Hampshire, will be applied to all employees at the yard who are vulnerable to the Selective Service and Training Act."[80] Captain Davis, always meticulous in his planning, had reduced the problem with the SSA to manageable proportions.

In July 1945 the *Portsmouth Periscope* reported, "As of 30 June, 5,033 workmen had shifted from war work to the fighting front" and "85 men from this Yard have died in action."[81] During the peak war years, when the average shipyard employment was about eighteen thousand, the average loss of employees to military service was well over a thousand employees per year. However, knowing in advance which critical skills would be lost, and when, the shipyard could hire replacements and schedule the necessary training to minimize the impact on production schedules.

—⚍—

In summary, Portsmouth Navy Yard was blessed with an intelligent and motivated workforce during the war that gave patriotism and teamwork very high priority. A cooperative spirit based on mutual respect and trust characterized employee-management relations. The result was harmony in the workplace and few disciplinary actions. Women played an increasingly important role in the yard as they gradually gained access to training programs that qualified them for more responsible positions. Their progress was impressive and their contributions were significant. Because of the personnel disruptions caused by employees leaving the yard for military service, the yard negotiated a precedent-setting agreement with the SSA that allowed for the orderly release of employees in accordance with a long-range plan that permitted the yard to train replacements in a timely manner. The employees, in short, were the keystone upon which the shipyard built its remarkable success.

Photo 1: Triple simultaneous launching of *Redfish*, *Ronquil*, and *Razorback*. (Courtesy of Milne Special Collection and Archives Department, University of New Hampshire Library, Durham)

Photo 2: *Redfish*, *Ronquil*, and *Razorback* building in dry dock #1. (Courtesy of Milne Special Collections, University of New Hampshire Library, Durham)

Photo 3: Free French submarine *Surcouf* in dry dock #2 (Summer 1941). (Courtesy of Milne Special Collections, University of New Hampshire Library, Durham)

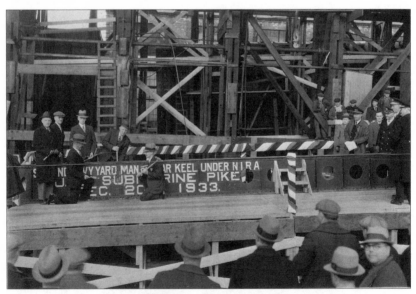

Photo 4: Keel laying for National Industrial Recovery Act submarine USS *Pike*. (Courtesy of Milne Special Collections and Archives Department, University of New Hampshire Library, Durham)

Photo 5: President Roosevelt touring the shipyard (August 1940). (Courtesy of Milne Special Collections, University of New Hampshire Library, Durham)

Photo 6: New fitting-out pier under construction (1942). (Courtesy of the Milne Special Collections, University of New Hampshire Library, Durham)

Photo 7: Rear Adm. Thomas Withers greeting managers during change of command, 10 June 1942. (Courtesy of Milne Special Collections, University of New Hampshire Library, Durham)

Photo 8: Shipyard civilian shop managers during World War II. Fred White, the master rigger and laborer interviewed for this volume, is shown in the upper left corner. (Courtesy of Milne Special Collections, University of New Hampshire Library, Durham)

Photo 9: Shipyard rally at start of the war, 15 December 1941. (Courtesy of Milne Special Collections, University of New Hampshire Library, Durham)

Photo 10: Submarine pressure hull sections in the building basin. (Courtesy of Milne Special Collections, University of New Hampshire Library, Durham)

Photo 11: USS *Pilotfish* and USS *Bang* preparing for launch in dry dock #1. (Courtesy of Milne Special Collections, University of New Hampshire Library, Durham)

Photo 12: Rear Admiral Withers and managers displaying "E" award. (Courtesy of Milne Special Collections, University of New Hampshire Library, Durham)

Chapter 5

Methods

Any present judgment of the organization, administration, and control procedures of the Navy Yard, Portsmouth, N.H. must give great weight to the development of the Yard, subordinating all other considerations to the demands of the war effort, into a specialized construction activity for submarines only. All operating units have been streamlined *for this sole purpose [emphasis added].*

—SecNav Industrial Survey #2,
6 November 1944

B y early 1942 several building blocks were in place upon which Portsmouth Navy Yard would raise a remarkable production record over the next few years. An impressive team of naval and civilian managers had been assembled, massive facility upgrades were in progress, orders had been received for dozens of new submarines, and employees were being hired at unprecedented rates. Organizationally, the yard had a free hand to manage its own growth and development. The final piece of the puzzle would be the implementation of industrial practices tailored to take maximum advantage of the shipyard's strengths, growing workforce, and expanding facilities.

Portsmouth Navy Yard employed a number of industrial practices during the war, either by design or necessity, that in some cases were years ahead of their time. Most notable of these were worker empowerment, small teams with specialized training, risk management, modular construction, and production assembly lines to the extent that they could be applied to submarine construction at the time.

This book argues that the yard's outstanding performance was the result of well-designed processes and practices that capitalized on all available resources. In the case of the most critically needed shipbuilding resource—building ways—Portsmouth Navy Yard was seriously under capacity immediately prior to the war, and it remained so challenged throughout the war. With only five building ways at the start of the war, the desired building rates could be achieved only if submarine hulls were forced off the ways very early in the construction schedule to free the ways for the next hulls. Submarines were launched at unprecedented rates, and much of the work normally done on the building ways had to be completed pier-side. Necessity was very much the mother of invention as the shipyard overcame the shortage of building ways by developing and optimizing techniques to build submarines side by side in the newly constructed dry dock and building basin.

Although quality of workmanship had always been a high priority at the Portsmouth Navy Yard, it was time and production efficiency, not perfection of product, that drove the yard during the war. It was the sacrifice of absolute quality for time that led to the production miracle at Portsmouth and other American shipyards during the war. This was in sharp contrast to the German approach to production, which was geared more toward optimum design and technical excellence than efficiency. Historian David Kennedy writes,

> In the inescapable trade-off between quality and quantity, the Germans characteristically chose the former, the Americans the latter. . . . Though the Americans also ultimately proved capable of some epochal scientific and technical breakthroughs, they innovated most characteristically in plant lay-out, production organization, economies of scale, and process engineering. If Germany aimed for the perfection of many things, America aspired to the commodification of virtually every thing. . . . [The United States placed] a premium on organizing production around simple repetitive tasks that did not demand technical adeptness or extensive training.[1]

As Kennedy suggests, a common theme throughout this chapter will be the streamlining of work at Portsmouth Navy Yard to enable the repetitive accomplishment of the same jobs on numerous successive submarines. It should also become evident that the shipyard excelled in those areas that, according to Kennedy, separated American industry from that of the enemy: plant layout, production organization, process engineering, and economies of scale.

An Assembly Line of Sorts

Fred White recalls that early in the war the shipyard managed to achieve an assembly line of sorts. Submarine sections, or modules, constructed in various buildings, were moved to the building sites to be welded together, and after launching, the submarines were moved from berth to berth for the completion of berth-specific tasks leading to machinery trials and completion. Granted, there was no assembly line as such, but the process did bear some resemblance to the automotive industry's conveyor belt that received subassemblies at various stations and moved on until a completed car was produced at the end of the line. At any rate, the submarine building process at the yard during the war was far removed from the custom building practices of the 1920s and early 1930s.

This assembly line of sorts began with the sectional construction process first used on NIRA submarine *Porpoise* in 1933. A discussion of the production methods used to build *Cachalot,* the last submarine delivered before *Porpoise,* will illustrate the important transition in production methods that occurred at that time. According to Adm. Stuart S. Murray, then Lieutenant Murray, the yard's assistant machinery superintendent and eventually the commanding officer of *Porpoise,* a "spit planning method" was used to build the *Cachalot*:

> The plans for the *Cachalot* were not as far ahead in the planning division as the actual production on the waterfront was—that is, the detailed plans of where the piping would go, where the wiring would go, where the auxiliary machinery would go. So on the waterfront we had to fix, or point out, and draw chalk marks as to where the pipelines would go and where the wiring would go and where the small auxiliary machinery would go. We facetiously called it the "spit" planning method. . . . One of the leading men said that I would stand in the engine room and spit, and where the spit landed was where a pipe would go. It wasn't quite that rough, but it wasn't scientific to say the least. The draftsmen would come down from the planning section when we had the pipe installed and draw their plans from where the pipes were rather than where they thought they were going.[2]

The shipyard working relationships that characterized the crude spit planning method eventually contributed to the successful wartime streamlining of the shipyard for the construction of new submarines. During the war, mutual trust and cooperation between skilled tradesmen on the waterfront and their counterparts in the Planning Department resulted in efficient construction methods that minimized paperwork and emphasized getting the job done.

Prior to *Porpoise* and *Pike,* flat steel plates were rolled to the desired cylindrical shapes in the structural shop and moved to the building site, where they were riveted together. Each submarine constructed was custom built at the building site. A Local Shore Station Development Board letter dated 30 July 1934 noted, "A new method has been developed for the construction of submarines." The letter explained, "The submarines *Porpoise* and *Pike* are being constructed in sections. A section of the boat weighing approximately twenty tons is constructed at Building 96 and after it has been riveted and welded the section is moved by crane and railroad cars and placed on the building ways in Building 115. This method of constructing a large section and moving it as one piece to the ways has proven economical and more rapid than the method which was formerly used."[3] The shipyard wanted approval for the continued use of Building 96 as a submarine section erection site instead of converting it to a storehouse as previously planned. This request, and others that followed, sought to continuously improve the sectional construction concept.

Another innovation, first used on *Porpoise* in 1933, further illustrates the yard's transition from custom-built submarines to methods and practices that would lead to increased production. After employing the spit planning method on *Cachalot*, the yard initiated a complete mock-up program on *Porpoise*. According to Admiral Murray,

> We made a complete mock-up, as it was called. That is, we built a wooden model of the submarine components, each individually, to exact scale. The shops could take their piping and all their machinery down there, and wooden models of it in the actual piping if they wanted to, to get the bends and actual locations in there, so that when it was taken down to the ship, it fitted in the right place. There was no more of the so-called spit alignment that there had been on the *Cachalot*.[4]

The fact that sectional construction and the use of wooden mock-ups began as early as 1934 illustrates the point made earlier that Portsmouth Navy Yard benefited from the continuous albeit limited stream of submarine construction orders during the 1920s and early 1930s. By directing new submarine orders to Portsmouth when Electric Boat and other yards were not getting orders, the Navy allowed Portsmouth to maintain a stable and trained workforce that knew how to build submarines. This core group went on to develop impressive new submarine construction techniques.

The shipyard developed and refined sectional construction during the latter half of the 1930s by creating other independent erection sites in various buildings convenient to the building sites. For example, the shipyard plan in 1937 for the expansion of facilities contained numerous features to accommodate sectional construction. These included a large addition to and alteration of the ship fitters shop, additional building ways, and cranes with greater lifting capacity.[5] Thus, Portsmouth planned for facilities that would support sectional construction, developed those facilities to the extent that limited funding was available, and acquired experience in this production technique. When orders skyrocketed and mass production became the order of the day, Portsmouth was poised to capitalize on the revitalized naval rebuilding program while other shipyards had to start from scratch or pick up where they left off years before.

Portsmouth Industrial Survey #2 (June 1942) concluded that more work should be done on the structural hull assemblies before they were placed in position on the ways.[6] The board recommended the installation of more equipment foundations, bulkhead valves, stuffing tubes, small structural bulkheads, and other miscellaneous items. Adding these components to the hull sections prior to moving them to the building ways accelerated the overall assembly schedule by reducing the time needed on the ways. This technique also provided better worksite access and reduced the number of workers needed in the confined spaces of tanks and compartments, either on the ways or after launch. Shipyard management recognized early on that the technique of maximizing sectional fabrication was critical to increased production.

The formula that Portsmouth Industrial Survey #2 (June 1942) outlined to increase submarine production was the same formula that other shipyards would use to deliver thousands of Liberty ships in record time a few years later. The process to build Liberty ships at the Southeastern Shipbuilding Corporation in Savannah, described by Tony Cope in *On the Swing Shift*, bore a striking resemblance to the submarine building process at Portsmouth Navy Yard: "Large sections of each Liberty ship were put on a concrete slab in front of the ways and then lifted into place by huge cranes. When the hull and superstructure were complete, the ship was launched and moved to a wet dock for fitting out. During the fitting out stage, some two hundred items were added, including the guns and all furnishings and equipment."[7] Frederic C. Lane made similar observations about the construction of liberty ships: "The phenomenal speed attained in [Liberty] shipbuilding during World War II consisted above all in reducing the length of time between keel layings and launchings. . . If the work of putting together the steel plates and shapes which formed the hull was all performed on the ways or building berths, then each building berth was occupied by one ship for a relatively long time. If, in contrast, the pieces were joined into large sections elsewhere than on the shipway, the time on the shipway could be reduced."[8] Working with much simpler systems and much roomier spaces, the builders of Liberty ships were able to accomplish more prefabrication and preassembly than was Portsmouth Navy Yard for the submarines it built. Nevertheless, Portsmouth continuously sought to increase the number of components—primarily foundations, hull fittings, bulkheads, and other structural components—that it could install in submarine sections prior to delivery to the building ways.

This is not to imply that Portsmouth Navy Yard was the only submarine building yard applying the process of sectional construction to submarines. The other submarine building yards used some form of the sectional assembly process. Electric Boat's process of sectional construction included an "upside-down" feature that rotated the pressure hull sections so that welders could "work upright instead of standing on their heads inside a rigid hull."[9] Portsmouth had the advantage of being first with the sectional construction process in 1934; thus the yard had more experience in perfecting the process and adding components to the hull sections. Portsmouth, with fewer building sites than other yards, had great motivation to perfect the sectional construction process as a way to accelerate the turnover of submarine hulls on the limited number of building sites. Without this process, Portsmouth might have been just another shipyard. With it, the yard was something special.

According to Fred White, thirteen steel cylinders were welded together to form a pressure hull. The sections were manufactured at various sites in the shipyard and then staged at the building ways, ready to be placed by crane onto the covered ways or lowered into a dock or the building basin. This would begin as soon as a launching occurred and the vacated space was available for the next hull. Photo 10 in the gallery shows two submarine pressure hull sections on parallel sets of blocks in the new building basin (subsequently renamed dry dock #3). Note that these modules include the surrounding tank frames and struts and the centerline keel section below the pressure hull on the centerline. The process of installing internal pressure hull components, such as equipment foundations and hull valves, had not yet begun when this photo was taken. Most of the outer tank plating is also absent, probably to provide better access for installing tank components (air flasks, vent valves, piping, etc.) and perhaps because of weight considerations and limited crane-lifting capacity.

On at least one occasion, White recalled, a double launching and the laying of two new keels occurred in the same dock on the same day. After a morning launch, the dock was pumped down, the blocks were recapped, and the thirteen prefabricated pressure hull sections were then lowered into place on the blocks that evening.[10] White and his crew of riggers were well aware of the shipyard's critical need to maximize the use of building sites in order to achieve full production capability. Photo 11 in the gallery shows two submarines being prepared for launch.

If the sectional construction process was part one of the pseudo–assembly line at the yard, part two was the stepping of the submarines through various berths for the completion of berth-specific jobs, many of which were accomplished by special teams. Referring to figure 4, White recalled that newly launched submarines from dry dock #1 were first berthed at Berth 11A to have the sail and topside superstructure finished. White's men then moved the submarine to Berth 11B for the installation of periscopes and masts and then on to Berth 11C, where the bow torpedo tubes were completed and tested by firing water slugs out into the Piscataqua River. The submarines were then moved around the corner to Berth 13, where the stern tubes were completed and tested, and then on up the berth for the completion of internal work and preparations for dock trials. Other work, of course, took place at each successive berth in the process. The end result was an assembly line, in which the submarine stepped from berth to berth and Portsmouth's work specialization teams reported to the same berth over and over again to accomplish repetitive tasks.[11]

Figure 4. World War II Berthing Arrangements

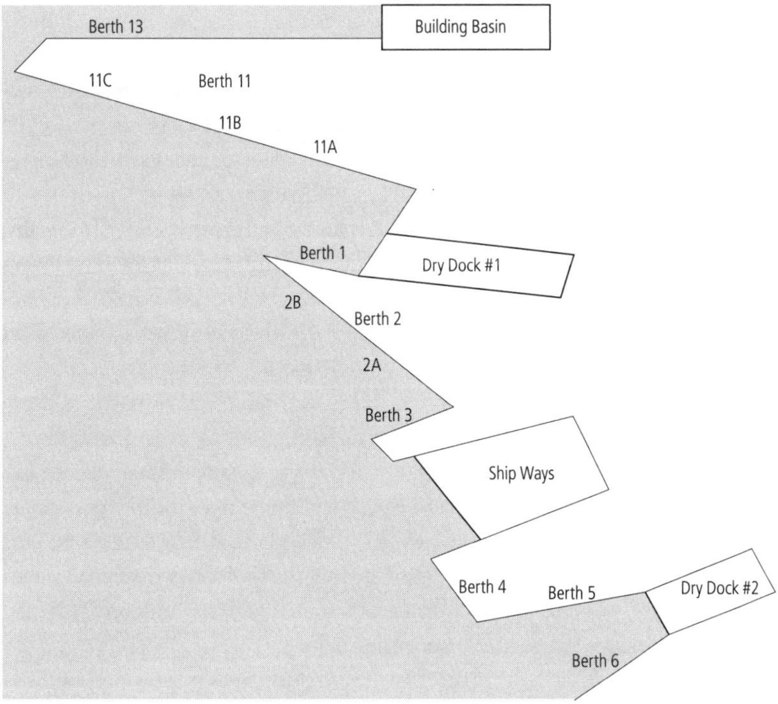

Source: NARA Waltham, RG 181, Portsmouth Naval Base Central Files, Box 18, Folder S-6, "Launching General."

Special Teams

A well-trained and self-motivated workforce with a homogeneous and repetitious workload, coupled with management concerns about the gradual loss of employees to the military services, was an environment made to order for the use of special teams. Special teams were made up of a small number of employees trained to accomplish a few specific tasks repetitively at successive work sites. A worker trained to accomplish the same job on submarine after submarine was both highly productive and an expert in performing that task. In addition, if he were drafted into the military, his replacement could be quickly trained to complete the specific task with minimal disruption to the building process. For all of these reasons, Portsmouth Navy Yard made maximum use of special teams.

Before the war, studies often associated management and productivity effectiveness with the correct corporate organizational diagram and gave little consideration to the efficiencies to be gained through revised workplace practices and employee motivation. During the war, increased production schedules and an influx of less experienced workers mandated that Portsmouth Navy Yard management maximize the potential of its workforce by turning toward employee empowerment and self-managing small teams.

Forty years later, Thomas J. Peters and others would herald worker empowerment as a revolutionary new management principle. Books by Peters, while lacking in academic rigor, spawned a management culture that rushed to implement employee empowerment, self-managing small teams, and other programs to advance employee participation and decision making in the workplace.[12] Ironically, given the World War II context of this study, many of the ideas put forth by Peters were adapted from Japan.

Peters' concepts gained popularity throughout the 1990s as the keys to increased productivity, quality, and worker satisfaction.[13] By the late 1990s the concepts had expanded from self-managing teams to self-managing organizations in which "there are no clear cut divisions between those who manage and those who are managed. Rather, everyone in the enterprise community is viewed as having full membership status, with a real share of the voice, and with a legitimate right to fully participate in the management of his or her own work."[14] While Portsmouth Navy Yard certainly was not a self-managing organization during the war, it did reap great benefits from the small specialized work teams that roamed the waterfront and skillfully performed their jobs with little or no supervision.

In the late twentieth century, as more and more companies empowered employees, numerous studies debated the concept. Studies by Chris Argyris, Bradley L. Kirkman, Benson Rosen, and others have confirmed the value of the concept when sincerely implemented with total dedication and commitment throughout the corporation.[15] Argyris, in particular, argues that anything less is a recipe for disappointing results. According to Argyris, superficial implementation of employee empowerment can bring more problems than progress. In normal peacetime industry, the creation, cultivation, and maintenance of the proper corporate environment are critical factors to the success of employee empowerment programs. At Portsmouth Navy Yard during World War II, there was no need to create and cultivate an environment to promote employee empowerment; it already existed. Shipyard managers and employees were focused on one goal—acceleration of wartime production. Commitment and dedication toward that end permeated the entire shipyard. Employee empowerment was not a management option; it was a necessity recognized and endorsed by all hands.

Mark Fenton-O'Creevy has argued that the success of self-managing teams hinges on the support of middle management. Roadblocks are experienced in companies in which middle management resists employee empowerment for selfish reasons, including concern for managerial job loss or management delayering.[16]

Wartime urgency and near unlimited job security ensured no such resistance by middle management at the Portsmouth Navy Yard.

A study by Bradley L. Kirkman and Benson Rosen has shown that the benefits of successful self-managing work teams can often exceed expectations for improved productivity, quality, and worker satisfaction. Kirkman and Rosen found that as self-managing teams gain experience and success, confidence, commitment, and even greater success follow. In addition, commitment to the concept, team, and organization increases. In time, employees develop a willingness to accept more responsibility for innovation on the job, improved customer relations, harmonious employee-management relations, accountability for results, and continuous improvement in production.[17] In effect, a cascading flood of good things happens when employees are well trained, trusted, empowered, and set free to do their jobs.

A seemingly never-ending stream of successes typified Portsmouth Navy Yard operations during the war. Many of the positive and highly desirable organizational attributes described in the previous paragraphs were included in those successes. This study augments the body of work that argues that employee empowerment, sincerely implemented with commitment and dedication, contributes significantly to outstanding production and other highly desirable corporate goals.

SecNav Industrial Survey #2 (1944) noted the widespread use of specialized teams at Portsmouth and reported, "Although the quality of the working force is at a high standard, there are many employees who have developed only specialized skills."[18] Pointing toward the need for a more uniformly trained workforce during reduced postwar operations, the survey report recommended that the specialists who were to be retained as shipyard employees after the war should receive more formal and extensive training. It was no accident that Portsmouth Navy Yard had a large number of employees with specialized skills. Shipyard management recognized early on that specialized training and specialized teams should be an integral part of the shipyard's industrial operation.

The team that Commandant Wainwright had assembled in November 1941 to study work practices and make recommendations for improvements highlighted the need for specialization. Recognizing that it would be difficult for the shipyard to obtain the numbers of skilled and trained mechanics needed to quickly ramp up production, the team reported, "While it is not possible to train skilled mechanics in short enough time to make them available in the near future, it is possible to train unskilled men who have suitable adaptability in a few of the operations of the various trades in short time. By assignment of these men to operations which they have been trained to perform and by placing them under the supervision of skilled mechanics, it is possible to get work done which could not be accomplished if only skilled men were used." Similarly, the team recommended that some shops discontinue their existing practice of assigning a group of men to custom build a single ship through completion in favor of using the same men to perform the same operations on different submarines. According to the team report, "It is obvious that a man or a group of men is better able to perform a task after having done it on another similar ship than is a different man or group of men . . . after they have completed this work on one ship, they be moved to the next ship and assigned the same work. This recommendation applies not only to mechanics, but also to shop supervisors and to ship superintendents."[19] Thus, on the day after the attack on Pearl Harbor, when the report was issued, the shipyard was already considering the need for specialized training and the advisability of assigning lesser skilled workers to repetitive tasks.

The production officer, Capt. S. E. Dudley, reinforced and formalized the recommendations of Portsmouth Industrial Survey #1 (1941) when he advised shop masters that new work methods were needed to achieve expected production increases and that the new methods should include a high degree of specialization: "We have 18 hulls to lay down. . . . Our previous methods produced good ships, but each vessel was a custom built job. Such methods will not meet the problem that we are now facing. . . . You can't run Subs down an assembly line, but for 'outside work' you can do the next best thing, that is, move men along from ship to ship to do the same work on each."[20] Similarly, in mid-January 1942 Captain Davis reminded the shops to use "repeat work teams for assembly, installation, erection, and test jobs in shops."[21] It was believed that completion dates on some ships might suffer from the effort to maximize specialization but that, in the aggregate, the result would be an optimum performance overall.[22] Production results proved this belief to be absolutely true.

Job specialization was by no means unique to Portsmouth Navy Yard. The practice was widespread in the shipyards that mass produced Liberty ships for the same reasons that it worked at Portsmouth. According to Frederic C. Lane, "When the work was planned so that the same crew had the same task every day, there was no need of teaching the new workmen the 40 or 70 operations which had formed part of the craft learned by an apprentice at Newport News. Instead, a man who had only one skill could be kept busy doing that one thing."[23] Although the repetitive task performed on a Liberty ship by a worker with limited skills was much simpler than the specialized tasks performed by a submarine construction worker at Portsmouth, the concept was the same.

William Tebo, the high school teenager employed at the navy yard in 1944, recalled how he traveled from submarine to submarine on the building ways performing the few electrical jobs for which he was the "expert installer" with minimal supervision. According to Tebo, he was a member of a small team of electricians assigned to a specific submarine compartment. One of his jobs was to wire the electrical distribution panel for the newly installed, and highly secret, shipboard radar. With the radar consoles and equipment concealed under wrappings and coverings, Tebo dutifully wired the radar electrical panels on submarine after submarine.[24] Thus, with limited electrical training, and minimal supervision, Tebo was able to provide a most useful and productive service to the yard during his six months of employment before he left for military service. Tebo was one of hundreds of specialists on small teams utilized throughout many of the trades. It is clear that specialized training, and the formation of specialized work teams, were part of the shipyard's mobilization agenda from the start of the war.

Other shipyards and industries must have shared with Portsmouth Navy Yard wartime environments and experiences that were especially conducive to increasing worker responsibilities. Yet, little has been written that explores the wartime contributions of worker empowerment. Numerous studies examine the post-war abandonment of the wartime production advantages experienced as women flooded the workplace. Perhaps new studies should be commissioned to address management's postwar abandonment of the wartime production advantages of worker empowerment. Fortunately, both women and worker empowerment made strong comebacks in the workplace in the latter half of the century.

Risk Management

The shipyard management team was aggressive and willing to assume reasonable risks to increase production. Portsmouth Navy Yard faced two major obstacles to increased production at the start of the war. The first—insufficient building ways—was satisfactorily resolved locally through aggressive and innovative management. The second—late deliveries of components supplied by contractors—was more difficult and frustrating for management to deal with because the solution required the support of external contractors and agencies. The yard could control its own fate on the first obstacle, but had much less say on the second. As the war progressed, more and more contractor-supplied components were not only late but also did not meet quality requirements and performance standards.

By December 1942 the shipyard had created a number of opportunities for increased production. One was using the new dry dock #1 for construction of two or three submarines at a time, instead of for the repair of submarines, as originally intended by the chief of naval operations (CNO). At the start of the war, the CNO placed the highest priority on the repair and maintenance of the existing fleet. He considered it an urgent matter to ensure that shipyard facilities and dry docks were available for that purpose. However, Portsmouth Navy Yard successfully challenged the original intent for the dock in the interest of maximizing submarine construction at the yard. The tension that existed between the CNO's interest in maintaining the existing fleet and the assistant secretary of the navy's interest in building new ships met in dry dock #1 at Portsmouth Navy Yard.

By way of background, the Greenslade Report on the Adequacy and Future Development of Naval Shore Establishments, dated 6 January 1941, concluded that Portsmouth Navy Yard should "handle 6% of the repair load of the entire U.S. Fleet." The Greenslade Board recommended that "a Twin Destroyer Dock [able to accommodate two destroyers at the same time] be built to enable the shipyard to carry its portion of the work level."[25] The Bureau of Ships authorized the shipyard to construct such a dock in March 1941.[26] The *Portsmouth Herald* of 20 March 1941 reported that the dock "will be big enough to handle destroyers as well as subs." At no point in the article did it say that the dry dock would be utilized for the construction of two or three submarines simultaneously, which was its ultimate use during the war.[27]

In early 1941 it was part of the Navy mobilization plan to assign Portsmouth Navy Yard a significant fleet repair workload that was not necessarily limited to submarine repair work. The Navy Department had authorized construction of the new dock to accommodate this work. Portsmouth management, however, wanted to avoid as much repair work as possible in order to streamline its operation for submarine construction. The shipyard could kill two birds with one stone if it could get the Bureau of Ships and the CNO to authorize the building of submarines in the new dry dock. The yard would gain two, possibly three, additional building ways for increased submarine construction and, at the same time, reduce the assignment of repair work to the yard.

Commandant Withers presented two options to Washington to obtain the additional building ways needed for increased production. Two side launching ways could be built at Berth 6 in four or five months for about $90,000, or the new dry dock could be used for new construction. The shipyard argued that the use of the new dry dock was far more efficient, more economical, and less risky than the side launching ways. The dock was the more efficient option because it was centrally located to the shops. It was the more economical option because the cost of preparing for and launching from the dry dock would require less timber and other materials than would a lateral launching. Finally, the launchings would be less risky from a dry dock because they involved merely an undocking evolution. On the other hand, "the side launching scheme required the second vessel to be skidded up into launching position," an operation that was by no means trivial.[28] A lateral launching evolution also required a higher stage of ship completion because a large roll would occur as the hull entered the water.

The management of Portsmouth Navy Yard had ulterior motives for the dry dock from the time construction was first authorized. Internal studies in December 1941 by Lt. (jg) H. A. Arnold and the hull superintendent, Capt. J. H.

Spiller, had proposed that the upper end of the new dry dock be used as a building basin for the construction of two submarines at the same time the caisson and dry dock machinery were being completed. Arnold and Spiller thought that the dry dock would be far enough along to start construction of two submarines in May 1942. Their study concluded, "By this method two vessels could be sufficiently far advanced to permit floating them near the same time that the dock is ready to go into operation [December 1942]."[29] In other words, in December 1941 some ship-yard managers were considering the option of starting construction of two subma-rines in a hole in the ground with no means of getting them waterborne until the remainder of the dry dock was completed. This proposal was never advanced to higher authorities for approval, but it does illustrate the aggressive thinking, and the willingness to accept risk, that came to characterize yard management dur-ing the war. From the start of the war, the shipyard managers seemed to hold little doubt that they would eventually use the new dry dock for construction of subma-rines. They merely needed to pick the right time to inform their superiors of their intentions to better ensure approval. In the meantime, construction moved for-ward on the dock, still officially intended for repairs and overhauls, through the summer and fall of 1942.

When the dock neared completion, the yard moved to realize its objective. On 27 November 1942 Commandant Rear Admiral Withers wrote a personal letter to Rear Adm. W. B. Farber in the Office of the Chief of Naval Operations to gain sup-port for the yard's plan to build submarines in the dock. Withers wrote, "The new twin dock is fitted for shipbuilding, and it is located just outside our Shipfitters' Shop, which is ideal for shipbuilding."[30] Withers noted further that approval would result in a $100,000 savings over the other option of building two side launch ways alongside one of the piers. Withers then asked his friend to assist in gaining quick approval for his official request, which would soon follow.

In December 1942 the yard pushed its proposal to a successful conclusion. Key to gaining approval was the shipyard's argument that the original shipyard graving dock (renamed dry dock #2) had sufficient capacity for emergency repairs and that it would be a waste of a valuable resource not to use the new dry dock for subma-rine construction.[31] Utilizing the new dry dock with two building ways increased the number of building ways to nine, giving a potential minimum annual build-ing rate of twenty-seven submarines. Higher building rates were possible if the time required on the building ways could be shortened to less than four months or if more submarines could be squeezed into the new dry dock.[32] Both possibili-ties were eventually realized, and the shipyard went on to achieve a building rate of over thirty submarines in one year.

How valid was the shipyard argument that dry dock #2 could handle all the anticipated submarine repair work? In retrospect, it was probably a stretch and somewhat risky to make such a case. An analysis of the 1943 weekly dry dock usage reports shows that the dock was rarely without a submarine and frequently had two submarines in dock.[33] As it turned out, when building dozens of submarines a year, a fair number of those required docking for repairs or inspections prior to final delivery. That workload alone kept dry dock #2 busy.

Dry dock #1 was first used as intended by the Navy for repairs to the USS *Marlin* in March 1943. After that, the dock was dedicated to new construction for the remainder of the war. The heavy use of dry dock #2 suggests that it may have been a marginal decision as to whether or not that dock could comfortably handle the repair workload. It appears that the chief of naval operations and the Bureau of Ships were content to let Portsmouth Navy Yard run its own show as long as it was delivering new submarines at record rates.

The risk management of dry dock #1 did not stop with the authorization to use it for construction of new submarines. The first two submarine keels, for USS *Bang* (SS 385) and USS *Pilotfish* (SS 386), were laid in the dock on 30 April and 15 May 1943, respectively. Those submarines were launched simultaneously on 20 August 1943. Determined to maximize use of the dock, the yard laid keels for three submarines, USS *Razorback* (SS 394), USS *Redfish* (SS 395), and USS *Ronquil* (SS 396), on 9 September 1943. The simultaneous launching of these submarines on 27 January 1944 was described in the vignette that opened the introduction.

The experiences with dry dock #1 illustrate the aggressiveness of the shipyard management team and a willingness to assume risks to achieve increased production. At the same time, a decision to limit submarine construction in dry dock #1 to only two at a time, after previously building three at one time, indicates that the shipyard was also quick to balance reason and risk. Recalling the triple simultaneous launching that occurred in January 1944, it can be speculated that, had the shipyard continued to successfully build three at a time in dry dock #1, the title of this study might well have been *36 in '44* instead of *32 in '44*.

—m—

This discussion turns now to the second example of risk management: the development of procedures to work around the receipt of late and unreliable contractor components. The emphasis of Portsmouth Industrial Survey #1 (December 1941) was on facility and personnel upgrades. By the time of the second survey report in June 1942, the personnel issue was of secondary importance, facility improvements were well under way, and the emphasis had shifted to material procurement and scheduling. The board's second report opened with an enthusiastic endorsement of the yard's exceptional performance during the first six months of the war: "The increase in the rate of building submarines has far exceeded not only the schedule but even the most optimistic hopes of everyone connected with it. . . . This [greatly reduced] length of time on the building ways seems phenomenal when compared to the best performances reached by other yards." The report then turned to the problem of material procurement: "The greatly accelerated rate of construction of submarines has brought to light certain additional factors which adversely affect the building program in various degrees. . . . Procurement under present conditions [a lack of orders far into the future] is one of the most critical factors in submarine construction. . . . A system has been formed and the method of scheduling has been changed radically . . . the system offers promise of more orderly construction and shorter building periods." The survey team believed that "the acquiring of a long-range construction program is of prime and critical importance" because it would allow bulk ordering and "lessen the difficulties of procurement which in itself would eliminate or minimize many other problems of management."[34] In other words, if the shipyard could order material for five or six submarines at a time, the first submarine on the schedule might suffer late deliveries, but the others would probably have a large percentage of ordered material sooner than needed.

Unfortunately, shipyard plans to bulk order material further aggravated a military procurement system that, according to David M. Kennedy, by the summer of 1942, had "abandoned any vestige of managerial discipline" as "military purchase orders became hunting licenses, unleashing a jostling frenzy of competition for materials and labor in the jungle of the marketplace."[35] In time, more disciplined priority systems would better integrate and coordinate interservice and civilian needs. However, at the start of the war, each service and each industrial community was looking out for itself. Portsmouth Navy Yard was no exception.

In late 1942 the shipyard reported that the only scheduling delays being experienced at the yard were associated with late component and material deliveries. In a 12 December 1942 letter to the Bureau of Ships, the commandant reported with confidence that Portsmouth Navy Yard could build submarines in 150 days. However, it was necessary to continue scheduling construction periods for 210 days because of problems with material deliveries, especially steel and main engines. The industrial manager, Captain Davis, wrote, "The steel situation calls for special comments. At the start, the [SS] 285 Class submarines were handicapped due to late receipts of high tensile steel and heavy plates for bulkheads. This same situation exists now for the [SS] 308 Class, serious delays are being encountered."[36] Late delivery of steel was a widespread problem in the shipbuilding industry. In *Ships for Victory*, Frederic C. Lane concluded that, by late 1942, "Facilities were adequate so that deliveries [of completed merchant ships] would have been higher in the last quarter of 1942 and throughout 1943 if more steel had been allocated to the yards." Ordering of steel for many submarines of the same class in bulk permitted Portsmouth Navy Yard to build thirty-two submarines in 1944, very close to the maximum capability of its facilities. Unfortunately, bulk ordering, such as employed by Portsmouth Navy

Yard, further exaggerated steel shortages at other shipyards. Lane noted, "It should be made clear that the limit to merchant ship production was set not by the nation's steel capacity alone, but by it in conjunction with the allocation of steel to Army, Navy, and other users."[37] Lane implied that excessive ordering of steel throughout the armed services, which enjoyed much higher priorities than the U.S. Maritime Commission, contributed to the detriment of merchant shipbuilding. Portsmouth Navy Yard may have been a guilty party, but the need to quickly bring the war in the Pacific to a conclusion by delivering more submarines was overriding, at least as far as the shipyard was concerned.

Late deliveries were not limited to steel. In April 1942 the yard reminded the Bureau of Ships that the delivery schedule for the submarine building program in progress depended on delivery of main propulsion machinery for which the bureau was responsible. The shipyard had not received delivery information from the bureau for these critical components.[38] In August 1943 the shipyard reported schedule delays resulting from late receipt of main power electrical control cubicles and electric motors for auxiliary equipment.[39] The next month the yard reported that delivery dates for auxiliary engines, main propulsion engines, and main propulsion generators were four to eight weeks too late to support orderly progress of construction.[40] Also, the delivery of radars, sound gear, and batteries was reported to be two to three weeks later than scheduled. As noted earlier, delivery of components for the first submarine on an order for several submarines was often in jeopardy. Components for the remainder of the submarines on the order were usually on hand well before scheduled installation dates.

The problem with late contractor components was highlighted at a conference at the Bureau of Ships on 13 and 14 August 1943. The conference had been convened in response to a request by Undersecretary of the Navy Forrestal to see what could be done to speed up submarine construction. The production officer, Captain Dudley, represented Portsmouth Navy Yard at the conference. His conference report shows that representatives from Portsmouth, Electric Boat, Manitowoc, Cramp, and Boston were "unanimous in their comments that the present difficulty was largely due to late delivery of component parts and that the situation was getting no better." Each yard identified other needs that, if met, might lead to improved production, but all other problems paled in comparison to late material deliveries. The Bureau of Ships suggested that perhaps a central procurement agent, like Electric Boat, might better coordinate deliveries to each shipyard. The Electric Boat representative responded that his company did not want the job, but "they would do it if it was decided upon."[41] The yards agreed that it would be better to continue with the present system rather than try to initiate a new ordering system that might further compound their problems.

At the conference, the shipyards were asked to predict annual submarine production capacities assuming the completion of necessary facility improvements and the achievement of satisfactory material deliveries. The representatives gave the following responses:[42]

	1944	1945
Portsmouth	30	35
Electric Boat	32	42
Manitowoc	13	15
Cramp	18	18
Boston	—	14

Indicative of the comprehensive understanding that Portsmouth management had of the yard's capabilities and processes, the yard came very close to achieving predicted maximum production in 1944 when thirty-two submarines were actually delivered, two more than predicted. All the other yards fell short of their predictions. A major reason for Portsmouth's success was the shipyard's ability to find ways to work around late material deliveries and to resolve problems with unreliable contractor-supplied components.

Portsmouth and the other yards had to continuously deal with poor quality and unreliable contractor-supplied components. The shipyard determined early on that certain pieces of critical contractor-supplied equipment were too unreliable to install shipboard in the condition as received. To do so would be to jeopardize completion schedules. If the equipment failed during testing and had to be removed from the tight confines of the submarine for shop repair, delay would incur. Worse yet, premature failure on sea trials or after could jeopardize lives. Not having the time and resources to satisfactorily engage and resolve all contractor issues in a timely manner, the shipyard routinely reworked critical components before they were installed. The additional cost for this rework was similar to an insurance premium; it was substantially less than the alternative. SecNav Industrial Survey #2 (1944) highlighted this practice: "Certain items of submarine equipment such as electric driven pumps and air compressors are invariably broken down after delivery from the manufacturer, and given a complete overhaul. This is justified by the Yard as economical in the long run since, earlier in the building program, defects developed after installation so that units had to be removed for overhaul."[43] By accomplishing this "insurance" work early in the schedule, the shipyard reduced the probability of experiencing costly disruptive work later when timely completion of the ship would be jeopardized. When multiple submarines in dry dock had to be launched simultaneously, a delay on one ship impacted the others. Risk management became an integral part of all routine shipyard planning, procurement, and production processes during the war.

Production Scheduling

The production scheduling system developed at Portsmouth Navy Yard early in the war to advance the sectional construction process also became a valuable tool for managing and working around material procurement problems. Faced with a rapidly expanding workload, it soon became obvious that work-scheduling practices, which had produced one or two custom-built submarines per year in the past, were outdated. In addition, the expected increase in the pace and number of production activities required much closer coordination between designers, material procurement agents and expeditors, schedulers, and those executing the work.[44]

At this point, it is important to note the advantage that Portsmouth and Electric Boat enjoyed as the principal designers of the submarines they were building. During the war, each new order for a group, or class, of submarines included the latest technical improvements, frequently developed as the result of feedback from battle-tested submarines. The accounting for the classes of submarines built during World War II can be confusing. Gary Weir explains, "Although the three principal classes of fleet submarines during World War II were *Gato, Balao,* and *Tench,* technical variations within each class often prompted submariners and BUSHIPS to refer to particular groups of submarines by more specific class names, like *Gunnel* or *Drum.*"[45] According to Cdr. John D. Alden, *Gato* was the basic World War II fleet submarine design. *Balao*'s primary technical variation was an increased test depth and *Tench*'s primary technical variation was increased torpedo stowage.[46] Portsmouth Navy Yard's administrative history of World War II notes that between June 1940 and June 1943 the yard received contracts for no less than 8 different classes totaling 106 submarines.[47] Thus, Portsmouth Navy Yard considered each new order for a group of submarines to be a new class of submarine. As a principal design agent, Portsmouth could incorporate the necessary changes, freeze the design, and promptly feed the changes to the yard scheduling system for advance bulk ordering of material and job order preparation for the next group of submarines to be built. This was all part of streamlining the design and production processes for new construction.

The improved scheduling system was known as the Portsmouth Material Control System. It was developed to further advance the yard's continual efforts to maximize hull section content in the shops prior to delivery to the building sites. This more formal system of subassembly, work scheduling, and material control was implemented in July 1942 with the specific purpose of "providing a better means of building more submarines in less time."[48] The basic building block of the system was a control unit, termed a "group," that was essentially the largest subassembly that could be efficiently put together prior to shipboard installation. Based on the shipyard's experience, the completion of "groups" was scheduled no more precisely than the specific week that the assembly was needed after a keel was laid. For example, a group that was required two weeks before a keel was laid would be labeled 2B (for *before*) and a tank required four weeks after keel laying would be identified as 4A (for *after*). This was a major advance over previous scheduling attempts at the yard. The scheduling system, designed and implemented in 1942, reflected eight years of experience with submarine sectional construction that had started in 1934 with the NIRA submarines. It was far removed from the "spit planning method" that Admiral Murray had observed on the *Cachalot* in the early 1930s.

Under the new Portsmouth Material Control System, the start date for construction or assembly of each group dictated need dates for all other activities that were required to support that event, such as the delivery of material, the issue of drawings and plans, the construction of temporary facilities, and the assignment of shop labor. A key step in the process was the verification that all material and support documents were on hand before the start of the job. The group schedule could be easily transferred from hull to hull for all submarines of the same class, permitting the bulk ordering of material for similar ships of the same class far in advance of actual need dates. Thus, the Portsmouth Material Control System became the prime tool that enabled the yard to circumvent the inefficiencies of the procurement system.

Portsmouth's Material Control System was a first step toward critical path scheduling. The locally designed and implemented system was one of the keys to success that enabled the shipyard to accelerate construction from mid-1942 through the end of the war. SecNav Industrial Survey #2 (1944) acknowledged the value of the Portsmouth Material Control System and recommended further enhancements to improve integration of material ordering activities with planned work schedules.[49]

Innovative Management

After reviewing Captain Davis' management attributes in chapter 3, one would suspect that any organization under his command would necessarily be rich in new ideas and innovative practices. Indeed, much of what shipyard management did to increase production during the war, and much of what has been presented so far in this chapter, can be grouped under the generic heading of innovative management. However, a few additional examples will make the argument for innovative management even more convincing. First, innovation was obviously present in August

1941 when the shipyard convinced the Bureau of Ordnance to permit the use of twenty obsolete Civil War–era muzzle-loading guns, then in storage at the yard, as mooring bollards on the new extension of Berth 6.[50]

Two other examples, much less pragmatic, were far more important to the shipyard's mission. The first involved finding transportation to and from the shipyard for thousands of new employees. The second involved delaying the arrival of submarine crews at the shipyard to minimize mutual interference between crews and shipyard workers during the final stages of construction. The latter was not as simple a matter as it might first appear. It required that the shipyard convince the chief of naval operations that the war effort would benefit from having the crews spend less time at the shipyard becoming familiar with their new submarines. As in the case of the plan to use dry dock #1 for new construction, Commandant Withers did not hesitate to challenge the decisions and policies of his superiors when needed to improve the productivity of his shipyard. Fortunately, the recommendations of the Portsmouth Navy Yard were usually well received in Washington because of the yard's recognized position of excellence in submarine technology and construction.

The rapid increase in yard employment at the beginning of the war required some innovation to transport thousands of employees to work at a time when automobiles were in short supply and gasoline was rationed. In March 1942 the yard contracted with Hill Transportation Company of Portland, Maine, to provide bus service within a sixty mile radius of the yard. The service continued until November 1944, when the yard began to run its own fleet of buses. Hill's fleet of over a hundred buses brought employees to work from as far away as Lowell, Massachusetts; Portland, Maine; and Manchester, New Hampshire. In a 1946 report, the shipyard estimated that during the peak employment period of the war, 10,000 employees arrived for work daily in 2,500 private vehicles (averaging 4 occupants per vehicle), 8,000 arrived by bus, and 2,500 walked to work. Vehicles and buses were usually filled to capacity to conserve gas and tires for the war effort.[51]

Mass bus transport for shipyard workers contributed to a significant reduction in local traffic during the war years, despite a doubling of the local population and a quadrupling of shipyard employees. Undoubtedly, the rationing of automobiles, tires, and gasoline was also a major contributing factor. At any rate, traffic surveys of vehicles crossing the interstate bridge connecting Portsmouth and Kittery showed the following:[52]

Period	Total Vehicle Count
12/1/41–8/1/42	785,870
12/1/42–8/1/43	520,925
12/1/43–8/1/44	316,327
12/1/44–8/1/45	498,429
12/1/45–8/1/46	830,860

It is interesting to note that at about the time that Portsmouth Navy Yard employment peaked at 20,445 in late 1943, the traffic crossing the bridge was less than half what it was at the start of the war. Employees were walking to work from nearby housing projects, sharing a ride with other employees, or taking the bus. The innovative and far-reaching bus system complemented the conservation efforts of the local communities and contributed to the shipyard's success.

Innovation was also evident when Commandant Withers approached the chief of naval operations in January 1943 with a request to delay submarine commissioning dates and, thus, the arrival of submarine crews at the shipyard. As previously stated, the shipyard considered this action necessary to minimize the mutual interference between crews and shipyard workers as the submarine approached completion.[53] Prior to the spring of 1943, this period of mutual interference varied from submarine to submarine but was typically between six and eight weeks. For example, the USS *Balao* (SS 285) was commissioned at Portsmouth Navy Yard two months before delivery on 4 April 1943.

The chief of naval operations approved Withers' request, obviously respecting the commandant's previous position as Commander Submarine Force U.S. Pacific Fleet. In that job, Withers had been responsible for crew training and the readiness of each submarine in his command. The next submarine to be completed at Portsmouth, the USS *Billfish* (SS 286), was commissioned just fifteen days prior to delivery. Thereafter during the war, submarines at Portsmouth Navy Yard were routinely commissioned between two and three weeks prior to delivery. Portsmouth Navy Yard's record of success and recognized expertise in submarine construction had paved the way for the fleet support that was needed to promote further success. Confident in the quality of Portsmouth-built submarines and the leadership of Commandant Withers, the chief of naval operations agreed to reduce the time that his submarine crews had to inspect and familiarize themselves with their submarines before they departed the shipyard. This action proved to be less controversial than one might think because, as the war progressed, the submarine commissioning crews included increased numbers of battle-experienced submarine sailors who required less time to familiarize themselves with a new submarine.

Open Communications

Earlier it was established that Commandant Withers had great people skills as a leader. He was personable and had a bent toward congeniality and open communications with his subordinates and employees. Assistant Secretary of the Navy Bard held similar views about the importance of open communication. In June 1943 Bard urged navy yard commandants to promote open lines of communication between management and employees. Bard believed, "Any team whether in sport, industry, or war, to be effective must have a common understanding of the game. To secure the highest degree of efficiency, each member of the team must at least understand the signals, the objective, the rules, and the part he is to play." Bard saw the process of open communication to be a win-win situation for both management and employees, "The process of taking employees into the confidence of management creates far greater respect for management and usually saves much time and energy for both groups."[54] Commandant Withers and his managers could not have agreed more.

There was no need to establish open lines of communication at Portsmouth Navy Yard, as the assistant secretary of the navy was suggesting, because they already existed. From Rear Admiral Withers' open leadership style to the civilian managers that Eileen Dondero Foley observed touring the industrial areas interacting with the employees, open communication was a way of life in the yard. As SecNav Industrial Survey #2 (1944) reported, the work was completed with minimum paperwork and written instructions and with few meetings. William Tebo did not see a job order during the six months that he worked at the yard in 1944.[55] He was well trained for the jobs he was assigned, and he performed them well. Obviously, most shipyard employees did the same. Open and efficient communications were by-products of the yards' "walk around" style of management and supervision.

Communications and Work Control Technology

The state of the shipyard communication and work control systems, those processes that transfer verbal and written work instructions and other information between shipyard support groups and waterfront work sites, were inadequate when mass production arrived at Portsmouth Navy Yard in 1940. They remained so for the duration of the war. If, as this study suggests, the shipyard utilized production processes that were well ahead of their time, then the yard managed to do so with rudimentary communication and work control tools. In reviewing the yard's unsuccessful attempts to acquire state-of-the-art communications and control technology, its wartime production performance becomes even more remarkable.

The massive infrastructure upgrades that accompanied mobilization included few improvements to the shipyard's communications and control systems. As will be seen, repeated shipyard requests to higher authority to upgrade these systems received little or no support. Considering the ease with which massive funding was obtained for dry docks, building ways, and other facilities, it is surprising that so little priority was given to upgrading the systems needed to communicate and transfer information throughout the shipyard. This may be because the need for better communications equipment was not appreciated at the start of mobilization. Later in the war, when the need became obvious and urgent, funds for navy yard facilities were being were redirected to armaments as discussed in chapter 2.

At the start of the war Portsmouth Navy Yard did not have the up-to-date internal systems of communication and work control that existed in other shipyards. These shortcomings included a grossly inadequate telephone system, ineffective means to transmit messages and work instructions throughout the yard, no "clock system" for the accounting of employee hours, and no "check system" for paying employees. In essence, Portsmouth was still a manual yard whereas other yards had taken the first steps toward automating various administrative tasks. Portsmouth, favored with workload prior to the war, had not been favored with any degree of automation. The custom building of one or two submarines per year was primarily based on experience and acquired skills, attributes that were not supported by any state-of-the-art communication and automation system or process.

The yard telephone system was outdated and did not have the required capacity at the start of the war. In 1936 it was reported that the shipyard's manual phone system had a capacity of 200 lines, 150 of which were then in service. It also had some thirteen pay stations for unofficial calls made to off-site locations. As the shipyard began to ramp up production in response to ever increasing orders in 1940 and 1941, shipyard management quickly realized that the shipyard phone system was not equipped to handle the increasing workload. Nonetheless, telephone upgrades were installed only on a piecemeal basis and complaints of poor service persisted throughout the war.

The late 1930s saw several advances in telephone technology that greatly increased the capacity and efficiency of telephone systems. Coaxial cable was introduced in 1937, as well as multiplexing techniques that allowed numerous calls to be simultaneously carried over a single cable. Switching technology also advanced in the late 1930s, becoming more rugged and reliable. More mundane improvements included the combined handset and spiral cord, both introduced in 1938. Transistor circuitry and electronic switching, developed for military applications during the war, found widespread civilian application immediately after the war. Telecommunications technology had made great strides by 1940, but the shipyard had benefited little from those advances.[56]

Rear Admiral Withers issued a shipyard notice on 10 December 1942 that urged employees to make as few telephone calls as possible because "the large expansion in personnel and work of the Yard has increased the volume of telephone business to the point where the present capacity of the Yard Telephone Exchange is overtaxed during certain hours of the day."[57] The industrial manager also believed, as late as January 1943, that "the Yard's steadily expanding building program, combined with the increasingly difficult problems of material procurement, has developed to a point where the existing telephonic communication between the material Planning Superintendent's desk and the Supply Department . . . is totally inadequate." Captain Davis wanted the shipyard to purchase one of the many interoffice communication systems that were appearing on the market about that time.[58]

The state of communications technology in the early 1940s is a study unto itself. Systems that the shipyard considered buying were quite rudimentary by today's standards. Those systems included SELECT-O-PHONE (an automatic telephone service that eliminated the need for an operator and provided for "hands-free" speaker communication), an exclusive Exec-U-Phone (a system for recording conversations on vinyl 78 RPM [revolutions per minute] records), a TelAutograph Telescriber (an interdepartmental communication system to eliminate phone calls between shipyard departments and provide for the efficient movement of material and supporting paper between departments), an RCA Paging and Public Address System, and an audible and visual call system for the shops. In the spring of 1943 the shipyard attempted to get approval to install an announcing system that would enable the commandant to readily communicate in a broadcast manner to many important buildings and worksites and industrial managers to better communicate within their buildings.[59] Despite the decentralization that reduced the Bureau of Ships' oversight of navy yards, purchase requests for such upgrades had to be approved by the bureau. The requests were denied.

The manual methods of transferring technical specifications and work instructions between the Supply and Industrial departments, which worked when the yard built one or two submarines per year, could not work efficiently when the shipyard was building one or two dozen submarines per year. In 1941 Portsmouth requested approval from the Bureau of Ships to purchase three teletype machines to improve the internal "handling of dispatches and other paper."[60] Again, the request was denied. According to the bureau, teletype machines were not cost-effective when compared to telephone rates and other means to transmit production instructions throughout the yard.[61] The Bureau of Ships appeared to be out of touch with the needs of the yard for state-of-the-art communications and production control systems.

The outdated infrastructure systems at Portsmouth Navy Yard were not limited to communications systems. When Captain Davis reported to the shipyard in 1941,

he was surprised at what he found in the way of support systems. "Unlike probably all [other] Navy Yards, Supervisors of Shipbuilding, Commercial Companies,
and Government Offices, Portsmouth does not have a clock system."[62] Instead,
employee time and attendance records were kept manually. Incredibly, the shipyard did not have the means to pay employees by check, as did most other shipyards. Instead, the employees lined up every Friday for a cash payday that was the
height of inefficiency and disorder.[63]

Hull Superintendent Tusler deplored the chaotic conditions that existed in the
yard on Fridays when large numbers of employees lined up to be paid in cash for
their weekly hours. He recommended that the shipyard "adopt a check method
of paying Yard employees in order to eliminate the delays now encountered on
Friday." Tusler also recommended that the yard "adopt a time-clock system of
checking employees in and out, and require employees to check in and out four
times a day as is customary in other Yards."[64] The Bureau of Supplies and Accounts
authorized the shipyard to install an employee clock system in June 1941,[65] but it
was not until 13 May 1942 that the time-clock system was completely installed and
operational. Only then was the shipyard able to eliminate the inefficient process of
paying employees in cash each Friday.[66] Cash paydays may have made sense when
the yard employment was only a few thousand, but by May 1942 employment was
about fifteen thousand, and chaos reigned on Friday afternoons. It was estimated
in May 1942 that the new check payment system would save seven thousand work
hours per week.[67]

As shipyard management did with most obstacles, be it building ways, unreliable contractor-supplied components, or antiquated communications and work
control systems, it found ways to get the job done with what was available. The
need for upgraded communications and control systems was reduced by task-
ing existing systems to the limit, reducing paperwork to a minimum, and relying
on jobsite supervision and worker empowerment. Here again, when faced with a
major impediment to orderly operations, the small yard with a repetitive workload
had a distinct advantage over larger yards with variable workloads.

Farm-Out Programs

The shipyard could not have achieved its production records without an extensive
farm-out program. This program involved a network of local, private-sector shops
able to accomplish the machining, welding, and electrical work that exceeded the
capacity of the shipyard shops. Before September 1941 the shipyard farmed out
only the machining of aluminum housings for electrical fixtures. By late 1941 the
inside machine shop's workload to support the increased number of submarines
under construction exceeded the shop's three-shift capacity. To work around the

overload, the shipyard contracted with the Industrial Development Company of Portland, Maine, to manufacture air compressor and pump parts. In March 1942 additional machine shop work was farmed out to Kidder Press Company of Dover, New Hampshire. Kidder Press eventually garnered $4.7 million of Portsmouth Navy Yard contracts. The company performed so well meeting those contracts that it received several government awards for excellence, under the recommendation of Portsmouth Navy Yard. Local welding companies were also used to relieve the overload in the shipyard welding shop.

Figure A-4, Portsmouth Navy Yard Man Hours per Submarine (1940–45) shows how the shipyard increased its farm-out program (shaded in the figure) beginning in late 1942 and continuing until mid-1945. Most noteworthy is the fact that when the yard achieved its maximum efficiency of 665,000 work hours per submarine in mid-1944, approximately 100,000 of those hours were attributed to farm-out work. Farm-out work was extensive until mid-1945, when new construction orders declined, reducing the workload and need for farm-out. Shipyard records for 1943–44 indicate, "The total value of contracts farmed out amounted to approximately $13,190,409. This represents a value greater than the entire Yard output during the fiscal years of 1939 and 1940."[68] In other words, the annual farm-out program during the two peak war years, 1943 and 1944, approximated the annual shipyard production for the two years immediately preceding the war.

The magnitude of the farm-out program highlights the value of the Portsmouth Material Scheduling System. The shipyard needed to coordinate a farm-out program that approximated the workload of another entire shipyard. It had to work around late material deliveries and rework new contractor-supplied components to resolve quality issues. It had to manage these problems as production schedules accelerated. The effectiveness and value of the Portsmouth Material Scheduling System is clear from the success that the shipyard achieved in this environment. One factor that undeniably contributed to this success was that most of the farm-out program contractors were reliable local vendors that essentially became an extension of the shipyard.

Training

With the hiring of hundreds of thousands of inexperienced workers, the nation's shipyards were severely challenged to turn new hires into productive employees. In this regard, the navy yards had an advantage over many of the private yards in that they had existing training and apprentice programs that could be upgraded and expanded while, in many cases, the private yards had to originate such programs.

According to Frederic C. Lane, the U.S. Maritime Commission's plan to mandate shipyard training by enforcing "the systematic training of workers before they were upgraded to first class mechanics" was largely ineffective because the commission failed to regulate the upgrading of mechanics at the start of the war. Consequently, "the Maritime Commission lost control" and was "unable to . . . force better training." Despite the commission's push for "in-plant training," in 1943 "the Kaiser companies [in Oregon] were still paying trainees to go to public schools for courses."[69]

Portsmouth Navy Yard did not have to be forced to implement training programs. Instead, training was recognized as crucial to the increased production of submarines. At the start of the war the yard immediately expanded its apprentice program and subsequently augmented it with other off-yard federally funded training programs.

The skilled labor base in the area could not immediately support the needed increase in shipyard employment. Even before the war skilled workers were in short supply, as evidenced by the fact that the Portsmouth area had not been able to attract much industry. Speaking to the local Rotary Club in January 1941, Mr. Lawrence M. Meyer, industrial agent of the New Hampshire Planning and Development Commission, noted that the area had in the past "lost not one but several industrial opportunities because we did not have sufficient skilled labor."[70]

It was essential that the shipyard have a large skilled labor pool from which to draw if it were to achieve its production expectations. The skill levels were achieved through three primary means of training. First, the Shipyard Apprentice Training Program, run by the shop masters for advancement of mechanics to the next class or to journeyman, achieved the successful integration of in-yard training with advancement that Lane found lacking in private shipyards. Second, free supplementary and preemployment vocational training courses were given at off-yard locations with the cooperation of the Federal War Production Training Program through New Hampshire's Department of Education. Finally, the Engineering Science Management War Training Program at the University of New Hampshire offered advanced technical and engineering courses.

The apprentice program was a well-established shipyard tradition by the late 1930s. Immediately prior to World War II, the program was functioning at near full capacity and successfully providing the skilled mechanics the shops needed at the time. For example, the program had 346 students enrolled in August 1941, 342 students on 1 December 1941, 336 students on 5 January 1942, and 391 students on 2 March 1942.[71] There was no reason to create new in-yard training programs to meet the increased needs for skilled tradesmen; the existing program was simply expanded.

The existing apprentice program consisted of approximately eighteen classes of about twenty students each that met for two hours a day, three days a week. A high school diploma was required for entry into the program. A minimum credit of 1,816 school hours or specialized shop training was required before a candidate could take the promotional exam that was routinely given twice a year prior to the war. However, by October 1941 the exam was being given more often because more workers had entered the apprentice program.[72] Percy Whitney, who had hired into the apprentice program after two and one half years at Bates College, remembered it as being academically demanding. In particular, he recalled having to pass classroom metallurgy, trigonometry, and other challenging technical courses while working as an apprentice in the shipyard foundry.[73]

The Federal War Production Training Program was run by the states, with machines and equipment provided by the federal government. This program provided supplemental trade and technical instruction necessary for employment at the shipyard or to become better qualified in a trade once employed. Fourteen similar training programs were run throughout the state of New Hampshire. The Portsmouth program, however, was "praised by the navy vocational officers as one of the finest in the country."[74]

By early 1941 a coordinated federal, state, and local effort had established machine operator classes at Portsmouth High School. In March 1941 the high school program was expanded to include a three-shift defense school for welders. The machine shop classes under way at the time added an extra session from 10:00 PM to 7:00 AM. The training program was subsequently expanded to include gas and electric welding classes at a local industrial firm, the Morley Company, to meet an urgent need for welders at the navy yard. As noted earlier, Captain Davis had identified a shortage of welders to be the most critical obstacle to increased production in early 1942. Classes at Morley Company grew to include training twenty-four hours a day for welders, sheet metal workers, pipe fitters, ship fitters, machinists, electricians, machine operators, blueprint machine operators, and copyist draftsmen. In 1943 the program trained nearly a thousand workers for positions at the navy yard.[75] During the three years of operations, the school employed as many as eighty instructors who trained over seven thousand people.[76]

William Tebo was a fifteen-year-old high school junior when he took four hundred hours of machine operator defense training at Portsmouth High School to gain employment at the shipyard. Once hired, he was further trained as an electrician in order to perform limited, but important, shipboard wiring jobs. According to Tebo, the shipyard employed hundreds of fifteen- and sixteen-year-old high school students during the war. They would go to school during the day and then work the 3:00 PM to 11:00 PM shift at the shipyard. Like Tebo, most of them passed through the shipyard for less than a year before they entered military service once they turned seventeen. Tebo was at the yard for about six months, beginning in early 1944. By maintaining good grades, he and other teenagers could be excused from the last two periods of the day at the high school, which gave them enough time to get to the yard for shift start.[77]

The University of New Hampshire Engineering Science Management War Training Program provided the more technical and professional training required for shipyard technicians, engineers, and managers. This curriculum included courses in mechanics, strengths of materials, metallurgy, and welding theory. Over five thousand employees took advantage of the free training offered by the state and the university.[78] The support provided by the nearby university was certainly of great benefit to the shipyard and the war effort.

As previously noted, some industries had avoided the seacoast area prior to the war because of a lack of skilled workers. The programs discussed above produced thousands of skilled workers during the war and turned a shortage of skilled labor into an abundance of the same in a few years. In addition, the conversion of the federal defense training program into a state vocational training school, immediately after the war, went a long way toward ensuring that the area had a long-term supply of skilled labor.

—∿—

The methods employed by Portsmouth Navy Yard during the war contained many of the same elements taught in management schools forty years later, especially employee empowerment and specially trained small teams. In addition, well-designed training programs, assembly lines, risk management, innovative management, open communications, and large farm-out programs were all in evidence at the yard during the war. Moreover, the implementation of those methods in conjunction with a competent management staff and an intelligent, self-motivated workforce proved to be a powerful force that produced submarines at unprecedented rates.

Chapter 6

Metrics

During the war and until recently the Yard's principal business has been the construction of submarines. . . . Production records covering man hours required to build those vessels . . . clearly indicate that costs were reduced progressively as the volume of production increased.

—REAR ADM. THOMAS WITHERS,
23 March 1945

N
o matter how competent the management, how dedicated the workforce, and how well conceived the industrial tactics and strategy, it is results that count. For manufacturing processes, quantifiable results are usually the most meaningful indicators of success or failure. These indicators are frequently referred to today as "metrics." Metrics might include total numbers produced, production rates achieved, or work hours expended per widget. The eye-catching production metrics, in terms of submarine delivery rates, motivated this study.

In the interest of consistency, Portsmouth Navy Yard's production numbers will be revisited and examined in more detail in this section. Two other indicators of success—cost and quality—will also be reviewed. In today's world of industry and shipbuilding, both of these are true metrics in every sense of the word. Both can be quantified and analyzed in detail to indicate performance trends. Such was not the case at the yard during the war. Records for cost and quality were often abbreviated or eliminated in the interest of production efficiency. However, other evidence is available to provide some indication as to how the yard performed in both of these areas. Remarkable production numbers lose much of their luster if costs are excessive or quality is poor. As it turns out, cost and quality were as much a part of the Portsmouth success story as was production.

Production

As noted in the introduction, Portsmouth Navy Yard delivered seventy-nine submarines between 1 July 1940 and 1 July 1945, after averaging less than two submarines per year in the 1930s.[1] Electric Boat delivered seventy-eight submarines during the same period. Portsmouth delivered 81 percent of the submarines constructed in navy yards and Electric Boat delivered 70 percent of the submarines constructed in private yards. For emphasis, the discussion that follows restates a few of the production records presented in earlier chapters, along with additional noteworthy achievements.

The remarkable string of firsts accomplished by Portsmouth began with the first double launching of U.S. submarines when the USS *Scamp* (SS 277) and *Scorpion* (SS 278) slid down their building ways on 20 June 1942.[2] Another first for the yard was the double launching of USS *Picuda* (SS 382) and USS *Pampanito* (SS 383) from the new building basin on 12 July 1943, marking the first time that submarines had been fabricated below sea level at Portsmouth Navy Yard.[3] This practice, of course, would become the key to Portsmouth's success once dry dock #1 was put into use for the construction of new submarines. The construction of multiple submarines below sea level in the building basin and dry dock #1 enabled the shipyard to dramatically increase production, despite the limited number of traditional building ways.

The yard improved on its dual launchings with the first triple submarine launching on 28 October 1943, when the USS *Sterlet* (SS 392) and USS *Pomfret* (SS 391) were floated in the new building basin and the USS *Piranha* (SS 389) was launched in the traditional manner from the building ways.[4] On 27 January 1944 the shipyard went one better and set another world record by launching four submarines on the same day. USS *Razorback* (SS 394), USS *Redfish* (SS 395), and USS *Ronquil* (SS 396) were floated in dry dock #1 and USS *Scabbardfish* (SS 397) slid down a building way.[5] A fifth submarine, USS *Segundo* (SS 398), was launched from a building way ten days later making it five launchings in eleven days.[6] Portsmouth was not the only shipyard achieving remarkable production during the war. The *Portsmouth Herald* of 2 March 1943 has a photograph of four new destroyers being launched in fourteen minutes at the Federal Shipbuilding and Dry Dock Company at Kearny, New Jersey, earlier that year.[7]

With much of the discussion that follows focused on the building periods achieved by Portsmouth and other yards during the war, it is appropriate to highlight a December 1941 change to the completion trials agenda that shortened building periods by several weeks. On 17 December 1941 the chief of naval operations eliminated builder's underway trials and substituted main propulsion and auxiliary machinery trials alongside the pier, subject to the acceptance of the Board of Inspection and Survey (Insurv Board).[8] Underway trials were eliminated to avoid any possibility of offshore enemy attacks. The process for submarine acceptance trials was simplified even more in October 1942, when the president of the Insurv Board requested shipyards to establish their own subboards to perform acceptance trials and inspections in cases in which workload prevented the participation of an Insurv Board team.[9] Any comparisons between World War II submarine building durations and prior building durations must take this change into account. Comparisons of building durations between competing submarine building yards during the war are legitimate as they all complied with the same completion requirements.

The time from keel laying to completion of a submarine at Portsmouth was cut to less than half between November 1941, when USS *Drum* (SS 228) was delivered in 469 days, and December 1942, when USS *Steelhead* (SS 280) was delivered in 222 days. Portsmouth would eventually reduce submarine building time to 173 days and set another record by launching USS *Cisco* (SS 290) just fifty-six days after laying the keel.[10] The production numbers leave little doubt that Portsmouth Navy Yard was exceeding all expectations in meeting the challenges brought about by a world at war.

Those numbers led Portsmouth to receive six Army-Navy Production "E" Awards between 10 August 1942 and 18 July 1945. Portsmouth Navy Yard had the distinction of being the first naval establishment to receive the award.[11] Assistant Secretary of the Navy Bard presented the initial award at a ceremony with two governors, two senators, a congressman, and ten thousand shipyard employees in attendance. The five awards that followed meant that the yard was continuously recognized throughout the war for superior production performance.[12] The yard won the award every time it was eligible for it. Photo 12 in the gallery shows Rear Admiral Withers and shipyard managers displaying one of the "E" awards.

Table 9 compares the World War II performance of Portsmouth Navy Yard with its primary competitors: Electric Boat in Groton, Connecticut; Mare Island Navy Yard in Vallejo, California; and Manitowoc Shipyard in Manitowoc, Wisconsin. Compared to its competitors, Portsmouth submarines spent remarkably less time on the building ways and were completed many months sooner. With only nine building ways at Portsmouth, Portsmouth-built submarines were launched at a rate that was over four times faster than those at Electric Boat, which had twenty-one ways. As has been repeatedly emphasized throughout this book, it was this incredibly high launch rate that tells the wartime success story of the Portsmouth Navy Yard.

Table 9: Submarine Shipyard Schedule Performance (World War II)

Shipyard	Subs Built 1940–45	No. Bldg. Ways 1941	1945	Shortest Bldg. Pd.‡	Shortest Time on Bldg. Ways‡
Portsmouth§	79	5	9	173 days	56 days
Electric Boat*	78	11	21	317 days	est. 8 mos.
Mare Island†	17	2	8	273 days	192 days
Manitowoc‡	28	Side Launches		269 days	117 days

§*Administrative History, Portsmouth Navy Yard in World War II*, Portsmouth Naval Shipyard Museum Archives, Kittery, ME, 73. Not shown in the table is Cramp Shipbuilding (ten submarines).

*John D. Horn, *Submarines and the Electric Boat Company*, V-3, V-5, Navy Department Library, Naval Historical Center, Washington, D.C. Electric Boat had eleven building ways in 1940. Ten building ways were added with the Victory Yard in 1941.

†Bureau of Ships, *United States Naval Administration in World War II*, 1946, Navy Department Library, Naval Historical Center, Washington, D.C., 635–37.

‡David Randall Hinkle, ed., *United States Submarines* (Annandale, VA: Navy Submarine League, 2002), 114–16. Manitowoc Shipyard in Wisconsin built submarines on cradles and launched them sideways into a river too shallow for endwise launchings.

Portsmouth-built USS *Kingfish* (SS 234), completed on 20 May 1942, was credited with the sinking of an enemy ship, a Japanese freighter off southern Kyushu, on 1 October 1942, just thirteen months after her keel had been laid.[13] At a time when other shipyards were having difficulty delivering submarines in thirteen months, *Kingfish* had been built, steamed halfway around the world, and had sunk Japanese shipping in that short period.

A comparison to the average time on the building ways for Liberty ships, which were simple structures by comparison, originally designed for rapid, modular construction, sheds even more light on Portsmouth's remarkable achievement. After averaging about 150 days on the ways in January 1942, Liberty ships were routinely launched in 40 days by late 1942, and that performance remained typical for the remainder of the war.[14] As noted earlier, the submarine USS *Cisco* (SS 290) was launched at Portsmouth in late 1942 after just 56 days on the ways. By late 1942 private shipyards had progressed well up the learning curve for Liberty ships, and the yards were mass-producing the ships needed to replace those being sunk at record rates by German U-boats. Portsmouth was making comparable progress toward the mass production of submarines that would eventually wreak similar havoc on the Japanese merchant fleet.

In April 1944 the vice chief of naval operations, Vice Adm. F. J. Horne, wrote a letter to Rear Admiral Withers expressing the fleet's appreciation for Portsmouth Navy Yard's performance:

The Secretary of the Navy revealed that the Japanese had lost one-third of their available tonnage up to 3 September 1943, and that seventy-seven percent of that tonnage loss was sunk by our submarines. Of the submarines contributing to these sinkings, forty percent were built by your Navy Yard. This is, indeed, a record of which you can be proud . . . congratulations to the Commandant, to the officers and men under him, and to the civilian employees who have contributed a part to the submarine building program. Their wholehearted cooperation and thorough workmanship, characteristic of all Portsmouth boats, is a factor that has contributed in no small part to our Navy's success in the submarine war to date.[15]

The remarkable production record of the shipyard and the quality of Portsmouth-built submarines were recognized and appreciated at the highest levels of the U.S. Navy.

Costs

It was not that Portsmouth Navy Yard management did not care about costs. Early on they had decided that costs were far less important than time when building submarines for national defense. The report issued by Captain McKee's industrial review team on 8 December 1941 concluded with a statement emphasizing the importance of time versus costs: "Time which is lost now can not later be made up no matter how great the effort. In comparison with time, cost is now of so little importance that it must be completely disregarded if thereby a loss of time can be avoided."[16] Thus, from the day the war started, the shipyard planned to essentially disregard costs for the sake of production and accelerated submarine completions. The analysis that follows will show that this management strategy, which placed extreme emphasis on production efficiency, also produced excellent cost performance as a by-product.

Any cost analysis of operations at Portsmouth Navy Yard during the war is difficult because of abbreviated and incomplete accounting records. However, there is sufficient information available to evaluate the cost performance of Portsmouth relative to other navy yards in selected areas. In addition, local records are available that show dramatic reductions in the number of work hours (labor costs) required to build a submarine as the war progressed.

Table 10 shows the average workday costs of productive labor and the indirect overhead expense as a percentage of productive labor for all navy yards for FY 1942. It can be seen that the average cost per workday at Portsmouth Navy Yard was slightly below the average at all navy yards, and the overhead expense was considerably less than the average. The labor costs are more reflective of competition for workers in geographical areas than anything else: the West Coast yards were the highest, the southern yards the lowest, and the East Coast yards were in the middle. Overhead expense, the indirect costs and support required for productive labor to accomplish its work, is more of an indicator of shipyard efficiency. Portsmouth is among the leaders in this category, far below the average of all navy yards. Streamlining shipyard operations for submarine construction, especially the utilization of small, independent teams that required little support, would have contributed to a lower overhead rate.

Table 10: Navy Yard Costs Performance (1 July 1942–30 June 1943)

	Avg. Workday Cost of Productive Labor ($)	Indirect Overhead Expense % P.L.
Portsmouth	8.32	39.8
Boston	8.41	37.7
New York	8.74	46.1
Philadelphia	8.48	42.7
Washington	8.15	83.0
Norfolk	7.65	43.7
Charleston	7.67	38.0
Mare Island	8.64	42.2
Puget Sound	8.77	54.9
Pearl Harbor	9.10	65.2
Average All Yards	8.38	47.2

Source: "Comparative Statement—Expense Trends at Navy Yards—Percentages of Productive Labor," NARA College Park, RG 24, Bureau of Naval Personnel General Correspondence 1941–45, Box 1601, Folder NY Jan. 1, 1943.

On a macro scale the above analysis indicates that in June 1943 Portsmouth Navy Yard was very competitive with other navy yards in terms of labor and overhead costs. The discussion that follows will show that the shipyard cost performance improved significantly between June 1943 and the end of the war. This is reflected in substantially reduced building periods and in the reduced number of direct labor workdays required to construct a submarine.

Determining the cost of a submarine built at Portsmouth Navy Yard during the war is not a simple matter. As part of the effort to streamline processes for new construction, job orders were issued by classes of submarines, and not for individual hull, because all submarines of the same class required the same set of jobs. Consequently, costs were not collected for individual submarines but rather for the entire order of a group of submarines. Thus, return costs were not available until the last submarine of the order was completed, and even then, much prorating of costs was involved. This practice prevented the use of return costs as a management tool. However, a popular maxim of the shipyard industry is "time is money," meaning ships require expenditures as long as they remain at the shipyard. At a minimum, ships require services and utilities, and because they are complicated pieces of machinery, they frequently require maintenance or repair. Thus, while Portsmouth was not monitoring and managing costs on an individual ship basis, the shipyard was certainly keeping costs under control by delivering a submarine to the fleet every few weeks during the height of the war.

In March 1945, responding to SecNav Industrial Survey #2 (1944), which noted a lack of production and cost control records, Rear Admiral Withers emphasized that the shipyard's first priority during the war had been production, and cost reduction was a direct result of that priority: "During the war and until recently the Yard's principal business has been the construction of submarines. The Yard completed 12 submarines in 1942, 19 in 1943, and 32 in 1944. Production records covering man hours required to build those vessels and most of their important components during the three years are available and clearly indicate that costs were reduced progressively as the volume of production increased."[17] This study uses the records cited by Withers to make his case. Figure A-4, Portsmouth Navy Yard Man Hours per Submarine (1940–45), illustrates the cost reduction to which Commandant Withers was referring. Note on Figure A-4 that the work hours required to complete a submarine decreased from nearly 2 million on 7 December 1941 to 665,000 during the second quarter of 1944. It can be concluded that the labor cost per submarine delivered in 1944 was about one-third the labor cost per submarine delivered in late 1941.

Portsmouth's ability to deliver submarines at the end of the war at 33 percent of the work-hour cost required at the start of the war compares favorably with the work-hour cost reductions experienced on Liberty ships. At the start of 1942 the first Liberty ships delivered required about 1.25 million work hours to construct. By mid-1945 the total had dropped to about 400,000 per ship, 32 percent of the initial cost.[18] One can conclude that Portsmouth Navy Yard achieved cost reductions on submarines during the war that were nearly identical to those achieved on Liberty ships, a product that was much less complicated than submarines and specifically designed for ease of construction. When examined in light of the well-documented efficiencies of Liberty ship construction, Portsmouth's war record is all the more impressive.

But how did Portsmouth's cost performance compare to its prime competitor, Electric Boat? Gary Weir writes, "Of the five building yards producing the Navy's submarines during the war, EB did the job more cheaply than the others." Citing an Electric Boat cost of $2,765,000 for SS 222, Weir states, "When compared by the Price Adjustment Board in the spring of 1942, EB's unit cost on the SS-222 fell below those recorded at Portsmouth and Mare Island by about $1 million [36 percent less]." Weir also cites a 1938 Navy Department study comparing the cost of building ships at private versus public yards that concludes private yards could build ships more cheaply for reasons that included lower pay rates and less generous leave policies. The study noted, however, that comparisons "could only be made in the most general terms."[19] Only general comparisons could be made because the cost accounting practices were different at public and private yards. However, at the start of the war, all evidence points to higher costs at Portsmouth than at Electric Boat.

Weir closes his analysis of construction costs by noting that in the spring of 1942 Electric Boat took an average of fourteen months to complete a submarine whereas Portsmouth took only nine and a half months, 32 percent less time.[20] The completion of a submarine in 32 percent less time at 36 percent more cost argues against the "time is money" hypothesis presented earlier. The analysis that follows will clarify this apparent discrepancy and show that, had the Price Adjustment Board done a similar review of submarine construction costs in 1944, during the peak production years of the war, Portsmouth's costs would have compared much more favorably to Electric Boat's costs.

World War II actual cost data for submarine construction is scarce at best. However, in early 1941 Captain Davis' staff provided him the following cost estimates for submarines under construction at Portsmouth: USS *Marlin* (SS 205), $3.6 million; USS *Grayling* (SS 209), $4.3 million; and USS *Drum* (SS 228) and USS *Runner* (SS 275), $4.5 million each.[21] The last three submarines are of the same class as the Electric Boat submarines that resulted in the average unit cost of $2.765 million reported earlier. Thus, an apples-to-apples comparison is possible. At first blush, it appears that the average cost differential between Portsmouth and Electric Boat was even greater than the $1 million reported by the Price Adjustment Board in the spring of 1942.

Analyzing figure A-4, showing the average work hours required per submarine at Portsmouth, will clarify the yard's cost performance. The high cost estimates provided to the industrial manager in early 1941 were most likely based on the yard's performance in 1940, when the yard required about 1.75 million work hours to complete a submarine. By the spring of 1942, when the Price Adjustment Board provided its comparison figures, Portsmouth had reduced its labor expenditures per submarine to about 1.4 million work hours. This 20 percent reduction in work hours would have reduced actual costs on SS 228 and SS 275 proportionately to about $3.6 million, roughly equal to the $1 million differential cited by the Price Adjustment Board. The question is, Is that a fair comparison of Portsmouth and Electric Boat costs for the remainder of the war years? When asking that question, one should keep in mind that almost all of the submarines built by Portsmouth (seventy-nine) and Electric Boat (seventy-eight) during the war were built after the Price Adjustment Board's report in the spring of 1942.

Another look at figure A-4 leads to the conclusion that the comparison is fair and accurate only if Electric Boat made the same dramatic labor savings as Portsmouth did throughout the remainder of 1942, 1943, and the first half of 1944. In other words, Electric Boat would have had to reduce labor costs by over 50 percent, as Portsmouth did, between the spring of 1942 and the summer of 1944 for the comparison to be valid in 1944.

Granted, Electric Boat probably experienced labor savings during those years. However, this is where the "time is money" argument reenters the picture. As it turns out, in the spring of 1942 Portsmouth was still delivering submarines in twelve or thirteen months and not the nine and a half months reported earlier by Weir. An addendum to *Portsmouth Navy Yard's Administrative History* provides a chart showing dates for keel laying, launching, and completion for all Portsmouth-built submarines between 1940 and 1945. This chart shows that in the spring of 1942 completions had been reduced to twelve or thirteen months. On 6 June 1942 Portsmouth Industrial Survey #2 (June 1942) reported, "The time required to build submarines between keel laying and completion has been reduced from 15 months for the fastest built ships at this yard before December 1, 1941 to a few days less than 12 months for the latest completed ship. To date the shortest building time at other yards has been 12 1/3 months at Groton and 14 months at Mare Island."[22] Thus, in the spring of 1942 shipyards were completing submarines in about one year.

By the summer of 1944 Portsmouth was routinely completing submarines in six months or less. Thus, between the spring of 1942 and the summer of 1944, Portsmouth reduced its average building period approximately 50 percent while reducing costs by about the same 50 percent. Electric Boat did not experience a similar reduction in building durations. As noted in Table 9, the shortest building period at Electric Boat was just over ten months. If one gives Electric Boat a generous credit of 25 percent reduction in building time, it seems reasonable to conclude that a cost comparison between the two yards in 1944, when both were operating at maximum efficiency, would have found Portsmouth comparing much more favorably than it did in the spring of 1942. Which brings one back to Commandant Withers' contention that the records "clearly indicate that costs were reduced progressively as the volume of production increased."[23]

Another factor should be considered when comparing the costs of Portsmouth and Electric Boat. It will be argued later in this chapter that Portsmouth-built submarines were typically more complete and better equipped with the latest design improvements than were submarines delivered by Electric Boat. That is to say that Portsmouth, a government shipyard, was more accommodating to contract modifications that added work than was Electric Boat, a private shipyard. Late work is often costly and disruptive to other planned work. Portsmouth's costs should have been driven up accordingly, but were not.

In Commandant Withers' response to SecNav Industrial Survey #2 (1944), he explained that the recent curtailment of orders for new submarines and the assignment of other miscellaneous work to the yard required the shipyard to pay closer attention to the forecasting of workload and labor requirements. Also, Withers explained that the yard was returning to former cost control and cost monitoring practices that included keeping material usage and tonnage records in the blacksmith shop and foundry, recording the rate of use of each type of welding rod, and issuing individual ship job orders.[24] Thus, in May 1945 the yard began to undo much of the streamlining for new construction that had carried it so successfully through the war.

In highlighting the return to cost control measures with the winding down of the war, the shipyard was confirming the assignment of secondary importance to such measures during the war. Portsmouth Navy Yard's emphasis was on maximum production during the war, not on keeping records. Returning to figure A-4, it can be noted that, with the reinstitution of record-keeping and cost-monitoring practices, the work hours expended per submarine increased noticeably in 1945. Many factors contributed to this increase, including a drop in orders for new construction, an increasing repair and miscellaneous workload, and the efficiency disruptions that typically accompany a dramatic reduction in workforce in an industrial environment. Even more difficult to measure, but definitely a factor, was the psychological return to normalcy and a more relaxed pace of work after working under supercharged wartime conditions for four years. If nothing else, the inefficiencies realized in late 1945 validated the golden era of production that Portsmouth Navy Yard had experienced during the war, when the decks had been cleared for new construction and processes had been streamlined toward that end.

Quality

Lacking modern quality control records, the quality of Portsmouth submarines built during World War II is best judged by Board of Inspection and Survey reports and by the testimonials of the men who sailed them to war. For example, the material condition of the USS *Trout* (SS 202), one of the first submarines that the yard delivered to the fleet after Pearl Harbor, was praised by the Board of Inspection and Survey: "The *Trout* was in an unusually advanced stage of completion and excellent operation condition. Workmanship is excellent. This vessel is an achievement that reflects credit upon the Portsmouth yard."[25] Inspection teams routinely praised Portsmouth-built submarines.

The vice chief of naval operations, in May 1944, sent Portsmouth the following excerpt from the war report of a recently returned U.S. submarine: "The officers and crew of this submarine heartily endorse the Navy Yard, Portsmouth, New Hampshire, as a builder of rugged submarines."[26] The choice of the adjective "rugged" to describe Portsmouth-built submarines was most likely made by a submarine commanding officer whose ship and crew had survived a depth charge attack, thanks at least in part to the skilled workmanship of Portsmouth employees.

Between 10 January 1944 and 7 July 1945, the commanding officers of ten different submarines commended the shipyard for the fine construction and workmanship on their Portsmouth-built boats.[27] Those compliments included one from Lt. Cdr. George Street, Medal of Honor recipient as commanding officer of Portsmouth-built USS *Tirante* (SS 420). Lieutenant Commander Street thanked Portsmouth Navy Yard "for building us such a crackerjack submarine." He reported that the "Japs tested the hull" and the "crew found it eminently satisfactory."[28] It was an accumulation of such accolades that caused the chief of naval operations to cite the "thorough workmanship, characteristic of all Portsmouth boats" in an April 1944 letter to the shipyard.[29]

SecNav Industrial Survey #2 (1944) confirmed what the fleet already knew when it concluded that the result of Portsmouth's efforts "has been an outstanding performance, not only in numbers of vessels produced, but in the satisfactory quality and performance of these vessels, as evidenced by favorable comments of Commanding Officers."[30] Indeed, the best measurement of the quality of a shipyard's workmanship is the favorable endorsement of the commanding officers and sailors who sailed its ships into harm's way.

A submarine sailor's perception of quality has much to do with the time and effort required of him to make repairs after leaving the shipyard. Submarines built in private yards apparently sailed from the yard with incomplete work left for sailors to finish. On the other hand, a Portsmouth-built boat left the yard a much more complete product. According to submarine historian Cdr. John D. Alden, "As a government yard, Portsmouth was quick to correct problems encountered during service, whereas the boats delivered from the private yards had to have more last-minute changes made at Pearl Harbor or other advanced bases before going on patrol."[31] From this standpoint alone, one can understand the fleet's appreciation for a Portsmouth-built boat.

In closing this discussion on quality, it is appropriate to highlight that Portsmouth maintained consistently high quality despite frequent first-time installations of important new design features on its submarines. With a career background steeped in submarine tactics and technical needs, Commandant Withers had a compelling interest in expediting the latest design upgrades to the fleet. The designers, draftsmen, and planners who worked for the planning officer, Captain

McKee, were responsible for working out the details and sending the upgrades to the production schedulers. As noted earlier, the yard was blessed with a cadre of experienced and talented designers who were able to expedite those upgrades. Captain McKee brought considerable experience and consistency to the process that hastened design changes to the fleet.

Lt. Cdr. George Street, the Medal of Honor recipient cited earlier, described how he and his executive officer, Lt. Cdr. Ned Beach, worked with McKee to install needed improvements on the USS *Tirante* (SS 420) when it was being built at Portsmouth. According to Street, "Captain Andy McKee was an outstanding submarine designer. Ned and I would take out a piece of paper. . . . We'd draw up this stuff . . . and he'd [McKee] gather one of his draftsman under his supervision and draw it up." These changes included moving the mechanism to rig out the bow planes to a less awkward location so that *Tirante* could dive a few seconds faster. Another change rotated the ladder between the conning tower and the control room ninety degrees to make it more accessible and to prevent knee injuries. Yet another change remounted the target bearing transmitter (TBT) on the bridge to make its use more convenient. With MeKee's help, these "back of the envelope" changes sketched out on site by Street and Beach were converted into formal design changes and installed immediately. Private shipyards were not as receptive to this type of unplanned work, which was not under contract, but it was obvious to Street that "we were operating in a creative environment" where "the shipyard emphasized team work—working together."[32]

Portsmouth Navy Yard, as the primary submarine design yard during the war, often delivered its submarines with state-of-the-art technical upgrades far in advance of other submarine shipyards. Shipyard records note, with considerable pride, the important technical features that the yard was able to progressively and routinely incorporate into the basic World War II fleet–type submarine design that existed at the start of the war: "Included in these changes were: the increase of hull strength, or maximum depth for submergence; addition of several types of radar; a change to direct drive with slow speed motors instead of noise-producing reduction gears; addition of considerable sonar equipment; equipment capable of withstanding the shock of depth-charge; sound isolation methods to minimize noise transmitted through the hull by auxiliary machinery and electrical equipment, and many others."[33] First-time installations of design changes require special attention and extra effort to ensure satisfactory performance and compatibility with other shipboard systems. They are typically costly and not trouble free. Portsmouth Navy Yard's ability to routinely install design upgrades, while achieving remarkable production rates and consistently high quality, reflects even more credit due to the shipyard management and employees. More importantly, submarine commanding officers could confidently go to sea in a Portsmouth-built submarine knowing that it was well built and technically superior to other submarines.

Portsmouth Navy Yard's remarkable production performance during the war was achieved with no sacrifice to cost and quality. The well-advertised production numbers speak for themselves and a closer look at cost and quality has shown equally impressive results.

Chapter 7

Transformations

You can thank God that you are in a Portsmouth boat.

—CDR. L. D. McGREGOR, Commanding
Officer USS *Redfish*, 19 December 1943, on the
Bottom of East China Sea

Portsmouth Navy Yard experienced a number of transformations during and immediately after the war. The most obvious was the physical transformation resulting from the major land reclamation projects and the infrastructure development that accompanied mobilization. The yard's workload, transformed to a specialization in submarine construction during the war, returned to a potpourri of work assignments at the end of the war. On a larger scale, the yard played a major role in the completion of the policy transformation that saw the Navy Department gain the technical control of submarine design and construction that was lacking during World War I. Finally, the yard was included in a postwar organizational change that gave the Bureau of Ships more responsibilities for navy yard operations.

The highlights of the yard's physical transformation included the reclamation projects that added the twelve-acre trapezoid-shaped fitting-out pier and the ammunition stowage area to Jamaica Island. Other major additions were dry dock #1 and the building basin, which were so critical to the yard's impressive building rates. Equally important were the upgraded building ways that were increased from three partially covered ways to five completely covered ways. These sites became the heart of submarine construction operations during the war. There were many other shop and infrastructure upgrades, but these were the most significant. The end result was a definite shift in the center of shipyard operations from the prewar activity in and around dry dock #2 to the southwest toward the new facilities that included dry dock #1, the fitting-out pier, and the building basin.

A significant physical transformation was avoided when a proposal to base a fleet of out-of-commission (mothballed) ships at Portsmouth Navy Yard was considered but never implemented. The mothball fleet would have included

"48 submarines, 2 tenders and certain minor craft." An October 1944 U.S. Coast and Geodetic Survey study concluded that a large portion of the waterfront space at the shipyard was developed but unavailable or unsuitable for berthing medium-draft vessels in quantity. Excessive tides and currents and winter ice conditions were also cited as undesirable elements for long-term berthing of ships or submarines. The only feasible alternative was to develop and dredge the more sheltered and protected back channel for berthing—a costly proposition. The survey recommended against this course of action and the proposal to base a mothballed fleet at Portsmouth went no further.[1] The mothballed East Coast submarine fleet was ultimately sent to Philadelphia Navy Yard.

During the war Portsmouth Navy Yard completed a long-term strategic transformation from a multipurpose shipyard to a shipyard streamlined for submarine construction. By 1944 the yard had become the preeminent designer and builder of submarines for the U.S. Navy. The end of the war quickly brought an end to that ultraefficient shipyard. The yard reverted to prewar conditions, with employment levels closer to six thousand than the peak in excess of twenty thousand in 1943. A potpourri of postwar work included orders for submarine repairs and overhauls, the manufacture of miscellaneous pontoons and yard craft, and preparation of submarines for the mothball fleet. Additional work was necessary to dispose of submarines or sell excess submarines to foreign nations. More and more, the building of new submarines was pushed to a secondary role. After building thirty-two in 1944, the yard built twelve submarines in 1945, three in 1946, none in 1947, one in 1948, none in 1949, and none in 1950.

By 1950 employment had fallen to a little over four thousand, about the same that the yard had in 1939. The shipyard had come full cycle, and its ultraefficient, streamlined processes receded into the past. Portsmouth kept remnants of the mass-production techniques it had developed and utilized, but for the most part, wartime innovations found less and less application as the workload dropped. The construction of multiple submarines was discontinued in dry dock #1 and the building basin, the stepping of submarines from berth to berth for specific work items lost its production advantages, and paperwork and record-keeping requirements returned. By the early 1970s the yard had acquired a specialty in the repair and overhaul of nuclear submarines that continues to this day.

Portsmouth Navy Yard's performance during the war validated the policy change that the U.S. Navy had initiated after World War I to gain technical control of submarine construction. Unlike during World War I, when it had little or no technical input into the design of the submarines built by private industry, the U.S. Navy directed and controlled all technical upgrades during World War II. The Navy not only gained control of submarine design and technology, it was also able to feed wartime experience back to the Design Division at Portsmouth Navy Yard and have the desired technical alterations installed on the next order of submarines. Portsmouth had played a key role in the Navy's strategy to gain control of the submarine design and construction process.

The establishment of the Bureau of Ships in June 1940, to replace the competing Bureau of Engineering and the Bureau of Construction and Repair, clarified many navy yard organizational and administration issues. However, other agencies and bureaus continued to direct various fragments of operations at navy yards. As late as December 1944 Secretary of the Navy Forrestal, who continued to be frustrated with the inefficient administration of the navy yards, wrote, "What I want is some man whose sole job is to examine the functions, to compare operations and handle difficulties [at navy yards.] We should have one man to go to."[2] With the war winding down in the summer of 1945, a move to improve the overall operating efficiency of navy yards by further clarifying organizational responsibilities and putting one person in charge developed. A survey conducted by the Industrial Survey Division in the Office of the Secretary of the Navy in July 1945 concluded, "The attainment of greater and enduring improvements in the operating efficiency of the Navy Yards and Naval Drydocks will be materially facilitated by a realignment and clarification of the organization and administration of these establishments . . . by concentrating full authority and responsibility for Departmental administration of these establishments in a single agency of the Navy Department."[3] By the end of 1945 a full-scale reorganization of navy yard administration and management that ultimately resulted in increased responsibilities for the Bureau of Ships was in progress, as was a reorganization of navy yards that gave the commandant full responsibility for all operations at his navy yard. Name changes accompanied the reorganization; commandants became commanding officers, and navy yards became naval shipyards. In December 1945 Portsmouth Navy Yard became Portsmouth Naval Shipyard, the title it holds today.[4]

—ᛡ—

USS *Redfish* (SS 395), one of the three submarines launched simultaneously on 27 January 1944, experienced its own transformation of sorts late in the war. After being the center of attention during flag-waving ceremonies and champagne toasts at Portsmouth Navy Yard early in 1944, the submarine found itself battle damaged and on the bottom of the East China Sea before the year was out. On 19 December 1944, after sinking the Japanese carrier *Unryu*, the submarine was the victim of a depth charge attack from Japanese destroyers.[5]

After returning to Pearl Harbor from the East China Sea, the crew learned that the submarine would have to transit halfway around the world to Portsmouth Navy Yard for repairs. Pearl Harbor and all the West Coast yards were full with ships needing emergency repairs. On 17 February 1945 the *Redfish* limped up the

Piscataqua River toward Portsmouth Navy Yard. TM2 Dan MacIsaac was on deck with the line handlers as the submarine steamed up the river. He and his shipmates never expected to be back in the yard so soon.[6]

MacIsaac had been in the Forward Torpedo Room, after the sinking of the *Unryu*, when three Japanese destroyers dropped seven depth charges off the starboard bow of the submerged *Redfish*. No one on board was closer to the explosions. MacIsaac was thrown to the forward end of the compartment, where he lay in the bilge, unconscious, for some period of time. The explosions cracked the pressure hull and damaged piping, torpedo tubes, and other equipment in the room. MacIsaac awoke to the sound of rushing water, realizing that he and his shipmates had to isolate the leaks quickly, and as best they could, if the submarine was to be saved. Using wrenches, rags, and whatever was available, MacIsaac and his mates stopped the leaks. *Redfish* rested on the bottom of the East China Sea for four hours to avoid detection and further attacks.

As soon as MacIsaac and his mates had gained control of the flooding, the commanding officer, Cdr. L. D. McGregor, came forward from the conning tower to assess the damage. Today, over sixty years later, MacIsaac remembers the captain's exact words to him and his shipmates, "You can thank God that you are in a Portsmouth boat." Such was Portsmouth Navy Yard's reputation for building quality submarines.

The *Redfish* was greeted at the pier by shipyard officials and hundreds of shipyard workers eager to inspect the damage and their workmanship. MacIsaac was responsible for the Torpedo Room, where most of the damage had occurred. He remembers worker after worker inspecting damaged pipes, tubes, and equipment to see if they could, or should, have done something differently. As MacIsaac pointed out the damage and told the story of the attack, the workers empathized with the crew and delighted in the fact that their work had held up to such a pounding. According to MacIsaac, the workers felt personally responsible for the fact that the submarine and crew had survived the attack. MacIsaac, who had gained considerable respect for Portsmouth workmanship while his submarine was being constructed, was more convinced than ever that the men and women at Portsmouth Navy Yard were an unusually dedicated and talented workforce.

The *Redfish* completed repairs in May 1945 and made the long transit back to the Pacific to resume war patrols until the end of the war. That same month, U.S. destroyers escorted four German submarines, U-805, U-873, U-1228, and U-234, to Portsmouth Navy Yard for observation, selective stripping, and processing of prisoners. A few months after the departure of the *Redfish*, the submarine action in the Pacific began to wind down, and more and more submarines found their way back to Portsmouth. The submarine traffic in the Piscataqua River was heavy in late 1945 and the first half of 1946. An average of eight U.S. submarines each month arrived at the yard for work.[7]

A conference was held at Portsmouth Naval Shipyard on 21 June 1946 "to discuss the availability of berthing facilities for additional naval craft." When Vice Adm. Thomas L. Gatch, Commander, Naval Surface Forces Atlantic, asked how many craft were presently moored at the yard, Cdr. A. K. Romberg responded that there were forty boats moored at the yard—"the greatest number of boats ever moored at Portsmouth at a single time."[8] It was quickly concluded that the shipyard had no berths available for additional naval craft.

By the summer of 1946 the shipyard was inundated with submarines and immersed in a wealth of miscellaneous work assignments. Orders for the construction of new submarines had stopped. The shipyard's finely tuned operation, which had pushed *Redfish* and seventy-eight other submarines to war in record numbers, had come to a grinding halt. Priorities had changed from the construction of submarines to the disposal of submarines, and a remarkable period of submarine construction had come to a close for the Portsmouth Navy Yard.

Conclusion

I n his classic treatment of World War II merchant shipbuilding, *Ships for Victory*, Frederic C. Lane attributes success, in part, to lessons previously learned, but "also on a readiness to learn new lessons from day-by-day experiences in new situations." Likewise, Lane urges caution when summarizing the lessons to be learned from the World War II mobilization because "the lessons that should be drawn from the experience of 1940–45 will depend on the situation to which they are to be applied."[1] Lane's observations are especially valid for the lessons to be learned from Portsmouth Navy Yard's World War II mobilization experience.

While Portsmouth Navy Yard had gained experience and accumulated lessons learned with sectional construction and the use of wooden machinery mock-ups prior to the war, the willingness to learn new lessons from day-to-day experiences in new situations at the start of the war proved to be the hallmark of the yard's success. Although the yard workers had never built a submarine below sea level before, a shortage of building ways quickly helped them to recognize building submarines in the new dry dock #1 and the new building basin as the key to increasing production.

Adapting to circumstances and less-than-optimum conditions for production goals became strengths of shipyard management. The prime example of this was the "push 'em off the ways" philosophy that compensated for the shortage of building ways. Another example was management's refusal to let late or unreliable contractor-supplied components affect production schedules by pretesting and rebuilding suspect components as necessary prior to shipboard installation. Schedules and contingency plans were adjusted on a day-to-day basis to compensate for shortages through a locally developed Portsmouth Scheduling System. Yet another example of adaptation was the refusal to let inadequate communication and work control systems affect production. That production challenge was overcome through open communications and informal work procedures that minimized the need for paperwork. Finally, the low industrial priority routinely assigned to submarines was overcome by the bulk ordering of material and components for entire classes of submarines. The yard's innovative scheduling system readily accommodated this practice.

Having crafted submarines one at a time with experienced and skilled workers before the war, the yard shifted to the mass production of submarines with inexperienced workers by equipping them with specialized skills and empowering them to work independently in small teams, doing the same job at repetitive worksites. It is to the credit of a competent cadre of naval leaders and experienced civilian managers that they had the vision to free the workforce of undue paperwork, record keeping, cost accounting, and other restrictions so that production was king. There were no mixed signals or distractions throughout the yard. All hands were focused on, and committed to, supporting waterfront operations to maximize submarine production.

After an initial reluctance to bring aboard large numbers of women workers or to assign them to the more responsible and demanding jobs, shipyard management eventually hired women in large numbers that approached, by the latter stages of the war, 20 percent of the workforce. Women were gradually hired for positions of increased responsibility, including the skilled trades. When the Selective Service Administration threatened orderly production by randomly siphoning off many of the younger and often more talented employees from critical trades, shipyard management negotiated a first-of-its-kind three-state deal that provided for accurate recruitment forecasts and allowed the yard to plan for the loss of employees and the timely training of replacements. An important lesson to be learned from Portsmouth's mobilization experience is that management's ability to rapidly adjust to changing conditions and needs is critical to successful mobilization.

It is also true that Portsmouth Navy Yard's operations during the war provided a window on several important management concepts. As noted earlier, the significant benefits realized from worker empowerment, specialized small teams, and the employment of women during the war all waned after the war before making a strong comeback a quarter century later. The advantages of decentralized management in the shipbuilding industry also took a step backward immediately after the war in both the Navy Department and the U.S. Maritime Commission. While decentralized management has resurfaced as an important industrial concept, Lane's caution about lessons learned "depending on the situation to which they are to be applied" rings especially true for the shipbuilding industry and, most notably, modern submarine construction. The decision-making independence given World War II shipyards to build Liberty ships and fleet submarines is far less applicable to current shipbuilding, especially the construction of nuclear-powered submarines. These technological marvels demand quality and safety controls that are best centrally managed and uniformly applied across all construction sites. This study does, however, suggest that selective application of decentralized management in any industry, including shipbuilding, has the potential to pay huge dividends.

One unqualified truth can be taken from the Portsmouth Navy Yard mobilization experience: Remarkable production success can be achieved when bold and enlightened management leads dedicated and motivated employees and both are zealously committed to a common objective. This is especially true when that objective is winning a war. The wartime environment may very well have been the lubricant that enabled all the shipyard's organizational pieces to fit together and run so efficiently. However, the environment would have mattered little had the shipyard employees and management not been up to the task at hand. Fortunately, as this study shows, all three factors meshed as never before to produce submarines at unprecedented production rates, including *32 in '44*.

Appendix:
Additional Figures

Figure A-1: Portsmouth Navy Yard (1939)

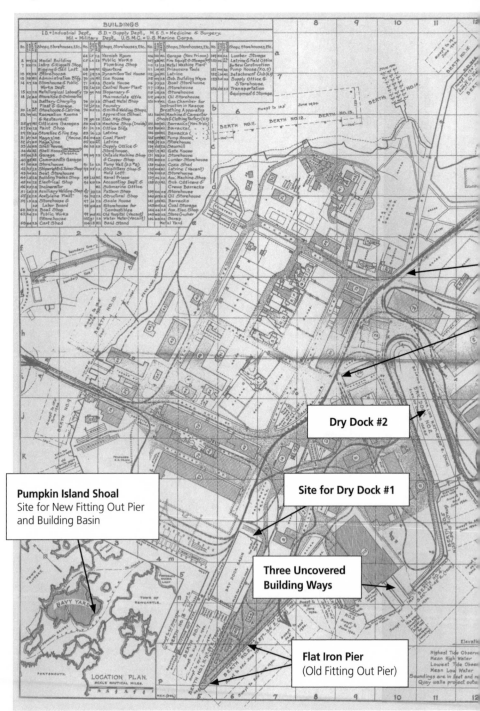

Source: NARA Waltham, RG 181, Portsmouth Naval Base Central Files, Box 20, Folder EE1, "President's Visit 1940."

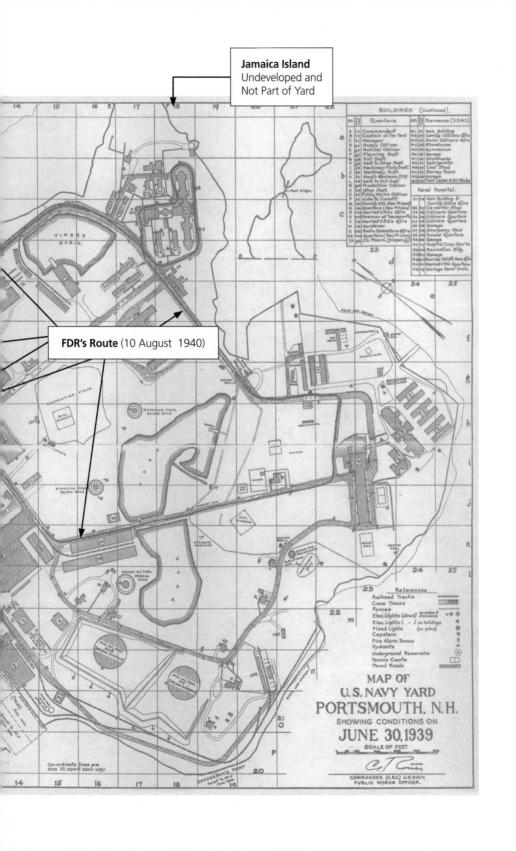

Jamaica Island
Undeveloped and
Not Part of Yard

FDR's Route (10 August 1940)

BUILDINGS (Continued).

Naval Hospital.

References
Railroad Tracks
Crane Tracks
Fences
Elec. Lights (street)
Elec. Lights ( ) on buildings
Flood Lights (on poles)
Capstans
Fire Alarm Boxes
Hydrants
Underground Reservoirs
Tennis Courts
Paved Roads

MAP OF
U.S. NAVY YARD
PORTSMOUTH, N.H.
SHOWING CONDITIONS ON
JUNE 30, 1939
SCALE OF FEET

COMMANDER (C.E.C.) U.S. NAVY,
PUBLIC WORKS OFFICER.

Co-ordinate lines are
200 ft. apart each way.

Figure A-2: Portsmouth Navy Yard (1945)

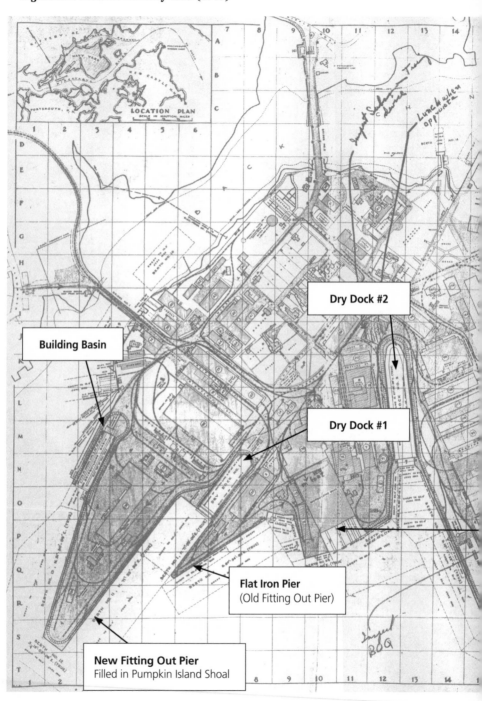

Dry Dock #2

Building Basin

Dry Dock #1

Flat Iron Pier
(Old Fitting Out Pier)

New Fitting Out Pier
Filled in Pumpkin Island Shoal

Source: NARA Waltham, RG 181, Portsmouth Naval Base Central Files, Box 20, Folder A1/Y1, "Portsmouth (1943–49)."

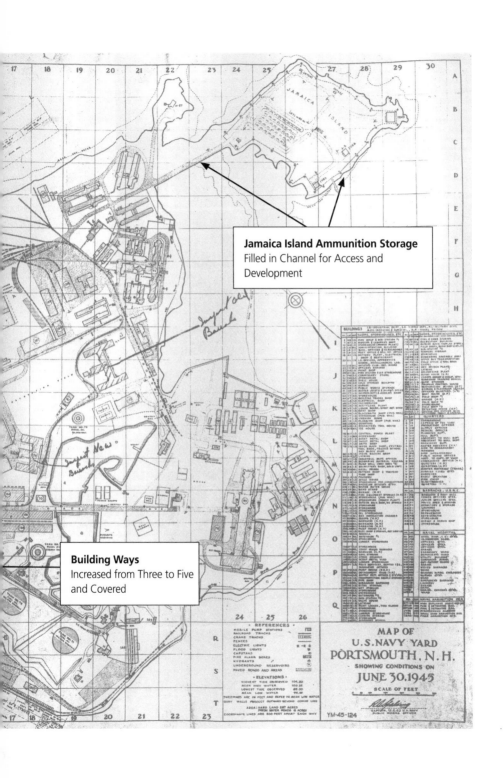

Jamaica Island Ammunition Storage
Filled in Channel for Access and
Development

Building Ways
Increased from Three to Five
and Covered

MAP OF
U.S. NAVY YARD
PORTSMOUTH, N.H.
SHOWING CONDITIONS ON
JUNE 30, 1945
SCALE OF FEET

YM-45-124

Figure A-3: Portsmouth Navy Yard Manpower Curves by Work Category (1940–45)

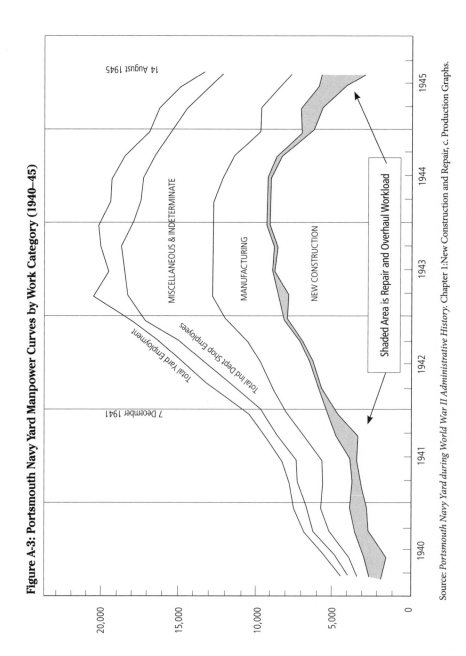

Source: *Portsmouth Navy Yard during World War II Administrative History*. Chapter 1:New Construction and Repair, c. Production Graphs.

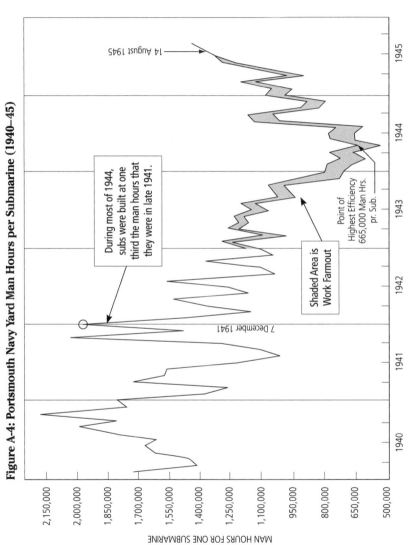

Figure A-4: Portsmouth Navy Yard Man Hours per Submarine (1940–45)

During most of 1944, subs were built at one third the man hours that they were in late 1941.

7 December 1941

14 August 1945

Point of Highest Efficiency 665,000 Man Hrs. pr. Sub.

Shaded Area is Work Farmout

MAN HOURS FOR ONE SUBMARINE

2,150,000
2,000,000
1,850,000
1,700,000
1,550,000
1,400,000
1,250,000
1,100,000
950,000
800,000
650,000
500,000

1940
1941
1942
1943
1944
1945

Source: *Portsmouth Navy Yard during World War II Administrative History*. Chapter 1:New Construction and Repair, c. Production Graphs.

Notes

INTRODUCTION

Epigraph source: Secretary of the Navy Frank Knox, ALNAV Dispatch to all Naval Stations, 11 December 1941, National Archives and Records Administration, Waltham, MA, Record Group 181, Portsmouth Naval Shipyard General Correspondence (Central Files), Box 24, Folder A14-6, "Status of Nations with Reference to War and Peace." Hereafter referred to as NARA Waltham, RG 181.

1. The thirty-two submarines credited to Portsmouth Navy Yard in 1944 are SS 387 through SS 410, SS 417 through SS 423, and the USS *Lionfish* (SS 298), as listed in *Administrative History: Portsmouth Navy Yard in World War II* (n.d., Portsmouth Naval Shipyard Museum Archives, Kittery, ME), 8–10. USS *Lionfish* was towed from Cramp Shipbuilding Company in Philadelphia on April 1944 to Portsmouth Navy Yard after it was 48.5 percent completed. USS *Manta* (SS 299), also towed from Cramp Shipbuilding in April 1944, was completed at Portsmouth on 20 January 1945. *Cradle of American Shipbuilding: Portsmouth Naval Shipyard, Portsmouth, New Hampshire* (Portsmouth: Portsmouth Naval Shipyard, 1978) lists thirty-four submarines commissioned at Portsmouth Navy Yard in 1944, including SS 298 and SS 299. Commissioning dates precede completion dates by several weeks and do not necessarily fall in the same year. In a letter to the Bureau of Ships dated 23 March 1945 (cited in ch. 6), the shipyard commandant, Rear Adm. Thomas Withers, credits the shipyard with completing twelve submarines in 1942, nineteen submarines in 1943, and thirty-two submarines in 1944. In addition, the shipyard history cited above notes on page 10, "During the calendar year [1944], the Navy Yard completed thirty-two submarines." This book and its title are consistent with the thirty-two submarines cited by Withers' letter and the shipyard history.

2. Fred White (master rigger and laborer at Portsmouth Navy Yard), interview by author, 3 April 2006, New Castle, NH.

3. Dan MacIsaac (crew member of USS *Redfish*), interview by author, 9 November 2006, Portsmouth Naval Shipyard Museum.

4. Secretary of the Navy James Forrestal, letter to Commandant Portsmouth Navy Yard, 27 January 1944, NARA Waltham, RG 181, Portsmouth Naval Shipyard General Correspondence (Central Files), Box 18, Folder S-6, "Launching General, Jan 1944–47."

5. "Yard Is Tops in Sub Production," *Portsmouth Herald*, 19 July 1945, 1.

6. Theodore Roscoe, *United States Submarine Operations in World War II* (Annapolis: U.S. Naval Institute, 1949), 527–65. This work accounts for enemy tonnage sunk by individual submarines. The 1.7 million tons is the author's count for Portsmouth-built subma-

135

rines from that work. Another source, John D. Horn, "Submarines and the Electric Boat Company," (A.B. thesis, Princeton University, 1948), 89, provides the following summary of sunk tonnage by shipyard: 80 Electric Boat submarines sunk 1,990,454 tons (38.5 percent), 69 Portsmouth submarines sunk 1,607,016 tons (32.8 percent), 22 Mare Island Submarines sunk 988,357 tons (22 percent), and 19 Manitowoc submarines sunk 494,737 tons (9.6 percent). Horn cited the source for these totals as "Figures courtesy Electric Boat Company." Thus, two independent accounts credit Portsmouth-built submarines with about 1.7 million tons of enemy tonnage sunk, representing about one-third of the total tonnage sunk.

7. Roscoe, *United States Submarine Operations in World War II.* A graph inside the back cover shows 5,329,000 tons of enemy shipping sunk by U.S. submarines.

8. "72 Port City Subs Launched in 44 Months Play Vital Role," *Portsmouth Periscope,* 27 August 1945, 1, Papers of Harold Caswell Sweetser, Portsmouth Navy Yard Supervisory Naval Architect, 1917–58, Sweetser Family Papers, Milne Special Collections, University of New Hampshire Library, Durham, NH.

9. Frederic C. Lane, *Ships for Victory: A History of Shipbuilding under the U.S. Maritime Commission in World War II* (Baltimore: Johns Hopkins University Press, 2001), 3.

10. Ibid., 830.

11. See Keith E. Eiler, *Mobilizing America: Robert P. Patterson and the War Effort 1940–45* (Ithaca: Cornell University Press, 1997); Robert H. Connery, *The Navy and Industrial Mobilization in World War II* (Princeton: Princeton University Press, 1951); and Robert G. Albion and Robert H. Connery, *Forrestal and the Navy* (New York: Columbia University Press, 1962).

12. See Lane, *Ships for Victory*; Christopher James Tassava, "Launching a Thousand Ships: Entrepreneurs, War, Workers, and the State in American Shipbuilding, 1940–45" (Ph.D. dissertation, Northwestern University, 2003); and Marilyn S. Johnson, *The Second Gold Rush: Oakland and the East Bay in World War II* (Berkeley: University of California Press, 1996).

13. Tony Cope, *On the Swing Shift: Building Liberty Ships in Savannah* (Annapolis: Naval Institute Press, 2009).

14. Tassava, "Launching a Thousand Ships," 17.

CHAPTER 1: BETWEEN THE WARS

1. Connery, *Navy and Industrial Mobilization in World War II,* 266.

2. Gary Weir, *Building American Submarines 1914–1940* (Washington, DC: Naval Historical Center, 1991), 114.

3. "History of the Electric Boat Company, 1899–1949," unpublished typescript, chapter 4, 1–18, Navy Department Library, Naval Historical Center, Washington, DC.

4. Ibid.

5. A. I. McKee, "Development of Submarines in the United States," *Historical Transactions 1893–1943,* by Society of Naval Architects and Marine Engineers (New York, 1945), 347.

6. Ibid.

7. Quoted in "Portsmouth Won Fame with First Sub It Built, Has Kept Proud Record," *Portsmouth Herald,* 23 April 1942, 1.

8. George C. Dyer, "Beginning of the S-Boats," in *Submarine Stories: Recollections from the Diesel Boats,* ed. Paul Stillwell (Annapolis: Naval Institute Press, 2007), 31–33.

9. David F. Boyd, "Continuation of Preble's History of the United States Navy Yard, Portsmouth, N.H. Covering the Years 1875–1930," unpublished typescript, Maine Room, Rice Public Library, Kittery, ME, 38.

10. William D. Irvin, "Oddball S-Boat," in Stillwell, *Submarine Stories*, 62–66.

11. *Administrative History: Bureau of Ships in World War II*, Naval Department World War II Admin History #89, 1946, Navy Department Library, Naval Historical Center, Washington, DC, 5.

12. Lane, *Ships for Victory*, 32.

13. *Cradle of American Shipbuilding*, 76, 78, 80.

14. Robert Dallek, *Franklin D. Roosevelt and American Foreign Policy, 1932–1945* (New York: Oxford University Press, 1979), 75.

15. Weir, *Building American Submarines*, 114.

16. "The *Herald's* Platform," Editorial, *Portsmouth Herald*, 30 December 1939.

17. According to the *Portsmouth Herald*, the shipyard's first blackout drill was conducted on Sunday, 8 September 1940, and the first Portsmouth blackout drill was on Sunday, 27 October 1940. See "Navy Blackout Tomorrow," *Portsmouth Herald*, 7 September 1940; and "City Has Practice to Prepare for War Emergency," *Portsmouth Herald*, 28 October 1940.

18. "Poll Continues to Show Trend against British Aid," *Portsmouth Herald*, 5 January 1940, 1.

19. "This is War," *Portsmouth Herald*, 18 March 1941, 4.

20. Editorial, *Portsmouth Herald*, 27 May 1941.

21. Dallek, *Franklin D. Roosevelt and American Foreign Policy*, 260.

22. *Administrative History: Portsmouth Navy Yard*, 1.

23. "Navy Says British Ships in U.S. Ports," *Portsmouth Herald*, 21 September 1941, 1.

24. Medical Officer, Portsmouth Navy Yard memorandum to the Commandant, 10 September 1941, NARA Waltham, RG 181, Portsmouth Naval Shipyard General Correspondence (Central Files), Box 43, Folder EP13/L9-3 (161), "British Empire, *Surcouf* 1941–42."

25. "*Parthian* Once Sank Italian Sub; Free French *Surcouf* Unlucky," *Portsmouth Herald*, 3 October 1941, 1 and 9.

26. Ibid.

27. "Free French Sub Surcouf Is Lost," *Portsmouth Herald*, 18 April 1942, 1.

28. Production Officer, memorandum to Manager, 15 June 1934, NARA Waltham, RG 181, Portsmouth Naval Shipyard General Correspondence (Central Files), Box 2, Folder A9/A1-3/ENR, "Reports of Projects NIRA to Y[ards] & D[ocks] 1933–35 [Shore Projects]."

29. Secretary of the Navy, letter to Commandant Portsmouth Navy Yard, 18 January 1936, NARA Waltham, RG 181, Portsmouth Naval Shipyard General Correspondence (Central Files), Box 1, Folder A1, "New Construction 27 Sep 1932 to 29 May 1940."

30. Commandant Portsmouth Navy Yard, letter to Bureau of Yards and Docks, 29 August 1935, NARA Waltham, RG 181, Portsmouth Naval Base General Correspondence, Box 1, Folder A-1, "Works Progress Administration (WPA)."

31. Commandant Portsmouth Navy Yard, letter to Chief Bureau of Yards and Docks, 30 January 1941, NARA Waltham, RG 181, Portsmouth Naval Base General Correspondence, Box 1, Folder A-1, "Works Progress Administration (WPA)."

32. Chief Bureau Yards and Docks, letter, 9 June 1939, NARA Waltham, RG 181, Portsmouth Naval Base General Correspondence, Box 1, Folder A-1, "Works Progress Administration (WPA)."

33. *Administrative History: Bureau of Ships*, 7.

34. Weir, *Building American Submarines*, 62–63.

35. Bureau of Construction and Repair and Bureau of Engineering, joint letter to Commandant Portsmouth Navy Yard and Commandant Mare Island Navy Yard, 25 October 1935, NARA Waltham, RG 181, Portsmouth Naval Base General Correspondence, Box 18, Folder S-1, "Design of Vessels, Specifications, Plans, etc. (1925–1947)."

36. Commandant Portsmouth Navy Yard, letter to Commandant Mare Island Navy Yard, 8 June 1940, NARA Waltham, RG 181, Portsmouth Naval Base General Correspondence, Box 18, Folder S-1, "Design of Vessels, Specifications, Plans, etc. (1925–1947)."

37. Commandant Portsmouth Navy Yard, letter to Cramp Shipbuilding Company, 20 June 1942, and Commandant Portsmouth Navy Yard, letter to Cramp Shipbuilding Company, no date (probably 13 November 1942), NARA Waltham, RG 181, Portsmouth Naval Base General Correspondence, Box 18, Folder S-1, "Design of Vessels, Specifications, Plans, etc. (1925–1947)."

38. Bureau Construction and Repair and Bureau of Engineering, joint letter to Secretary of the Navy, 10 August 1938, NARA Waltham, RG 181, Portsmouth Naval Base General Correspondence, Box 1, Folder A1, "New Construction 27 Sep 1932 to 29 May 1940."

39. Secretary of the Navy, letter to Chiefs of Bureaus and Continental Shipyards, 30 December 1938, NARA Waltham, RG 181, Portsmouth Naval Base General Correspondence, Box 20, Folder FS, "Ships, Nov 1925 to 15 Nov 1939."

40. Commandant Portsmouth Navy Yard, Rear Adm. C. W. Cole, letter to Secretary of the Navy, 11 January 1939, NARA Waltham, RG 181, Portsmouth Naval Base General Correspondence, Box 20, Folder FS, "Ships 14 Nov 1925 to 15 Nov 1939."

41. For accounts of the *Squalus* recovery see *Portsmouth Herald*, 23 May–5 July 1939; Nathaniel Barrows, *Blow All Ballast! The Story of the Squalus* (New York: Dodd, Mead, 1940); Carl LaVo, *Back from the Deep: The Strange Story of the Sister Subs* Squalus *and* Sculpin (Annapolis: Naval Institute Press, 1988); and recorded eyewitness testimonies in the Portsmouth War Records, Cummings Library and Archives, Strawbery Banke Museum, Portsmouth, NH, MS 96, Box 1, Folder 3, "U.S. Navy Yard."

42. See "Naval Expansion Act, 14 June 1940," Frequently Asked Questions, Naval Historical Center, 30 June 1999, http://www.history.navy.mil/faqs/faq59-20.htm; and "Naval Expansion Act, 19 July 1940," Frequently Asked Questions, Naval Historical Center, 30 June 1999, http://www.history.navy.mil/faqs/faq59-21.htm (both accessed on 3 October 2010).

CHAPTER 2: RAMP-UP

Epigraph source: Secretary of the Navy, ALNAV 1, 1 January 1942, NARA Waltham, RG 181, Portsmouth Naval Shipyard General Correspondence (Central Files), Box 24, Folder A14-6, "Status of Nations with Reference to War and Peace."

1. Dallek, *Franklin D. Roosevelt and American Foreign Policy*, 224.

2. David M. Kennedy, *Freedom from Fear: The American People in Depression and War, 1929–1945* (New York: Oxford University Press, 1999), 431.

3. Quoted in Samuel Eliot Morison, *The Two-Ocean War: A Short History of the United States in the Second World War* (Boston: Little, Brown, 1963), 30.

4. "Naval Expansion Act, 14 June 1940," Frequently Asked Questions, Naval Historical Center, 30 June 1999, http://www.history.navy.mil/faqs/faq59-20.htm.

5. "Naval Expansion Act, 19 July 1940," Frequently Asked Questions, Naval Historical Center, 30 June 1999, http://www.history.navy.mil/faqs/faq59-21.htm.

6. Dallek, *Franklin D. Roosevelt and American Foreign Policy*, 232.

7. Connery, *Navy and the Industrial Mobilization in World War II*, 293.

8. Maurice H. Rindskopf, "*Drum* at War," in Stillwell, *Submarine Stories*, 107–112.

9. Industrial Officer, memo to Shop Masters, 24 December 1941, NARA Waltham, RG 181, Portsmouth Naval Shipyard General Correspondence (Central Files), Box 14, Folder A3-2/LC, PKG 6, "Orders to Shop Foremen."

10. Commandant Portsmouth Navy Yard John D. Wainwright, memo to Manager and Captain of the Yard, 5 February 1942, NARA Waltham, RG 181, Portsmouth Naval Base General Correspondence, Box 18, Folder S-7, "Docking—General."

11. Chief of Bureau of Construction and Repair, letter to Commandant Portsmouth Navy Yard, 28 November 1939, NARA Waltham, RG 181, Portsmouth Naval Shipyard General Correspondence (Central Files), Box 1, Folder A1/Y1, PKG 1, "Local Development Boards."

12. Commandant Portsmouth Navy Yard, letter to Chief Bureau of Construction and Repair, 28 December 1939, NARA Waltham, RG 181, Portsmouth Naval Shipyard General Correspondence (Central Files), Box 1, Folder A1/Y1, PKG 1, "Local Development Boards."

13. The details of the president's visit are from "Crowds Line Streets to Greet Chief Executive," *Portsmouth Herald*, 10 August 1940, 1, and an untitled one-page summary of the visit held at NARA Waltham, RG 181, Portsmouth Naval Base General Correspondence, Box 20, Folder EE "President's Visit, 1940."

14. Chief Bureau of Yards and Docks, letter, 7 October 1940, NARA Waltham, RG 181, Portsmouth Naval Base General Correspondence, Box 1, Folder A1, "New Construction 1930–1950."

15. Industrial Manager H. F. D. Davis, letter to Congressman Carl Vinson, Chairman of Committee on Naval Affairs, 15 March 1941, NARA Waltham, RG 181, Portsmouth Naval Shipyard General Correspondence (Central Files), Box 2, Folder A1-3, PKG 3, "General Building Program."

16. Manager, memo, 9 November 1936, NARA Waltham, RG 181, Portsmouth Naval Shipyard General Correspondence (Central Files), Box 1, Folder A1/Y1, PKG 1, "Local Development Boards."

17. Portsmouth War Records, Cummings Library, Strawbery Banke Museum, MS 96 Box 1, Folder 19, "Harbor Defense."

18. Senior Member, Shore Station Development Board, letter, 19 September 1941, NARA Waltham, RG 181, Portsmouth Naval Shipyard General Correspondence (Central Files), Box 1, Folder A1/Y1, PKG 1, "Local Development Boards."

19. Public Works Officer, memo to Commandant Portsmouth Naval Base, 19 May 1947, NARA Waltham, RG 181, Portsmouth Naval Base General Correspondence, Box 15, Folder L-5, "Inspection Naval Yard, 1945–48."

20. *Administrative History: Bureau of Yards and Docks in World War II*, Naval Department World War II Admin History #108, n.d., Navy Department Library, Naval Historical Center, Washington, DC, 1:175.

21. Ship Hull Superintendent, Flatiron Pier memo, 22 October 1941, NARA Waltham, RG 181, Portsmouth Naval Shipyard General Correspondence (Central Files), Box 2, Folder A1-3, PKG 3, "General Building Program."

22. Connery, *Navy and the Industrial Mobilization in World War II*, 135.

23. Commandant Portsmouth Navy Yard, letter to Bureau of Yards and Docks, 29 January 1942, NARA Waltham, RG 181, Portsmouth Naval Shipyard General Correspondence (Central Files), Box 1, Folder A1/Y1, PKG 1, "Local Development Boards."

24. Senior Member Shore Station Development Board, letter to Secretary of the Navy, 11 January 1942; and Secretary of the Navy, letter, 14 January 1942, NARA Waltham, RG 181, Portsmouth Naval Shipyard General Correspondence (Central Files), Box 36, Folder N15-8, "Slips and Basins."

25. White interview.

26. The new building basin was redesignated dry dock #3 after the war. The original shipyard graving dock was redesignated dry dock #2 when plans were approved to construct dry dock #1.

27. "Use of Dry Dock #1 for Building Submarines," Portsmouth Navy Yard, unsigned memo, 1 December 1942, NARA Waltham, RG 181, Portsmouth Naval Shipyard General Correspondence (Central Files), Box 2, Folder A1-3, PKG 4, "Building Program."

28. Lt. (jg) H. D. Arnold, memo to Hull Superintendent, 12 December 1941, NARA Waltham, RG 181, Portsmouth Naval Shipyard General Correspondence (Central Files), Box 2, Folder A1-3, PKG 3, "General Building Program."

29. *Administrative History: Bureau of Yards and Docks*, 1:172.

30. Lane's *Ships for Victory* is a classic summary of commercial shipbuilding during World War II that includes considerable discussion of the mobilization of private shipyards. Other mobilization sources include Connery, *Navy and the Industrial Mobilization in World War II* and Eiler, *Mobilizing America*.

31. *Administrative History: Bureau of Yards and Docks*, 1:196.

32. Horn, "Submarines and the Electric Boat Company," 92.

33. *Administrative History: Bureau of Ships*, 132.

34. Secretary of the Navy, letter to All Shore Activities, 25 June 1942, NARA Waltham, RG 181, Portsmouth Naval Shipyard General Correspondence (Central Files), Box 36, Folder N23-5, "Acetylene and Oxyacetylene."

35. Secretary of the Navy Frank Knox, letter to All Naval Activities, 4 November 1942, NARA Waltham, RG 181, Portsmouth Naval Shipyard General Correspondence (Central Files), Box 36, Folder N23-5, "Acetylene and Oxyacetylene."

36. Commandant First Naval District, letter to All Activities, First Naval District, 4 November 1942, NARA Waltham, RG 181, Portsmouth Naval Shipyard General Correspondence (Central Files), Box 13, Folder A3-2, "General Management 1932–1940."

37. Lane, *Ships for Victory*, 343.

38. Commandant T. Withers, memo to Heads of Division, Masters, Senior Office Supervisors, 24 December 1942, NARA Waltham, RG 181, Portsmouth Naval Shipyard General Correspondence (Central Files), Box 2, Folder A1-3, PKG 4, "Building Program."

39. Commandant Portsmouth Navy Yard, letter to Dr. W. B. Johnston, 14 January 1941, NARA Waltham, RG 181, Portsmouth Naval Base General Correspondence, Box 10, Folder N1-13, "Lands."

40. Commandant Portsmouth Navy Yard, letter to Chief Bureau of Yards and Docks, 10 October 1941, NARA Waltham, RG 181, Portsmouth Naval Base General Correspondence, Box 10, Folder N1-13, "Lands."

41. Judge Advocate General, Washington, D.C., U.S. naval message to Navy Yard Portsmouth, N.H., 7 December 1941, NARA Waltham, RG 181, Portsmouth Naval Base General Correspondence, Box 10, Folder N1-13, "Lands."

42. Rodney K. Watterson, "'32 in '44: A Management and Environmental Study of Submarine Construction at Portsmouth Navy Yard during World War II" (Ph.D. diss., New Hampshire University, 2007), 276, 286.

43. *Administrative History: Portsmouth Navy Yard*, 43.

44. Ibid., 20.

45. Commandant Portsmouth Navy Yard, letter to Bureau of Yards and Docks, 9 April 1946, NARA Waltham, RG 181, Portsmouth Naval Base General Correspondence, Box 15, Folder N1-13, "Lands Somersworth."

46. "Navy Takes Over Gypsum Plant to Make Sub Parts," *Portsmouth Herald*, 3 December 1943, 1.

47. "First Shipload of Gypsum Rock in Over 2 Years Arrives at Local Plant," *Portsmouth Herald*, 18 October 1945, 1.

48. Commandant Portsmouth Navy Yard, letter to Assistant Secretary of the Navy (Shore Establishment Division), 2 October 1939, NARA Waltham, RG 181, Portsmouth Naval Shipyard General Correspondence (Central Files), Box 2, Folder A1-2/NY, "Government Policies."

49. Hull Superintendent F. A. Tusler, memo to Production Officer, 3 February 1941, NARA Waltham, RG 181, Portsmouth Naval Shipyard General Correspondence (Central Files), Box 26, Folder A19, "Conferences, Congresses, and Conventions." Tusler's memo was in response to the industrial manager's request for items in preparation for his appearance before the Naval Subcommittee of the House Appropriations Committee concerning navy yard work.

50. Connery, *Navy and the Industrial Mobilization in World War II*, 269.

51. War Plans Officer, memo, 26 August 1940, NARA Waltham, RG 181, Portsmouth Naval Shipyard General Correspondence (Central Files), Box 24, Folder A16-11, "National Defense."

52. Industrial Manager H. F. D. Davis, letter to Congressman Carl Vinson, Chairman of Committee on Naval Affairs, 15 March 1941, NARA Waltham, RG 181, Portsmouth Naval Base General Correspondence, Box 2, Folder A1-3, PKG 3, "General Building Program."

53. Commandant Portsmouth Navy Yard, letter to Chief of Naval Operations, 2 January 1942, NARA College Park, Formerly Security Classified General Correspondence of the CNO/Secretary of the Navy, 1940–1947, RG 80, Box 442, File L9-3/NY-L9-3/NY1.

CHAPTER 3: MANAGEMENT

1. Industrial Relations Counselors Inc., letter to Assistant Secretary of the Navy Ralph A. Bard, 8 September 1942, NARA College Park, RG 19, Bureau of Ships General Correspondence, 1940–45, Box 151, Folder NY1, 1 July 1942–30 June 1943. Hereafter referred to as SecNav Industrial Survey #1 (1942).

2. Assistant Secretary of the Navy Ralph A. Bard, "Survey of Industrial Department, Navy Yard, Portsmouth, N.H.—Report No. 2 of Industrial Survey Division," 6 November 1944, NARA College Park, RG 19, Bureau of Ships General Correspondence, 1940–45, Box 785, Folder NY1/A3. Hereafter referred to as SecNav Industrial Survey #2 (1944).

3. Board of Shipbuilding Construction, "New Construction—Progress and Administration to Expedite Work," report for Commandant Portsmouth Navy Yard, 8 December 1941, NARA Waltham, RG 181, Portsmouth Naval Shipyard General Correspondence (Central Files), Box 2, Folder A1/3, PKG 4, "Building Program." Hereafter referred to as Portsmouth Industrial Survey #1 (December 1941).

4. Board of Shipbuilding Construction, "New Construction—Progress and Administration to Expedite Work," report to Commandant Portsmouth Navy Yard, 6 June 1942, NARA Waltham, RG 181, Portsmouth Naval Base General Correspondence, Box 1, Folder A1, "Construction June 1940 to Dec 1943." Hereafter referred to as Portsmouth Industrial Survey #2 (June 1942).

5. Secretary of the Navy, letter, 24 September 1941, NARA Waltham, RG 181, Portsmouth Naval Shipyard General Correspondence (Central Files), Box 2, Folder A1-3, PKG 4, "General Building Program."

6. "Adm. H. E. Yarnell Here to Inspect Local Navy Yard," *Portsmouth Herald*, 5 November 1941, 1.

7. Commandant Portsmouth Navy Yard Rear Adm. John D. Wainwright, memo, 7 November 1941, NARA Waltham, RG 181, Portsmouth Naval Shipyard General Correspondence (Central Files), Box 2, Folder A1-3, PKG 4, "General Building Program."

8. Connery, *Navy and the Industrial Mobilization in World War II*, 31.

9. Alfred D. Chandler Jr., "Management Decentralization: An Historical Analysis," in *The History of American Management: Selections from the Business History Review*, ed. James P. Baughman (Englewood Cliffs, NJ: Prentice Hall, 1969), 239, 212.

10. See Alfred D. Chandler Jr., *Strategy and Structure: Chapters in the History of the Industrial Enterprise* (Cambridge, MA: MIT Press, 1962) for a thorough discussion of the evolution of industrial corporate organizations and practices during the first half of the twentieth century. Also applicable are Chandler's *The Visible Hand: The Managerial Revolution in American Business* (Cambridge: Harvard University Press, 1977) and *Scale and Scope: The Dynamics of Industrial Capitalism Business* (Cambridge: Harvard University Press, 1977); David Hounshell, *From the American System to Mass Production, 1800–1932: The Development of Manufacturing Technology in the United States* (Baltimore: Johns Hopkins University Press, 1984); Thomas K. McCraw, ed., *The Essential Alfred Chandler: Essays Toward a Historical Theory of Big Business* (Boston: Harvard Business School Press, 1988); Alfred D. Chandler and Herman Daems, eds. *Managerial Hierarchies: Comparative Perspectives on the Rise of the Modern Industrial Enterprise* (Cambridge, MA: Harvard University Press, 1980).

11. Lane, *Ships for Victory*; Tassava, "Launching a Thousand Ships."

12. Tassava, "Launching a Thousand Ships," 1.

13. *Administrative History: Bureau of Ships*, 135.

14. SecNav Industrial Survey #2 (1942), 1.

15. Organization Planning and Procedures, "Review of the Organization and Administration of Navy Yards and U.S. Naval Drydocks," letter to Assistant Secretary of the Navy Ralph A. Bard, 13 July 1945, NARA College Park, RG 19, Bureau of Ships General Correspondence, 1940–45, Box 785, Folder NY1/A3. This survey provides a summary of the history of navy yard organization and administration with recommendations for improvements.

16. *Administrative History: Bureau of Ships*, 135.

17. Ibid., 25.

18. Quoted in ibid., 29–30.

19. Ibid., 42.

20. Quoted in Organization Planning and Procedures, letter to Assistant Secretary of the Navy Ralph A. Bard, Enclosure A, 3c, 13 July 1945, NARA College Park, RG 19, Bureau of Ships General Correspondence, 1940–45, Box 785, Folder NY1/A3.

21. *Administrative History: Bureau of Ships*, Table 5, "Personnel On-board by Months, 1933–45."

22. Ibid., 201–2.

23. Connery, *Navy and Industrial Mobilization in World War II*, 74.

24. Ibid.

25. Secretary of the Navy Frank Knox, "National Defense Shipbuilding Program—Expedition and Prosecution of Work," letter to Chief Bureau of Ships and Commandants All Navy Yards, 15 January 1941, NARA College Park, RG 24, Bureau of Naval Personnel General Correspondence, 1941–45, NY1 (66-176) to NY2 (551-661), Box 1601, Folder NY 166-176.

26. *Administrative History: Bureau of Ships*, 327.

27. Chief of the Office of Procurement and Material Admiral S. M. Robinson, memo to the Undersecretary of the Navy, 31 July 1942, quoted in full in *Administrative History: Bureau of Ships*, 201–2.

28. Ibid., 331, 333.

29. Ibid., 324, 326.

30. Ibid., 162.

31. Albion and Connery, *Forrestal and the Navy*, 61.

32. Chief Bureau of Ships, confidential letter, 18 September 1943, NARA Waltham, RG 181, Formerly Confidential Correspondence, Portsmouth Naval Shipyard, 1930–50, Box 3, Folder L6-3, "Progress Reports."

33. David Lawrence, article with Washington date line, undated, NARA Waltham, RG 181, Portsmouth Naval Base General Correspondence, Box 1, Folder A1, "New Construction June 1940–December 1943." At the time, Lawrence was the editor and founder of the *United States News*, a newspaper that was combined in 1948 with another of his initiatives, the *World Report*, to form the popular magazine, *U.S. News and World Report*.

34. Roscoe, *United States Submarine Operations in World War II*, 10.

35. COMSUBPAC, "Mission Orders," December 1941, *Submarines Pacific Fleet*, http://www.subsowespac.org/comminiques/orders-cycle-02.pdf (accessed 3 October 2010).

36. *The Lucky Bag*, Vol. 13 (Annapolis: U.S. Naval Academy, 1906).

37. "Submarine Pioneers," *Chief of Naval Operations Submarine Warfare Division*, http://www.navy.mil/navydata/cno/n87/history/pioneers2.html (accessed 6 November 2009).

38. The front page of the *Portsmouth Herald* from 19 June 1939 has a picture of the board of inquiry that includes Captain Withers.

39. "Withers Takes Command of Portsmouth Navy Yard," *Portsmouth Herald*, 11 June 1942, 1.

40. *Commander Submarine Force Pacific Fleet*, http://www.csp.navy.mil/admirals/withers.htm (accessed 1 May 2007).

41. Weir, *Building American Submarines*, 40.

42. White interview.

43. Other officers reporting to the commandant included the medical officer, the officer in charge of the prison, the officer in charge of the Marines, and the communications officer.

44. At the start of the war, the public works officer and the disbursing officer also reported to the industrial manager. "Industrial Department Organizational Chart—1940," NARA Waltham, RG 181, Portsmouth Naval Shipyard General Correspondence (Central Files), Box 10, Folder A3/NY1, "Organizational Charts for Officer Personnel Under Manager, 1934–43."

45. Stan Davis (grandson of Capt. H. F. D. Davis), interview with author via e-mail, 3 October 2007.

46. *The Lucky Bag*, vol. 15 (Annapolis: U.S. Naval Academy, 1908).

47. Commandant Rear Admiral Thomas Withers, "Economy in Naval Expenditures," memo, 28 August 1943, NARA Waltham, RG 181, Portsmouth Naval Shipyard General Correspondence (Central Files), Box 14, Folder A3-2/LC, PKG 8.

48. "General Programs, Purpose, and Specific Problems for Next Meeting," 21 June 1943, NARA Waltham, RG 181, Portsmouth Naval Shipyard General Correspondence (Central Files), Box 13, Folder A3-2, "General Management."

49. Davis interview.

50. Manager, memo, 13 June 1943, NARA Waltham, RG 181, Portsmouth Naval Shipyard General Correspondence (Central Files), Box 36, Folder N5 14, "Welding Shop."

51. Ibid.

52. White interview.

53. McKee, "Development of Submarines in the United States."

54. Harry Jackson, "The Whale-Shaped Albacore," in Stillwell, *Submarine Stories*, 235–38.

55. Robert Whittaker, *Portsmouth-Kittery Naval Shipyard in Old Photographs* (Stroud, Gloucestershire: Alan Sutton, 1993), 108.

56. *Portsmouth Periscope*, 13 October 1945, 8, and 20 October 1951, 4, Papers of Harold Caswell Sweetser.

57. Navy Department, SOSED (Industrial Manpower Section), letter to Distribution List, 1 May 1943, NARA College Park, RG 38, Chief of Naval Operations General Correspondence, Box 151, Folder NY1, 1 July 1942 to 30 June 1943.

58. SecNav Industrial Survey #1 (1942), 2.

59. Horn, "Submarines and the Electric Boat Company," V-3–V-5.

60. SecNav Industrial Survey #1 (1942), 1–2.

61. SecNav Industrial Survey #2 (1944), 3.

62. *Cradle of American Shipbuilding*. The USS *Hudson* is listed near the back of the booklet as the last surface ship built at Portsmouth Navy Yard.

63. *Administrative History: Portsmouth Navy Yard*, ch. Ic, Production Graphs.

64. Jeffrey M. Dorwart, *The Philadelphia Navy Yard: From the Birth of the U.S. Navy to the Nuclear Age* (Philadelphia: University of Pennsylvania Press, 2001), 186.

65. Vice Chief of Naval Operations F. J. Horne, letter, 12 July 1943, NARA College Park, RG 80, Records of the Navy Department, 1798–1947, Formerly Security Classified General Correspondence of the CNO/Secretary of the Navy 1940–1947, Box 897, File L9-3/NY-NY1.

66. *Administrative History: Bureau of Ships*, Table 40, 599.

CHAPTER 4: EMPLOYEES

1. Stuart S. Murray, "Developing the Fleet Boats," in Stillwell, *Submarine Stories*, 67–71.

2. Fred White, oral interview by Linda White in conjunction with the Music Hall Shipyard Project, 19 April 1996, New Castle, NH. A tape of the interview is held at the Portsmouth Athenaeum.

3. "Navy Yard Workers Give a Day to Aid National Defense," *Portsmouth Herald*, 16 December 1941, 1.

4. "Ranger Lodge Machinists Hit Navy Yard Hours," *Portsmouth Herald*, 21 April 1942, 1.

5. "Navy Yard Shift Goes into Effect," *Portsmouth Herald*, 21 April 1942, 6.

6. "Portsmouth Navy Yard Bond-Buying Record Set as Goal for Hub Drive," *Portsmouth Herald*, 9 November 1942, 1.

7. "Admiral Lauds Cooperation of Labor, Management Here," *Portsmouth Herald*, 14 January 1946, 1.

8. SecNav Industrial Survey #2 (1944), 8.

9. Percy Whitney (apprentice program student and foundry employee at Portsmouth Navy Yard), interview by the author, 23 March 2006, New Castle, NH.

10. Eileen Dondero Foley (paint shop employee at Portsmouth Navy Yard), interview by the author, 30 August 2006, Portsmouth, NH.

11. SecNav Industrial Survey #2 (1944), 8.

12. Ibid., 4.

13. Portsmouth Industrial Survey #1 (1941), 11.

14. SecNav Industrial Survey #2 (1944), 11–12.

15. Ibid., 10.

16. SecNav Industrial Survey #1 (1942), 1.

17. Lane, *Ships for Victory*, 305.

18. William Tebo (apprentice program student and electrical shop employee at Portsmouth Navy Yard), interview by the author, 3 November 2006, Portsmouth Naval Shipyard Museum, Kittery, ME.

19. "Groton Strikers Deadlocked with Company," *Portsmouth Herald*, 15 August 1944, 1.

20. "7,500 Strike at Sub Yard in Groton," *Portsmouth Herald*, 16 August 1944, 1.

21. Foley interview.

22. Tebo interview.

23. Lorraine McConaghy, "Wartime Boomtown: Kirkland, Washington, A Small Town during World War II," *Pacific Northwest Quarterly* 80 (1989): 45.

24. Kennedy, *Freedom from Fear*, 14–15.

25. Watterson, "32 in '44," 187.

26. "History of the Electric Boat Company," V-9.

27. Watterson, "32 in '44," 359–60.

28. Tebo interview.

29. Lane, *Ships for Victory*, 301.

30. "May Inspect More Yards," *Portsmouth Herald*, 23 January 1945, 1.

31. Portsmouth Industrial Survey #1 (December 1941), 5.

32. Foley interview.

33. SecNav Industrial Survey #2 (1944), 10.

34. Tebo interview.

35. SecNav Industrial Survey #2 (1944), 10.

36. Alice Kessler-Harris, *Out to Work: A History of Wage-Earning Women in the United States* (New York: Oxford University Press, 1982), 275–76.

37. Lane, *Ships for Victory*, 257.

38. Navy Department (Industrial Manpower Section), "Employment of Women—Continental Navy Yards," letter to Distribution including All Navy Yards, 1 May 1943, NARA College Park, RG 38, Chief of Naval Operations General Correspondence, Box 151, Folder NY1, 1 July 1942 to 30 June 1943.

39. Manager, memo, 30 September 1942, NARA Waltham, RG 181, Portsmouth Naval Shipyard General Correspondence (Central Files), Box 8, Folder A2-11/NY2, "Circular Letter Navy Yard."

40. *Administrative History: Portsmouth Navy Yard*, 33.

41. *Boston Navy Yard Commandant's Circular No. 398*, 13 January 1942, NARA Waltham, RG 181, Portsmouth Naval Shipyard General Correspondence (Central Files), Box 2, Folder A2-11/NY2, "Circular Letter Navy Yard—Boston."

42. Manager, memo, 15 September 1942, NARA Waltham, RG 181, Portsmouth Naval Shipyard General Correspondence (Central Files), Box 8, Folder A2-11/NY2, "Circular Letter Navy Yard."

43. Manager, memo, 30 September 1942, NARA Waltham, RG 181, Portsmouth Naval Shipyard General Correspondence (Central Files), Box 14, Folder A3-2LC, PKG 7, "Orders to Shop Foremen."

44. Foley interview.

45. Tebo interview; and MacIsaac interview.

46. Dorwart, *Philadelphia Navy Yard*, 178.

47. Kessler-Harris, *Out to Work*, 275–76.

48. Manager, memo, 30 September 1942, NARA Waltham, RG 181, Portsmouth Naval Shipyard General Correspondence (Central Files), Box 14, Folder A3-2LC, PKG 7, "Orders to Shop Foremen."

49. Assistant Secretary of the Navy Ralph A. Bard, letter to Commandants All Continental Navy Yard, 25 May 1943, NARA College Park, RG 24, Bureau of Naval Personnel General Correspondence, 1941–45, Box 1601, Folder NY January 11, 1943.

50. Foley interview.

51. Kessler-Harris, *Out to Work*, 268.

52. Valerie Cunningham and Mark J. Sammons, *Black Portsmouth: Three Centuries of African-American Heritage* (Durham: University of New Hampshire Press, 2004), 168, 170–71.

53. Kessler-Harris, *Out to Work*, 278–79.

54. Manager, "Toilet Facilities for Women in Shops and Shop Offices," memo to Public Works Officer, 2 September 1942, NARA Waltham, RG 181, Portsmouth Naval Shipyard General Correspondence (Central Files), Box 36, Folder N4-14, "Latrines."

55. Lane, *Ships for Victory*, 257.

56. White interview.

57. Foley interview.

58. Kennedy, *Freedom from Fear*, 776–79.

59. "Survey of Health and Welfare in the Portsmouth Defense Area, August 1943," 35, 67, Cumings Library, Strawbery Banke Museum, Portsmouth, NH, Box 2, Folder 14, "S.C.D. Survey of Health and Welfare in Portsmouth."

60. Ibid., 36.

61. "Feminine Detail Takes Over Bus Service to Navy Yard," *Portsmouth Herald*, 18 May 1942, 1.

62. "Exeter Girls Study Mechanics: Some Will Turn Lathes in Portsmouth Navy Yard Soon, *Portsmouth Herald*, 18 June 1942.

63. "Woman's Place Is Back of the Monkey Wrench, Says Lady Machinist," *Portsmouth Herald*, 22 March 1943.

64. "School Aids Production of Navy Submarines," *Portsmouth Herald*, 12 May 1943.

65. "And More Are Needed," *Portsmouth Herald*, 11 November 1943, 1.

66. Quoted in "Yard Graduates Largest Group; Four Women," *Portsmouth Herald*, 10 May 1944, 1.

67. *Administrative History: Portsmouth Navy Yard*, 89.

68. Foley interview. Eileen Dondero Foley is the daughter of Mary C. Dondero.

69. *Portsmouth Herald*, 1 January 1945, 1.

70. "Women Juror Bill to Get New Action," *Portsmouth Herald*, 10 February 1945, 1.

71. White interview.

72. Kessler-Harris, *Out to Work*, 286.

73. Kennedy, *Freedom from Fear*, 459, 632, 635.

74. SecNav Industrial Survey #2 (1944), 10.

75. *Administrative History: Portsmouth Navy Yard*, 36.

76. Whitney interview.

77. Commandant Portsmouth Navy Yard, letter to Assistant Secretary of the Navy (Shore Establishment Division), 2 November 1939, NARA Waltham, RG 181, Portsmouth Naval Shipyard General Correspondence (Central Files), Box 36, Folder N5-14, "Welding Shop."

78. Manager, memo to Production Officer, 22 April 1942, NARA Waltham, RG 181, Portsmouth Naval Shipyard General Correspondence (Central Files), Box 36, Folder N5-14, "Welding Shop."

79. Charles Downing, interview by Susan Frankel in conjunction with the Portsmouth Music Hall Project, 15 August 1996, York Beach, ME.

80. "They Agreed on Navy Yard Employee Induction Plan," *Portsmouth Herald*, 5 February 1943, 1.

81. *Portsmouth Periscope*, 10 July 1945, 1, 6, Papers of Harold Caswell Sweetser.

CHAPTER 5: METHODS

1. Kennedy, *Freedom from Fear*, 648–49.

2. Murray, "Developing the Fleet Boats," 67–71.

3. Local Shore Station Development Board, letter to Senior Member of the Departmental Shore Station Development Board, 30 July 1934, NARA Waltham, RG 181, Portsmouth

Naval Shipyard General Correspondence (Central Files), Box 1, Folder A1/Y1, PKG 1, "Local Development Boards."

4. Murray, "Developing the Fleet Boats."

5. Commandant First Naval District, letter to Commandant Portsmouth Navy Yard, 10 December 1936, NARA Waltham, RG 181, Portsmouth Naval Shipyard General Correspondence (Central Files), Box 1, Folder A1-Y1, "Local Development Boards."

6. Portsmouth Industrial Survey #2 (June 1942), 14.

7. Cope, *On the Swing Shift*, 63.

8. Lane, *Ships for Victory*, 207.

9. "New Method Puts Subs into Mass Production," *Portsmouth Herald*, 16 May 1942, 1.

10. White interview.

11. Ibid.

12. Thomas J. Peters, *In Search of Excellence: Lessons from America's Best Run Companies* (New York: Harper & Row, 1982); *A Passion for Excellence: The Leadership Difference* (New York: Random House, 1985); *Thriving on Chaos: Handbook for Management Revolution* (New York: A. A. Knopf, 1994); *Liberation Management: Necessary Disorganization for the Nanosecond Nineties* (New York: A. A. Knopf, 1992). Peters' first work, *In Search of Excellence* (1982), advanced the principle that increased management trust and confidence in employees would lead to increased production. Several works later, Peters had progressed to the belief that "The self-managing team should be the basic organizational building block" (*Thriving in Chaos*, 297).

13. William C. Byham and Jeff Cox, *Zapp! The Lightning of Empowerment: How to Improve Productivity, Quality, and Employee Satisfaction* (New York: Harmony Books, 1990); Thomas A. Potterfield, *The Business of Employee Empowerment: Democracy and Ideology in the Workplace* (Westport, CT: Quorum Books, 1999).

14. Ronald E. Purser and Steven Cabana, *The Self-Managing Organization: How Leading Companies Are Transforming the Work of Teams for Real Impact* (New York: Free Press, 1998).

15. Chris Argyris, "Empowerment: The Emperor's New Clothes," *Harvard Business Review* 76: 3 (May/June 1998), 98–105; Bradley L. Kirkman and Benson Rosen, "Beyond Self-Management: Antecedents and Consequences of Team Empowerment," *Academy of Management Journal* 42: 1 (February 1999), 58–74; and Mark Fenton-O'Creevy, "Employee Involvement and the Middle Manager: Evidence from a Survey of Organizations," *Journal of Organizational Behavior* 19:1 (January 1998): 67–84.

16. Fenton-O'Creevy, "Employee Involvement and the Middle Manager," 67–84.

17. Kirkman and Rosen, "Beyond Self-Management," 59–64.

18. SecNav Industrial Survey #2 (1944), 10.

19. Portsmouth Industrial Survey #1 (December 1941), 3, 9.

20. Production Officer, memo to Masters, all Shops, 23 December 1941, NARA Waltham, RG 181, Portsmouth Naval Shipyard General Correspondence (Central Files), Box 14, Folder A3-2/LC, PKG 7, "Orders to Shop Foremen."

21. Manager, memo to Shop Masters, 16 January 1942, NARA Waltham, RG 181, Portsmouth Naval Shipyard General Correspondence (Central Files), Box 14, Folder A3-2/LC, PKG 6, "Orders to Shop Foremen."

22. Production Officer, memo to Masters, all Shops, 23 December 1942, NARA Waltham, RG 181, Portsmouth Naval Shipyard General Correspondence (Central Files), Box 14, Folder A3-2/LC, PKG 7, "Orders to Shop Foremen."

23. Lane, *Ships for Victory*, 238.

24. Tebo interview.

25. Chief Bureau of Ships, letter to Chief of Naval Operations, 30 December 1942, NARA College Park, RG 19, Bureau of Ships General Correspondence, 1940–45, Box 18, Folder P2-4 (vol. 3).

26. Bureau of Ships, letter, 14 March 1941, NARA College Park, RG 19, Bureau of Ships General Correspondence, 1940–45, Box 18, Folder P2-4 (vol. 3).

27. "New Basin Here Will Be Big Enough for Destroyers as Well as Subs," *Portsmouth Herald*, 20 March 1941.

28. Bureau of Ships, letter, 14 March 1941, NARA College Park, RG 19, Bureau of Ships General Correspondence, 1940–45, Box 18, Folder P2-4 (vol. 3).

29. Lt. (jg) H. A. Arnold, memo to the Hull Superintendent, 12 December 1941, NARA Waltham, RG 181, Portsmouth Naval Shipyard General Correspondence (Central Files), Box 2, Folder A1-3, PKG 4, "Building Program."

30. Commandant Portsmouth Navy Yard Rear Adm. Thomas Withers, personal letter to Rear Adm. W. B. Farber, 27 November 1942, NARA Waltham, RG 181, Portsmouth Naval Shipyard General Correspondence (Central Files), Box 2, Folder A1-3, PKG 4, "Building Program."

31. Commandant Portsmouth Navy Yard Rear Adm. Thomas Withers, letter to Vice Chief of Naval Operations, 7 December 1942, NARA Waltham, RG 181, Portsmouth Naval Shipyard General Correspondence (Central Files), Box 2, Folder A1-3, PKG 4, "Building Program."

32. Backup memo for above letter, 1 December 1942, NARA Waltham, RG 181, Portsmouth Naval Shipyard General Correspondence (Central Files), Box 2, Folder A1-3, PKG 4, "Building Program."

33. Commandant Portsmouth Navy Yard Rear Admiral Thomas Withers, letter to Chief of Naval Operations, 30 March 1943, NARA College Park, RG 80, Records of the Navy Department, 1798–1947, Formerly Security Classified General Correspondence of the CNO/Secretary of the Navy, 1940–47, Box 897, File L9-3/NY-NY1.

34. Portsmouth Industrial Survey #2 (June 1942), 1, 5.

35. Kennedy, *Freedom from Fear*, 626–27.

36. Commandant Portsmouth Navy Yard, letter to Bureau of Ships, 12 December 1942, NARA Waltham, RG 181, Portsmouth Naval Shipyard General Correspondence (Central Files), Box 1, Folder A1, "New Construction 1941–1943."

37. Lane, *Ships for Victory*, 343–46.

38. Commandant Portsmouth Navy Yard, letter to Bureau of Ships, 6 April 1942, NARA College Park, RG 24, Bureau of Naval Personnel General Correspondence, 1941–45, Box 1601, Folder NY/P-16-1, January 1944.

39. Commandant Portsmouth Navy Yard, letter to Bureau of Ships, 11 August 1943, NARA Waltham, RG 181, Portsmouth Naval Base General Correspondence, Box 1, Folder A1, "New Construction."

40. Portsmouth Navy Yard Progress Report, September 1943, NARA College Park, RG 24, Bureau of Naval Personnel General Correspondence, 1941–45, Box 1601, Folder NY1.

41. Capain Dudley, report on BuShips Conference of 13 and 14 August 1943, 17 August 1943, NARA Waltham, RG 181, Portsmouth Naval Shipyard General Correspondence (Central Files), Box 1, Folder A1, "New Construction Jan 1940 to Dec 1943."

42. Ibid.

43. SecNav Industrial Survey #2 (1944), 8.

44. Industrial Manager, Report of Manager's Conference, 22 June 1943, NARA Waltham, RG 181, Portsmouth Naval Shipyard General Correspondence (Central Files), Box 13, Folder A3-2, "General Management 1932–1940."

45. Weir, *Forged in War*, 16, n. 30

46. John D. Alden, "Victorious Submarines of World War II," in *United States Submarines*, ed. David Randall Hinkle (Annandale, VA: Navy Submarine League, 2002), 116.

47. *Administrative History: Portsmouth Navy Yard*, 1.

48. Ibid., 23.

49. SecNav Industrial Survey #2 (1944), 11.

50. The Chief of the Bureau of Ordnance, letter to Commandant Portsmouth Navy Yard, 2 August 1941, NARA Waltham, RG 181, Portsmouth Naval Shipyard General Correspondence, Central Files, Box 36, Folder N20-5, "Bollards Mooring."

51. *Administrative History: Portsmouth Navy Yard*, 38.

52. "Survey of Health and Welfare in the Portsmouth Defense Area."

53. Commandant Portsmouth Navy Yard, letter to Vice Chief of Naval Operations, 16 January 1943, NARA Waltham, RG 181, Formerly Confidential Correspondence, Portsmouth Naval Shipyard, 1930–50, Box 4, Folder SS/S8 Trials.

54. Assistant Secretary of the Navy Ralph A. Bard, letter to Commandants and Commanding Officers Concerned, 5 June 1943, NARA Waltham, RG 181, Portsmouth Naval Shipyard General Correspondence (Central Files), Box 13, Folder A3-2, "General Management 1932–1940."

55. Tebo interview.

56. Susan E. McMaster, *The Telecommunications Industry* (Westport, CT: Greenwood Press, 2002), 68–71.

57. Portsmouth Navy Yard, Notice, 10 December 1942, NARA Waltham, RG 181, Portsmouth Naval Shipyard General Correspondence (Central Files), Box 13, Folder A3-2, "General Management 1932–1940."

58. Manager, memo to Public Works Officer, 14 January 1943, NARA Waltham, RG 181, Portsmouth Naval Shipyard General Correspondence (Central Files), Box 13, Folder A3-2, "General Management 1932–1940."

59. Industrial Manager Capt. H. F. D. Davis, memo, 1 April 1943; and Portsmouth Navy Yard, letter to the Chief of Yards and Docks, 18 May 1943, NARA Waltham, RG 181, Portsmouth Naval Shipyard General Correspondence (Central Files), Box 13, Folder A3-2, "General Management 1932–1940."

60. Navy Yard Portsmouth, Dispatch 261600 to Bureau of Ships, 26 June 1941, NARA College Park, RG 19, Bureau of Ships General Correspondence, 1940–1945, Box 791, NY1/L11-3 vol. 2 to C-NY1/N6, Folder NY1/N36.

61. Chief Bureau of Ships, letter to Commandant Portsmouth Navy Yard, 25 August 1941, NARA College Park, RG 19, Bureau of Ships General Correspondence, 1940–1945, Box 791, NY1/L11-3 vol. 2 to C-NY1/N6, Folder NY1/N36.

62. Capt. H. F. D. Davis, letter to Capt. Claude A. Jones, Bureau of Ships, 24 May 1941, NARA College Park, RG 19, Bureau of Ships General Correspondence, 1940–1945, Box 791, NY1/L11-3 vol. 2 to C-NY1/N6, Folder NY1/N36.

63. Hull Superintendent (F. A. Tusler), memo to Production Officer, 3 February 1941, NARA Waltham, RG 19, Portsmouth Naval Shipyard General Correspondence (Central Files), Box 26, Folder A19, "Conferences, Congresses, and Conventions."

64. Hull Superintendent (F. A. Tusler), memo 3N/WJS to Production Officer, 3 February 1941, NARA Waltham, Record Group 181, Navy Yard Portsmouth General Correspondence, Box 26, Folder A19, "Conferences, Congresses, and Conventions."

65. Bureau Supplies and Accounts, letter, 19 June 1941, NARA College Park, RG 19, Bureau of Ships General Correspondence, 1940–45, Box 791, NY1/L11 3 vol. 2 to C NY1/N6, Folder NY1/P18-2.

66. Portsmouth Naval Base, Order No. 15-42, 5 May 1942, NARA Waltham, RG 181, Portsmouth Naval Base General Correspondence, Box 8, Folder "Navy Yard Orders 1942."

67. "Portsmouth Navy Yard Makes First Payment by Check," *Portsmouth Herald*, 14 May 1942, 8.

68. *Administrative History: Portsmouth Navy Yard*, 31.

69. Lane, *Ships for Victory*, 676–79.

70. "Navy Yard Workers Asset for City's Future," *Portsmouth Herald*, 30 January 1941, 1.

71. Shop Superintendent, memos, 26 August, 27 November, 30 December 1941, and 25 February 1942, NARA Waltham, RG 181, Portsmouth Naval Shipyard General Correspondence (Central Files), Box 14, Folder A3-2/LC, PKG 6, "Orders to Shop Foremen."

72. Ibid.

73. Whitney interview.

74. "Free Training Courses Offer Top Opportunities," *Portsmouth Herald*, 12 March 1944, 1.

75. "Start School for Welders Next Week," *Portsmouth Herald*, 20 March 1941, 1.

76. "Free Training Courses Offer Top Opportunities," *Portsmouth Herald*, 12 March 1944, 1.

77. Tebo interview.

78. *Administrative History: Portsmouth Navy Yard*, 47.

CHAPTER 6: METRICS

Epigraph source: Commandant Portsmouth Navy Yard, letter to Bureau of Ships, 23 March 1945, NARA Waltham, RG 181, Portsmouth Naval Base General Correspondence, Box 15, Folder L-5, "Inspection Naval Yard, 1945–48."

1. "Yard Tops in Sub Production," *Portsmouth Herald*, 19 July 1945, 1.

2. "Marks Yard's 6th, 7th Sub of 1942," *Portsmouth Herald*, 21 June 1942, 1.

3. "Two Subs Launched at Yard," *Portsmouth Herald*, 13 July 1943, 1.

4. "Three-Sub Launching Wednesday," *Portsmouth Herald*, 25 October 1943, 1.

5. "4 New Subs Launched for World's Record," *Portsmouth Herald*, 27 January 1944, 1.

6. "5th Sub Here in Ten Days," *Portsmouth Herald*, 5 February 1944, 1.

7. "Launch 4 Destroyers in 14 Minutes," *Portsmouth Herald*, 2 March 1943.

8. Chief of Naval Operations, "New Construction Submarines-Early Completion and Procedure after Completion," 17 December 1941, NARA Waltham, RG 181, Portsmouth Naval Base General Correspondence, Box 19, Folder S-8, "Trials."

9. President, Board of Inspection and Survey, "Acceptance and Inspection of Naval Vessels during Existing Emergency," 13 October 1942, NARA Waltham, RG 181, Portsmouth Naval Base General Correspondence, Box 19, Folder S-8, "Trials."

10. *Administrative History: Portsmouth Navy Yard*, 69.

11. "Navy Yard Hailed for 'Practical Patriotism'; Gets E Award Monday," *Portsmouth Herald*, 8 August 1942, 1.

12. Hinkle, *United States Submarines*, 114–15.

13. Roscoe, *United States Submarine Operations in World War II*, 175.

14. Lane, *Ships for Victory*, 174.

15. Chief of Naval Operations, letter to Commandant Portsmouth Navy Yard, 26 April 1944, NARA College Park, RG 38, Chief of Naval Operations General Correspondence, Box 1182, Folder NY1, 1 July 1943–30 June 1944.

16. Portsmouth Industrial Survey #1 (December 1941), 15.

17. Commandant Portsmouth Navy Yard, letter to Bureau of Ships, 23 March 1945, NARA Waltham, RG 181, Portsmouth Naval Base General Correspondence, Box 15, Folder L-5, "Inspection Naval Yard, 1945–48."

18. Lane, *Ships for Victory*, 231, fig. 19.

19. Weir, *Forged in War*, 34, 34n. 70.

20. Ibid., 35.

21. "Estimate of Statistical Cost of Submarines Under Construction," memorandum to manager, 5 February 1941, NARA Waltham, Portsmouth Naval Shipyard General Correspondence (Central Files), Box 26, Folder A19, "Conferences, Congresses, and Conventions."

22. Portsmouth Industrial Survey #2 (June 1942).

23. Commandant Portsmouth Navy Yard, letter to Bureau of Ships, 23 March 1945, NARA Waltham, RG 181, Portsmouth Naval Base General Correspondence, Box 15, Folder L-5, "Inspection Naval Yard, 1945–48."

24. Ibid.

25. "Commends Navy Yard on Sub *Trout*," *Portsmouth Herald*, 19 February 1941, 1.

26. Chief of Naval Operations, letter to Commandant Portsmouth Navy Yard, 27 May 1944, NARA College Park, RG 38, Chief of Naval Operations General Correspondence, Box 79, Folder Portsmouth, 1 July 1943–30 June 1944.

27. *Administrative History: Portsmouth Navy Yard*, 69.

28. Portsmouth Naval Base Notice, 8 May 1945, NARA Waltham, RG 181, Portsmouth Naval Base General Correspondence, Box 9, Folder A7-1, "Notices Navy Yard and Naval Base Jan 1 1945 to 1950."

29. Chief of Naval Operations, letter to Commandant Portsmouth Navy Yard, 26 April 1944, NARA College Park, RG 38, Chief of Naval Operations General Correspondence, Box 1182, Folder NY1, 1 July 1943–30 June 1944.

30. Secretary of the Navy, letter to Commandant Portsmouth Navy Yard, 6 November 1944, NARA College Park, RG 19, Bureau of Ships General Correspondence, 1940–45, Box 785, Folder NY1/A3.

31. Alden, "Victorious Submarines in World War II," 115.

32. Capt. George Street, USN (Ret.), interview by Claire Spellman in conjunction with the Music Hall Shipyard Project, 2 November 1995, Laman Club, Andover, MA. A tape of the interview is held by the Portsmouth Athenaeum.

33. *Administrative History: Portsmouth Navy Yard*, 2.

CHAPTER 7: TRANSFORMATIONS

Epigraph source: MacIsaac interview.

1. R. D. Spalding of the U.S. Coast and Geodetic Service, "Hydrographic Conditions at the Navy Yard and in Great Bay Area in Connection with Berthing of Vessels out of Commission," memo to the Commandant, 13 October 1944, NARA Waltham, RG 181, Portsmouth Naval Base General Correspondence, 1930–50, Box 18, Folder 3-7, "Docking—General."

2. Secretary of the Navy James Forrestal, "Organization Planning and Procedures," letter to Assistant Secretary of the Navy Ralph A. Bard, 13 July 1945, NARA College Park, RG 19, Bureau of Ships General Correspondence, 1940–45, Box 785, Folder NY1/A3.

3. Industrial Survey Division, Office of the Secretary of the Navy, "Review of the Organization and Administration of Navy Yards and Drydocks," 13 July 1945, NARA College Park, RG 38, Chief of Naval Operations General Correspondence, Box 1182, Folder NY/A3-1.

4. Secretary of the Navy James Forrestal, ALNAVSTA #38, 5 December 1945, NARA College Park, RG 24, Bureau of Naval Personnel General Correspondence, 1941–45, Box 1601, Folder NY.

5. See Roscoe, *United States Submarine Operations in World War II*, 407–8, for details of the *Redfish* sinking of the *Unryu*.

6. MacIsaac interview. The events witnessed by the *Redfish* that follow are all from the interview.

7. "U.S. Naval Shipyard, Portsmouth, N.H. Schedule of Ship Repair, Alteration, and Decommissioning," 21 January 1946, NARA Waltham, RG 181, Portsmouth Naval Base General Correspondence, 1930–50, Box 18, Folder 3-7, "Docking—General."

8. "Report of Conference Held at U.S. Naval Shipyard, Portsmouth, N.H. on 21 June 1946, in Connection with Berthing Facilities for Additional Naval Craft," NARA Waltham, RG 181, Portsmouth Naval Base General Correspondence, Box 18, Folder S-7, Docking—General.

CONCLUSION

1. Lane, *Ships for Victory*, 829, 830.

Bibliography

PRIMARY SOURCES

Archival and Special Collections

Cumings Library and Archives, Strawbery Banke Museum, Portsmouth, NH.
    MS 96 Portsmouth War Records.
Milne Special Collections, University of New Hampshire, Durham, NH.
    Papers of Harold Caswell Sweetser, Portsmouth Navy Yard Supervisory Naval
        Architect, 1917–58, including selected copies of the *Portsmouth Periscope*
        (Portsmouth Navy Yard's weekly newspaper), Sweetser Family Papers.
    Portsmouth Naval Shipyard Photographs Folders (Vols. 1–4).
National Archives and Records Administration, College Park, MD.
    Record Group 19, Bureau of Ships General Correspondence, 1940–45.
    Record Group 24, Bureau of Naval Personnel General Correspondence, 1941–45.
    Record Group 38, Chief of Naval Operations General Correspondence.
    Record Group 52, Bureau of Medicine and Surgery General Correspondence,
        1842–1951.
    Record Group 80, Records of the Navy Department, 1798–1947.
National Archives and Records Administration, Waltham, MA.
    Record Group 181, Formerly Confidential Correspondence, Portsmouth Naval
        Shipyard, 1930–50.
    Portsmouth Naval Base General Correspondence, 1930–50.
    Portsmouth Naval Shipyard General Correspondence (Central Files), 1925–50.
Navy Department Library, Naval Historical Center, Washington, D.C.
    Administrative History: Commandant First Naval District in World War II.
        Naval Department World War II Admin History # 109. Vol. 9. N.d.
    Administrative History: Bureau of Ships in World War II. Naval Department
        World War II Admin History #89. Vol. 1. 1946.

Administrative History: Bureau of Yards and Docks in World War II. Naval Department World War II Admin History #108. Vol. 1. N.d.

"History of the Electric Boat Company 1899–1949." Unpublished Typescript. N.d.

Portsmouth Naval Shipyard Museum Archives, Kittery, ME.

Administrative History: Portsmouth Navy Yard during World War II.

Cultural Resources Survey, Portsmouth Naval Shipyard, U.S. Department of Defense, Legacy Resource Management Program, April 2003. Prepared by the Louis Berger Group Inc. for the Engineering Field Activity Northeast Naval Facilities Engineering Command.

Portsmouth Public Library, Portsmouth NH.

Portsmouth Herald (Front pages and editorial pages for all issues between 1 January 1939 and 31 December 1946.)

Rice Public Library, Kittery, ME

Boyd, David F. "Continuation of Preble's History of the United States Navy Yard, Portsmouth, N.H. Covering the Years 1875–1930," typescript with handwritten corrections and additions. Maine Room.

Interviews

Interviews of Portsmouth Naval Shipyard retirees who worked at the yard during World War II:

Stan Davis, grandson of Capt. H. F. D. Davis, e-mails, September 2007, 3 October 2007, and 25 February 2008.

Eileen Dondero Foley, paint shop employee during World War II, 30 August 2006, Portsmouth, NH.

Dan MacIsaac, crew member of USS *Redfish* during World War II, 9 November 2006, Portsmouth Naval Shipyard Museum, Kittery, ME.

William C. Tebo, apprentice program student and electrical shop employee during World War II, 3 November 2006, Portsmouth Naval Shipyard Museum, Kittery, ME.

Fred White, master rigger and laborer during World War II, 3 April 2006, New Castle, NH.

Percy Whitney, apprentice program student and foundry employee during World War II, 23 March 2006, New Castle, NH.

SECONDARY SOURCES

Books

Albion, Robert G., and Robert H. Connery. *Forrestal and the Navy.* New York: Columbia University Press, 1962.

Barrows, Nathaniel. *Blow All Ballast! The Story of the Squalus.* New York: Dodd, Mead, 1940.

Bass, Bernard M. *Leadership and Performance beyond Expectations.* New York: Free Press, 1985.

Bolster, W. Jeffrey, ed. *Cross-Grained & Wily Waters: A Guide to the Piscataqua Maritime Region.* Portsmouth, NH: Peter E. Randall, 2002.

Bonnet, Wayne. *Build Ships! San Francisco Wartime Shipbuilding Photographs.* Sausalito, CA:Windgate Press, 2000.

Brooks, John. *Telephone: The First Hundred Years.* New York: Harper & Row, 1976.

Buckley, Thomas H. *The United States and the Washington Conference, 1921–1922.* Knoxville: University of Tennessee Press, 1970.

Buckley, Thomas H., and Edwin B. Strong. *American Foreign and National Security Policies, 1914–1915.* Knoxville: University of Tennessee Press, 1970.

Burns, James MacGregor. *Leadership.* New York: Harper & Row, 1978.

Byham, William C., and Jeff Cox. *Zapp! The Lightning of Empowerment: How to Improve Productivity, Quality, and Employee Satisfaction.* New York: Harmony Books, 1990.

Chandler, Alfred D. *Pioneers in Modern Factory Management.* New York: Arno Press, 1979.

———. *Precursors of Modern Management.* New York: Arno Press, 1979.

———. *Scale and Scope: The Dynamics of Industrial Capitalism Business.* Cambridge, MA: Harvard University Press, 1977.

———. *Strategy and Structure: Chapters in the History of the Industrial Enterprise.* Cambridge, MA: MIT Press, 1962.

———. *The Visible Hand: The Managerial Revolution in American Business.* Cambridge, MA: Harvard University Press, 1977.

Chandler, Alfred D., and Herman Daems, eds. *Managerial Hierarchies: Comparative Perspectives on the Rise of the Modern Industrial Enterprise.* Cambridge, MA: Harvard University Press, 1980.

Connery, Robert H. *The Navy and Industrial Mobilization in World War II.* Princeton: Princeton University Press, 1951.

Cope, Tony. *On the Swing Shift: Building Liberty Ships in Savannah.* Annapolis: Naval Institute Press, 2009.

Cradle of American Shipbuilding: Portsmouth Naval Shipyard, Portsmouth, New Hampshire. Portsmouth: Portsmouth Naval Shipyard, 1978.

Cunningham, Valerie, and Mark J. Sammons. *Black Portsmouth: Three Centuries of African-American Heritage*. Durham: University of New Hampshire Press, 2004.

Dallek, Robert. *Franklin D. Roosevelt and American Foreign Policy, 1932–1945*. New York: Oxford University Press, 1979.

Davis, George T. *A Navy Second to None: The Development of Modern American Naval Policy*. New York: Harcourt, Brace, 1940.

DeButts, John D. *The Telephone's First Century—and Beyond: Essays on the Occasion of the 100th Anniversary of Telephone Communication*. New York: Crowell, 1977.

Dingman, Roger. *Power in the Pacific: The Origins of Naval Arms Limitation, 1914–1922*. Chicago: University of Chicago Press, 1977.

Dorwart, Jeffrey M. *The Philadelphia Navy Yard: From the Birth of the U.S. Navy to the Nuclear Age*. Philadelphia: University of Pennsylvania Press, 2001.

Duis, Perry, and Scott LaFrance. *We've Got a Job to Do: Chicagoans and World War I*. Chicago: Chicago Historical Society, 1992

Eiler, Keith E. *Mobilizing America: Robert P. Patterson and the War Effort 1940–45*. Ithaca: Cornell University Press, 1997.

Fussell, Paul. *Wartime: Understanding and Behavior in the Second World War*. Oxford: Oxford University Press, 1989.

Gluck, Sherna Berger. *Rosie the Riveter Revisited: Women, the War, and Social Change*. Boston: Twayne Publishers, 1987.

Goldin, Claudia. *Understanding the Gender Gap*. New York: Oxford University Press, 1990.

Guyol, Philip N. *Democracy Fights: A History of New Hampshire in World War II*. Hanover: Dartmouth Publications, 1951.

Hinkle, David Randall, ed. *United States Submarines*. Annandale, VA: Navy Submarine League, 2002.

Hounshell, David. *From the American System to Mass Production, 1800–1932: The Development of Manufacturing Technology in the United States*. Baltimore: Johns Hopkins University Press, 1984.

Johnson, Marilyn S. *The Second Gold Rush: Oakland and the East Bay in World War II*. Berkeley: University of California Press, 1996.

Kennedy, David M. *Freedom from Fear: The American People in Depression and War, 1929–1945*. New York: Oxford University Press, 1999.

Kessler-Harris, Alice. *Out to Work: A History of Wage-Earning Women in the United States*. New York: Oxford University Press, 1982.

Lane, Frederick C. *Ships for Victory: A History of Shipbuilding under the U.S. Maritime Commission in World War II*. Baltimore: Johns Hopkins University Press, 2001.

LaVo, Carl. *Back from the Deep: The Strange Story of the Sister Subs Squalus and Sculpin*. Annapolis: Naval Institute Press, 1988.

Lawry, Nelson H., Glen M. Williford, and Leo K. Polaski. *Portsmouth Harbor's Military and Naval Heritage*. Portsmouth, NH: Arcadia Publishing, 2004.

Lotchin, Roger W., ed. *The Way We Really Were: The Golden State in the Second Great War.* Chicago: University of Illinois Press, 2000.

McMaster, Susan E. *The Telecommunications Industry.* Westport, CT: Greenwood Press, 2002.

McCraw, Thomas K., ed. *The Essential Alfred Chandler: Essays Toward a Historical Theory of Big Business.* Boston: Harvard Business School Press, 1988.

Milkman, Ruth. *Gender at Work: The Dynamics of Job Segregation by Sex during World War II.* Urbana: University of Illinois Press, 1987.

Morison, Samuel Eliot. *History of U.S. Naval Operations in World War II.* 15 vols. Boston: Little, Brown, 1947–62.

———.*The Two-Ocean War: A Short History of the United States in the Second World War.* Boston: Little, Brown, 1963.

Nash, Gerald D. *The American West Transformed: The Impact of the Second World War.* Bloomington: Indiana University Press, 1985.

——— . *World War II and the West: Reshaping the Economy.* Lincoln: University of Nebraska Press, 1990.

O'Connor, Raymond G. *Perilous Equilibrium: The United States and the London Naval Conference of 1930.* New York: Greenwood Press, 1962.

Palmer, David. *Organizing the Shipyards: Union Strategy in Three Northeast Ports.* Ithaca: Cornell University Press, 1998.

Peters, Thomas J. *In Search of Excellence: Lessons from America's Best Run Companies.* New York: Harper & Row, 1982.

———. *Liberation Management: Necessary Disorganization for the Nanosecond Nineties.* New York: A. A. Knopf, 1992.

———. *A Passion for Excellence: The Leadership Difference.* New York: Random House, 1985.

———. *Thriving on Chaos: Handbook for Management Revolution.* New York: A. A. Knopf, 1994.

Potter, E. B., and Chester W. Nimitz. *Sea Power: A Naval History.* Englewood Cliffs, NJ: Prentice Hall, 1960.

Potterfield, Thomas A. *The Business of Employee Empowerment: Democracy and Ideology in the Workplace.* Westport, CT: Quorum Books, 1999.

Purser, Ronald E., and Steven Cabana. *The Self-Managing Organization: How Leading Companies Are Transforming the Work of Teams for Real Impact.* New York: Free Press, 1998.

Roscoe, Theodore. *United States Submarine Operations in World War II.* Annapolis: U.S. Naval Institute, 1949.

Shubert, Paul. "How Is the Navy Organized to Fight the War?" In *America Organizes to Win the War: A Handbook on the American War Effort.* New York: Harcourt, Brace, 1942.

Society of Naval Architects and Marine Engineers. *Historical Transactions 1893–1943.* New York, 1945.

Stillwell, Paul, ed. *Submarine Stories: Recollections from the Diesel Boats*. Annapolis: Naval Institute Press, 2007.

Vatter, Harold G. *The U.S. Economy in World War II*. New York: Columbia University Press, 1985.

Weir, Gary. *Building American Submarines 1914–1940*. Washington, D.C.: Naval Historical Center, 1991.

———. *Forged in War: The Naval-Industrial Complex and American Submarine Construction, 1940–1961*. Washington, DC: Naval Historical Center, 1993.

Whittaker, Robert. *Portsmouth-Kittery Naval Shipyard in Old Photographs*. Stroud, Gloucestershire: Alan Sutton, 1993.

Winslow, Richard E., III. *Constructing Munitions of War: The Portsmouth Navy Yard Confronts the Confederacy, 1861–1865*. Portsmouth, NH: Portsmouth Marine Society, 1995.

———. *"Do Your Job": An Illustrated Bicentennial History of the Portsmouth Naval Shipyard, 1800–2000*. Portsmouth, NH: Portsmouth Marine Society, 2000.

———. *Portsmouth-Built: Submarines of the Portsmouth Naval Shipyard*. Portsmouth, NH: Portsmouth Marine Society, 1985.

Zeitlin, Jonathan, and Charles F. Sabel, eds. *World of Possibilities: Flexibility and Mass Production in Western Industrialization*. New York: Cambridge University Press, 1997.

Zeitlin, Jonathan, and Gary Herrigel. *Americanization and Its Limits: Reworking US Technology and Management in Post-war Europe and Japan*. New York: Oxford University Press, 2004.

Articles

Argyris, Chris. "Empowerment: The Emperor's New Clothes." *Harvard Business Review* 76:3 (May/June 1998): 98–105.

Barnett, Carole K., and Michael G. Pratt. "From Threat-Rigidity to Flexibility: Toward a Learning Model of Autogenic Crisis in Organizations." *Journal of Organizational Change Management* 13:1 (2000): 74–88.

Bonnet, Wayne. "Mare Island Naval Shipyard: World War II in the San Francisco Bay Area." In *Build Ships! San Francisco Wartime Shipbuilding Photographs*. Sausalito, CA: Windgate Press, 2000. http://www.cr.nps.gov/nr/travel/wwIIbayarea/mar.htm.

Chandler, Alfred C. "Management Decentralization: An Historical Analysis." In *The History of American Management*, edited by James P. Baughman, 187–243. Englewood Cliffs, NJ: Prentice Hall, 1969.

Dyer, George C. "Beginning of the S-Boats." In *Submarine Stories: Recollections from the Diesel Boats*, edited by Paul Stillwell, 31–35. Annapolis: Naval Institute Press, 2007.

Fenton-O'Creevy, Mark. "Employee Involvement and the Middle Manager: Evidence from a Survey of Organizations." *Journal of Organizational Behavior* 19:1 (January 1998): 67–84.

Irvin, William D. "Oddball S-Boat." In *Submarine Stories: Recollections from the Diesel Boats*, edited by Paul Stillwell, 62–66. Annapolis: Naval Institute Press, 2007.

Jackson, Harry. "The Whale-Shaped Albacore." In *Submarine Stories: Recollections from the Diesel Boats*, edited by Paul Stillwell, 235–38. Annapolis: Naval Institute Press, 2007.

Kirkman, Bradley L., and Benson Rosen. "Beyond Self-Management: Antecedents and Consequences of Team Empowerment." *Academy of Management Journal* 42:1 (February 1999): 58–72.

Lotchin, Roger W. "The Historians' War or the Home Front War? Some Thoughts for Western Historians." *Western Historical Quarterly* 26:2 (Summer 1995): 185–96.

McConaghy, Lorraine. "Wartime Boomtown: Kirkland, Washington, A Small Town during World War II." *Pacific Northwest Quarterly* 80 (1989): 42–51.

McKee, A. I. "Development of Submarines in the United States." In *Historical Transactions 1893–1943*, by Society of Naval Architects and Marine Engineers, 344–55. New York, 1945.

Murray, Stuart S. "Developing the Fleet Boats." In *Submarine Stories: Recollections from the Diesel Boats*, edited by Paul Stillwell, 67–71. Annapolis: Naval Institute Press, 2007.

Rindskopf, Maurice H. "*Drum* at War." In *Submarine Stories: Recollections from the Diesel Boats*, edited by Paul Stillwell, 107–12. Annapolis: Naval Institute Press, 2007.

Waldman, David A., and Francis J. Yammarino. "CEO Charismatic Leadership: Levels of Management and Levels-of-Analysis Effects." *Academy of Management Review* 24:2 (April 1999): 266–85.

Unpublished Theses

Douglas, Dean C. "Submarine Disarmament: 1919–1936." Ph.D. dissertation, Syracuse University, 1969.

Hirshfield, Deborah Ann. "Rosie Also Welded: Women and Technology in Shipbuilding during World War II." Ph.D. dissertation, University of California–Irvine, 1987.

Horn, John D. "Submarines and the Electric Boat Company." A.B. thesis, Princeton University, 1948.

Tassava, Christopher James. "Launching a Thousand Ships: Entrepreneurs, War, Workers, and the State in American Shipbuilding, 1940–45." Ph.D. dissertation, Northwestern University, 2003.

Watterson, Rodney K. "32 in '44: A Management and Environmental Study of Submarine Construction at Portsmouth Navy Yard during World War II." Ph.D. dissertation, New Hampshire University, 2007.

West, Michael A. "Laying the Legislative Foundation: The House Naval Affairs Committee and the Construction of the Treaty Navy, 1926–1934." Ph.D. dissertation, Ohio State University, 1980.

Speeches

Healy, Thomas. "The Outlook for Disarmament." Presented at All Souls Unitarian Church, Washington, DC, 3 March 1932. NARA Waltham, RG 181, Portsmouth Navy Yard General Correspondence (Central Files), 1925–1950, Box 24, Folder A14-7. "Scrapping of Ships."

Walsh, David L. "The Decline and Renaissance of the Navy, 1922–1944." Presented to the 78th Congress, 2nd Session, 7 June 1944. http://www.ibiblio.org/pha/USN/77-2s202.html.

Web Sites

Commander Submarine Force Pacific Fleet. http://www.csp.navy.mil/admirals/withers.htm.

National Park Service. "Mare Island Naval Shipyard." *World War II Shipbuilding in the San Francisco Bay Area.* http://www.cr.nps.gov/nr/travel/wwIIbayarea/shipbuilding.htm.

"Naval Expansion Act, 14 June 1940," Frequently Asked Questions, Naval Historical Center, 30 June 1999, http://www.history.navy.mil/faqs/faq59-20.htm.

"Naval Expansion Act, 19 July 1940," Frequently Asked Questions, Naval Historical Center, 30 June 1999, http://www.history.navy.mil/faqs/faq59-21.htm.

"Report of the Naval Inspector General Regarding Irregularities Connected with the Handling of Surrendered German Submarines." *U-Boat Archive, U-873.* http://www.uboatarchive.net/U-873NIGReport.htm.

"Submarine Pioneers." *Chief of Naval Operations Submarine Warfare Division,* http://www.navy.mil/navydata/cno/n87/history/pioneers2.html

Weir, Gary E. "Mobilization, Expansion, Integration: Building American Submarines, 1940–1943." Colloquium on Contemporary History Project, Naval Historical Center, 11 July 2003. http://www.history.navy.mil/colloquia/cch5d.htm.

Index

About the Author

CAPTAIN ROD WATTERSON is a graduate of the U.S. Naval Academy (BS), MIT (MS naval architecture and marine engineering and a naval engineer's degree), and the University of New Hampshire (PhD history). During his thirty-year naval career he was involved with shipyards and the design, construction, and maintenance of submarines. Following his naval career he worked for Textron Automotive Company for ten years as a program and industrial plant manager. In retirement he has been pursuing his lifelong love of history, a path that has led to this book, which marries that love with his extensive submarine, shipyard, and industrial management experience.